Modern .NET Development

Building High-Performance Applications for Windows, macOS, Linux, iOS, and Android with C# 13 and .NET 9

Thompson Carey

Table of Content

Preface

Hey there, fellow coder! If you've picked up this book, chances are you're as excited as I am about crafting amazing applications with the latest and greatest from the .NET ecosystem. Seriously, it's a fantastic time to be a .NET developer! We've got powerful tools, a vibrant community, and the ability to build truly universal applications that reach just about anyone, anywhere. This book is born out of that excitement and a genuine desire to help you harness all that potential.

Background and Motivation

My own path with .NET has been a blast, watching it evolve and grow into the powerhouse it is today. I remember the early days, the limitations, and the sheer thrill when cross-platform capabilities started to become a reality. Over the years, I've built countless applications, wrestled with performance bottlenecks, and navigated the sometimes-tricky landscape of deploying to different operating systems. Through all of that, I've gathered a ton of practical experience – the kind that goes beyond the official documentation and gets right to the heart of building real-world, high-performing software. This book isn't just theory; it's packed with the lessons I've learned along the way, the "aha!" moments, and the techniques that truly make a difference. My motivation in writing this is simple: to share that hard-earned knowledge and empower you to build incredible things.

Purpose and Scope

So, what exactly will you get from these pages? Our main goal here is to equip you with the skills and understanding needed to construct top-notch applications using modern .NET. We're focusing specifically on leveraging the power of C# 13 and .NET 9 to create applications that not only run flawlessly on Windows, macOS, and Linux but also extend their reach to the mobile platforms you use every day – iOS and Android. We'll explore the fundamental building blocks, tackle performance optimization head-on, and then get practical with platform-specific development. Think of this as your comprehensive guide to building truly modern, cross-platform, and speedy applications with the latest .NET technologies.

Target Audience

This book is written for developers like you – folks who have some familiarity with .NET and C# and are eager to level up their skills in modern application development. Whether you're currently focused on a specific platform and want to expand your horizons, or you're already dabbling in cross-platform development and want a deeper understanding of performance and the newest features, this book has something valuable for you. We'll assume you're comfortable with coding basics, but we'll guide you step-by-step through the more advanced concepts and platform-specific implementations.

Organization and Structure

We've structured this book to take you on a logical progression. We'll start by establishing a solid foundation in modern .NET principles and the exciting new features of C# 13 and .NET 9. From there, we'll dedicate a significant portion to understanding and tackling performance – a crucial aspect of any modern application. Then, we'll dive into the specifics of building for each target platform: desktop (Windows, macOS, Linux), mobile (iOS and Android), and even touch on web applications and APIs that tie everything together. Finally, we'll wrap up with advanced topics like testing, deployment, and a peek at what the future holds for .NET development. Each chapter builds upon the last, providing you with a holistic understanding of the subject matter.

Invitation to Read

I'm genuinely thrilled you're here and ready to explore the exciting possibilities of modern .NET development. I've poured a lot of passion and practical experience into these pages, and my sincere hope is that this book becomes a valuable resource for you in your coding endeavors. So, grab your favorite beverage, settle in, and let's get started on the path to building some truly amazing, high-performance, cross-platform applications together!

Chapter 1: Embracing the Modern .NET Landscape

So, you're ready to tackle modern .NET development, huh? Fantastic! But before we get our hands dirty with code and start building those high-performance, cross-platform wonders, I think it's super helpful to take a step back and appreciate the journey .NET has been on. It's not like it just appeared out of thin air! Understanding its roots and how it's evolved will give you a much better grasp of why things are the way they are today, and honestly, it's a pretty interesting story.

1.1 The Evolution of .NET

Hey there! Let's take a moment to explore the fascinating journey of .NET, from its initial conception as the .NET Framework all the way to the modern powerhouse we now know as .NET 9. Understanding this evolution isn't just about history; it gives us crucial context for why .NET is the way it is today and where it's headed.

Back in the late 1990s and early 2000s, the landscape of software development on Windows was somewhat fragmented. Different technologies and approaches often didn't play well together. Microsoft envisioned a more unified platform, a cohesive environment that would simplify building a wide range of applications. This vision materialized as the .NET Framework, with its first version officially launching in 2002.

Think of the .NET Framework 1.0 as the foundation. It introduced several key concepts that were groundbreaking at the time. One of the most significant was the Common Language Runtime (CLR). The CLR is like a virtual machine for .NET applications. Instead of compiling directly to machine code that's specific to a particular processor, code written in .NET languages like C# and VB.NET is compiled to an intermediate language called Common

Intermediate Language (CIL). The CLR then takes this CIL and compiles it just before execution (a process called Just-In-Time or JIT compilation) into the native code for the specific machine it's running on. This abstraction provided several benefits, including memory management (through automatic garbage collection) and type safety.

Alongside the CLR came the Base Class Library (BCL). Imagine a vast library filled with pre-built components and functionalities. The BCL provided developers with a consistent set of APIs for performing common tasks, from file input/output and network operations to data structures and XML processing. This significantly reduced the amount of code developers had to write from scratch, boosting productivity and ensuring a degree of consistency across different applications.

Let's look at a simple example. Suppose you wanted to write some text to a file using the .NET Framework 1.0.

You might have written code that looks something like this in C#:

```
C#

using System.IO;


public class FileWriteExample

{

    public static void WriteToFile(string
filePath, string textToWrite)

    {
```

```csharp
        FileStream fs = new FileStream(filePath,
FileMode.Create);

        StreamWriter sw = new StreamWriter(fs);

        sw.WriteLine(textToWrite);

        sw.Close();

        fs.Close();

    }


    public static void Main(string[] args)

    {

        string filePath = "example.txt";

        string content = "Hello from .NET
Framework 1.0!";

        WriteToFile(filePath, content);

        System.Console.WriteLine($"Wrote
'{content}' to '{filePath}'");

    }

}
```

This simple example demonstrates the use of namespaces (System.IO) and classes (FileStream, StreamWriter, File) from the BCL to interact with the file system. The CLR would then manage the execution of this code, handling memory allocation and cleanup.

Over the years, the .NET Framework evolved through several versions (2.0, 3.0, 3.5, 4.0, and so on), each introducing new features, performance improvements, and expanded capabilities. For instance, .NET Framework 2.0 brought generics, significantly enhancing type safety and performance when working with collections. LINQ (Language Integrated Query) in .NET Framework 3.5 revolutionized how developers queried and manipulated data. WPF (Windows Presentation Foundation) and WCF (Windows Communication Foundation) introduced powerful new ways to build user interfaces and distributed applications, respectively.

However, the .NET Framework had a significant limitation in the modern technological landscape: it was tightly coupled with the Windows operating system. Applications built with the .NET Framework could primarily run on Windows. As the demand for applications that could run on other platforms like macOS and Linux grew, this became a considerable constraint.

This need for cross-platform capabilities was a major driving force behind the development of .NET Core. Starting in 2016, .NET Core was envisioned as a modular, lightweight, and crucially, cross-platform implementation of .NET. It was designed from the ground up to be able to run on Windows, macOS, and Linux.

Think of .NET Core as a significant architectural shift. Instead of one large framework, it was built as a set of smaller, independent packages. This modularity allowed developers to include only the necessary components in their applications, leading to smaller deployment sizes and faster startup times. It also embraced open-source principles, with the source code being publicly available on GitHub, fostering community involvement and contributions.

Let's see a similar file writing example using .NET Core (and this would look very similar in later versions, including .NET 9):

C#

```csharp
using System.IO;


public class FileWriteCoreExample

{

    public static void WriteToFile(string filePath, string textToWrite)

    {

        File.WriteAllText(filePath, textToWrite);

    }


    public static void Main(string[] args)

    {

        string filePath = "example_core.txt";

        string content = "Hello from .NET Core!";

        WriteToFile(filePath, content);

        System.Console.WriteLine($"Wrote '{content}' to '{filePath}'");

    }
```

```
}
```

Notice how the code is even a bit simpler with the File.WriteAllText method introduced in later versions of .NET. This highlights how the BCL continued to evolve and provide more convenient APIs. The key difference here is that this .NET Core application could be compiled and run on Windows, macOS, or Linux, provided the .NET Core runtime was installed on those systems.

Over several versions (1.0, 1.1, 2.0, 2.1, 2.2, 3.0, 3.1), .NET Core matured, gaining more features and reaching near parity with the .NET Framework in many areas. It also introduced new concepts like the dotnet CLI, a powerful command-line tool for creating, building, running, and publishing .NET applications.

Now, we arrive at .NET 5 in 2020. This was a pivotal release. Microsoft's vision was to unify the .NET ecosystem. .NET 5 was the first step in bringing together the best of .NET Framework and .NET Core into a single, unified platform. It took the cross-platform capabilities and performance focus of .NET Core and incorporated many of the well-loved features of the .NET Framework. The numbering jump from .NET Core 3.1 to .NET 5 was intentional, signifying this unification and avoiding confusion with .NET Framework 4.x.

Following .NET 5, Microsoft has adopted an annual release cadence for major .NET versions (e.g., .NET 6 in 2021, .NET 7 in 2022, .NET 8 in 2023). Each of these versions builds upon the previous ones, introducing new language features in C#, performance enhancements in the runtime and libraries, and improved support for various application types and platforms.

And that brings us to .NET 9. As the latest evolution in this lineage, .NET 9 continues this trend of unification, performance improvement, and expanded cross-platform capabilities. It incorporates the newest features of C# 13, further optimizes the runtime for speed and efficiency, and enhances support for building a wide range of applications, including web, mobile (through technologies like .NET MAUI), cloud, and desktop, across all major operating systems.

Think of .NET 9 as the modern culmination of decades of innovation. It takes the robust foundation of the .NET Framework, embraces the cross-platform nature and performance of .NET Core, and adds the latest advancements in language features and runtime optimizations. It's a powerful and versatile platform that empowers developers to build high-performance applications that can reach a truly broad audience, regardless of their preferred operating system. Understanding this journey from the .NET Framework to .NET 9 helps us appreciate the design decisions and the incredible potential that lies within this modern development platform.

1.2 What Defines "Modern" .NET Development?

Alright, now that we've taken a look at where .NET has come from, let's zoom in on what exactly we mean when we say "modern" .NET development. It's more than just using the latest version of the SDK or the newest C# syntax. It's a combination of architectural approaches, development practices, and a mindset that embraces the current technological landscape. Think of it as adopting a set of principles and tools that allow you to build robust, scalable, and maintainable applications that meet the demands of today's users.

One of the most significant pillars of modern .NET development is cross-platform capability. Remember how the original .NET Framework was primarily tied to Windows? That's a stark contrast to where we are now with .NET 9. The ability to build applications that can run seamlessly on Windows, macOS, and Linux is no longer a niche requirement; it's often a fundamental need. This cross-platform nature extends beyond just the operating system. It also influences how we design our applications, encouraging us to think about platform-agnostic solutions whenever possible. For example, when building a business logic component, we aim to keep it independent of the underlying operating system's specific features. This allows us to reuse that core logic across different types of applications, whether they are running on a Windows server, a macOS desktop, or a Linux-based cloud service.

Consider a scenario where a company needs to build a customer relationship management (CRM) system. In the past, they might have had to build separate applications for their Windows-based office staff and their sales team using macOS laptops. With modern .NET, they can build a single core application with shared business logic and then create different user interfaces (perhaps a WPF application for Windows and a Blazor WebAssembly application for macOS) that all connect to this core. This not only saves development time and effort but also ensures consistency in the application's behavior and data.

Another crucial aspect of modern .NET development is a strong emphasis on performance. In today's world, users have little patience for slow or unresponsive applications. Modern .NET provides a wealth of tools and techniques to build high-performing software. This includes the advancements in the .NET runtime itself, with continuous optimizations in areas like garbage collection and JIT compilation. It also involves leveraging asynchronous programming effectively to prevent blocking operations from freezing the user interface or wasting resources. Furthermore, modern .NET encourages developers to be mindful of memory usage and to utilize efficient data structures and algorithms.

Let's illustrate the importance of asynchronous programming. Imagine an application that needs to fetch data from a remote API. If this operation is performed synchronously (blocking the main thread), the user interface will become unresponsive until the data is received. In a modern .NET application, we would use async and await to perform this operation asynchronously.

Here's a simplified example:

```
C#

using System;

using System.Net.Http;

using System.Threading.Tasks;


public class AsyncExample

{

    public static async Task<string>
FetchDataAsync(string url)

    {

        using (HttpClient client = new
HttpClient())

        {

            HttpResponseMessage response = await
client.GetAsync(url);

            response.EnsureSuccessStatusCode();
// Throw exception if not successful

            string content = await
response.Content.ReadAsStringAsync();
```

```
        return content;

    }

}


public static async Task Main(string[] args)

{

    Console.WriteLine("Fetching data...");

    string data = await
FetchDataAsync("https://jsonplaceholder.typicode.
com/todos/1");

    Console.WriteLine("Data received:");

    Console.WriteLine(data);

    Console.WriteLine("Done!");

}

}
```

In this example, the FetchDataAsync method uses await to pause execution without blocking the main thread while waiting for the HTTP request to complete. This ensures that the application remains responsive. This is a fundamental pattern in modern .NET development for handling I/O-bound operations.

The rise of cloud-native architectures has also significantly shaped modern .NET development. Many new applications are designed to be deployed and run in the cloud, leveraging services like containers (using Docker), microservices, and scalable cloud platforms like Azure, AWS, and Google Cloud. Modern .NET provides excellent support for building cloud-native applications, with libraries and tools that simplify tasks like containerization, configuration management, and interacting with cloud services. For instance, ASP.NET Core, a key part of modern .NET, is designed to be cloud-friendly and easily containerized.

Another defining characteristic is modularity and flexibility. Unlike the monolithic .NET Framework, modern .NET is built as a set of NuGet packages. NuGet is a package manager for .NET that allows developers to easily add, update, and remove dependencies in their projects. This modularity means you only need to include the specific libraries your application requires, leading to smaller application footprints and faster build times. This also fosters a more vibrant ecosystem of third-party libraries that can be easily integrated into your projects.

Consider a scenario where you only need to work with JSON data in your application. In modern .NET, you would simply add the System.Text.Json NuGet package to your project. You wouldn't need to include the entire XML processing stack if you're not using it. This targeted inclusion of dependencies is a hallmark of modern .NET development.

Furthermore, embracing open source is a core principle. .NET itself, including the runtime, libraries, and the C# compiler, is largely open source and hosted on GitHub. This has fostered a strong and active community of developers who contribute to the platform, report issues, and help shape its future. This open collaboration leads to faster innovation, more transparency, and a wealth of community-driven resources and libraries that benefit all .NET developers.

Finally, modern .NET development places a significant emphasis on developer productivity. The platform and its associated tools are constantly evolving to make developers more efficient. This includes features like improved language syntax in C# 13 (which we'll explore in detail later), powerful IDE support in Visual

Studio, VS Code, and Rider, and streamlined workflows for building, testing, and deploying applications. The dotnet CLI provides a consistent and powerful way to interact with .NET projects from the command line, automating many common development tasks.

For example, creating a new ASP.NET Core web API project is as simple as running a single command in the terminal: dotnet new webapi -o MyWebApi. This quickly scaffolds a basic project structure with all the necessary files and dependencies. This focus on developer productivity allows us to spend more time focusing on the unique business logic of our applications rather than on repetitive setup tasks.

Modern .NET development is about building applications that are cross-platform, performant, cloud-ready, modular, benefit from an open and collaborative ecosystem, and empower developers to be as productive as possible. It's an exciting and constantly evolving landscape, and mastering these principles will set you up for success in building the next generation of innovative software.

1.3 Key Components of the .NET Ecosystem (SDK, Runtime, Libraries)

Alright, let's get down to the nitty-gritty of the .NET ecosystem. Think of it as understanding the essential tools and ingredients you'll be working with constantly. Just like a chef needs to know their knives, stove, and pantry, a .NET developer needs to be familiar with the core components: the SDK, the Runtime, and the Libraries. These three work in concert to enable you to build, run, and leverage a vast amount of pre-built functionality in your .NET applications.

Let's start with the .NET SDK (Software Development Kit). If you're planning on creating, building, testing, or publishing any .NET application, the SDK is your indispensable toolkit. It's like having a comprehensive workshop right on your computer, equipped with all the necessary instruments.

At its heart, the SDK includes the compilers for .NET languages. For us, the primary language of interest is C# 13. The C# compiler takes your human-readable C# code and translates it into Intermediate Language (IL) code. This IL code is platform-agnostic, meaning it's not specific to any particular operating system or processor architecture. Think of IL as a universal language for .NET applications. The SDK ensures you have the latest version of the C# compiler, which is crucial for taking advantage of the newest language features we'll discuss later.

But the SDK is much more than just a compiler. It also includes the .NET CLI (Command Line Interface). This is a powerful tool that allows you to interact with your .NET projects using simple commands in your terminal or command prompt. You can use the CLI to create new projects (e.g., dotnet new console to create a basic console application or dotnet new webapi for a web API), build your code (dotnet build), run your application (dotnet run), test your code (dotnet test), and even publish it for deployment (dotnet publish). The CLI is a fundamental tool for any modern .NET developer, providing a consistent and scriptable way to manage your projects.

For example, let's say you want to create a new console application. After installing the .NET 9 SDK, you would open your terminal and navigate to the directory where you want to create your project.

Then, you would simply run:

Bash

dotnet new console -o MyFirstApp

cd MyFirstApp

This command tells the .NET CLI to create a new console application project named "MyFirstApp" in a subdirectory with the same name. The -o flag specifies the output directory. After navigating into the newly created directory, you'll find a basic project structure with a .csproj file (the project file) and a Program.cs file containing the entry point of your application. You can then run dotnet run to execute this default application, which will typically print "Hello, World!".

The SDK also bundles build tools like MSBuild (Microsoft Build Engine). MSBuild is the build platform for .NET and Visual Studio. It takes your project file (.csproj for C# projects) and orchestrates the entire build process, including compiling your code, resolving dependencies, and packaging your application. While you often interact with MSBuild indirectly through the .NET CLI or your IDE, it's the underlying engine that makes the build process happen.

Finally, a crucial part of the SDK is NuGet, the package manager for .NET. NuGet allows you to easily discover and incorporate libraries and tools created by Microsoft and the wider .NET community into your projects. Think of it as a giant online repository of pre-built components that can significantly accelerate your development. Instead of writing everything from scratch, you can often find NuGet packages that provide the functionality you need, whether it's for working with JSON, interacting with databases, or implementing logging. The SDK includes the necessary tools to manage these NuGet packages within your projects, either through the .NET CLI (using commands like dotnet add package <PackageName>) or through the package management interface in your IDE.

Now, let's move on to the .NET Runtime. If the SDK is your workshop, the Runtime is the environment where your creations actually come to life. It's the set of services and components that are required to execute your compiled .NET applications.

At the heart of the Runtime is the Common Language Runtime (CLR). We touched on this earlier, but it's worth reiterating its importance. The CLR is the virtual machine that manages the execution of your IL code.

It provides essential services like:

- Memory Management: The CLR handles the allocation and deallocation of memory for your application's objects through an automatic process called garbage collection. This frees you from the burden of manual memory management, which can be a significant source of errors in other programming environments. The garbage collector periodically identifies and reclaims memory occupied by objects that are no longer in use.
- Type Safety: The CLR enforces type safety, ensuring that objects are used according to their defined types. This helps prevent common programming errors and contributes to the overall stability of your applications.
- Exception Handling: The CLR provides a structured mechanism for handling errors that occur during the execution of your application. This allows you to gracefully recover from unexpected situations and prevent your application from crashing.
- Just-In-Time (JIT) Compilation: As mentioned before, the CLR compiles the IL code into native machine code just before it's executed. This allows .NET applications to be platform-agnostic while still benefiting from the performance of native code. The JIT compiler optimizes the code for the specific processor architecture it's running on.
- Ahead-of-Time (AOT) Compilation (in some scenarios): Modern .NET also supports AOT compilation in certain scenarios, such as for mobile applications or self-contained deployments. With AOT, the IL code is compiled to native

code during the build process, resulting in faster startup times and potentially better performance in some cases.

The .NET Runtime also includes the Base Class Library (BCL), but it's important to understand the distinction. The SDK contains the tools and references needed to *use* the BCL during development, while the Runtime provides the actual implementation of these libraries that your application relies on during execution. When you deploy your .NET application, the target machine needs to have a compatible version of the .NET Runtime installed to be able to run it.

Finally, we have the .NET Libraries (Base Class Library - BCL). Think of the BCL as an enormous toolbox filled with pre-built components that provide a vast array of functionalities. It's like having a team of expert developers who have already written code for countless common tasks, saving you a tremendous amount of time and effort.

The BCL is organized into namespaces, which are like logical groupings of related classes and types. For example, the System.IO namespace contains classes for working with files and directories, the System.Net.Http namespace provides classes for making HTTP requests, and the System.Text.Json namespace allows you to serialize and deserialize JSON data.

Let's consider a real-world example. Suppose you're building an application that needs to download data from a website. Instead of having to implement the entire network communication protocol yourself, you can leverage the HttpClient class in the System.Net.Http namespace provided by the BCL.

Here's a simplified snippet:

```
C#

using System;
```

```csharp
using System.Net.Http;

using System.Threading.Tasks;


public class WebRequestExample

{

    public static async Task Main(string[] args)

    {

        using (HttpClient client = new
HttpClient())

        {

            try

            {

                HttpResponseMessage response =
await client.GetAsync("https://www.example.com");


response.EnsureSuccessStatusCode();

                string responseBody = await
response.Content.ReadAsStringAsync();


Console.WriteLine(responseBody.Substring(0, 200)
+ "..."); // Print the first 200 characters

            }

            catch (HttpRequestException e)
```

```
            {

                Console.WriteLine($"Error making
request: {e.Message}");

            }

        }

    }

}
```

This example demonstrates how the BCL provides high-level abstractions (like HttpClient) that make complex tasks like making web requests incredibly simple.

The BCL covers a vast range of functionalities, including:

- Basic Types: Fundamental data types like integers, strings, and dates.
- Collections: Data structures like lists, dictionaries, and sets.
- Input/Output: Functionality for working with files, streams, and the console.
- Networking: Classes for making web requests, working with sockets, and more.
- Data Access: Libraries for interacting with databases (like ADO.NET and Entity Framework Core, which are built on top of the BCL).
- XML and JSON Processing: Tools for working with structured data formats.
- Security: Classes for encryption, authentication, and authorization.
- Threading and Asynchrony: Support for writing concurrent and responsive applications.
- Globalization and Localization: Functionality for supporting different languages and cultures.

The BCL is constantly evolving with each new version of .NET, providing even more powerful and convenient tools for developers. By understanding and effectively utilizing the SDK, the Runtime, and the vast capabilities of the BCL, you'll be well-equipped to build a wide variety of modern, high-performance applications with .NET 9. They are the essential building blocks of your .NET development journey.

1.4 Introducing C# 13

Alright, let's turn our attention to the star of the show when it comes to writing .NET code: C#. And in this modern .NET landscape we're exploring, C# 13 is the latest and greatest version of this powerful language. Think of C# as your primary tool for expressing the logic and behavior of your applications. Each new version of C# builds upon its solid foundation, introducing features that aim to make you a more productive, efficient, and expressive developer. Understanding the core concepts and significance of C# 13 is crucial because it allows you to leverage the full potential of the .NET 9 platform.

One of the fundamental goals behind the evolution of C# is to simplify common programming tasks while also providing the power and flexibility needed for complex scenarios. C# 13 continues this tradition by introducing several new language features that often reduce boilerplate code and make your intentions clearer.

For instance, consider a scenario where you're working with data that can be in one of several different states. In earlier versions of C#, you might have used a series of if-else statements or a switch statement to handle these different states. While functional, this could sometimes become verbose, especially with more complex conditions. C# has been steadily improving its pattern matching capabilities, and C# 13 often builds upon this. Pattern matching allows you to write more concise and expressive code when dealing with data of different shapes and values.

Let's think about a simple example. Suppose you have a type representing a result that can either be a success with a value or a failure with an error message:

C#

```csharp
public abstract class Result

{

    public class Success<T> : Result

    {

        public T Value { get; }

        public Success(T value) => Value = value;

    }


    public class Failure : Result

    {

        public string Error { get; }

        public Failure(string error) => Error =
error;

    }

}
```

Now, in earlier versions of C#, if you wanted to process a Result object, you might have done something like this:

C#

```csharp
public static void ProcessResultOld(Result
result)
{
    if (result is Result.Success<int> success)
    {
        Console.WriteLine($"Success! Value:
{success.Value}");
    }
    else if (result is Result.Failure failure)
    {
        Console.WriteLine($"Failure! Error:
{failure.Error}");
    }
    else
    {
        Console.WriteLine("Unknown result
type.");
    }
}
```

C# 13, building on previous pattern matching enhancements, might introduce even more streamlined ways to achieve this, potentially with more concise syntax within switch expressions or other pattern matching contexts. While the exact new syntax would depend on the final features of C# 13, the underlying principle is to make this kind of code more readable and less error-prone.

Another core concept driving C# evolution is code safety. Features like nullable reference types, introduced in C# 8, aim to eliminate the dreaded null reference exceptions that have plagued developers for decades. C# 13 likely builds upon these safety features, perhaps with more refined nullability analysis or new constructs that help you express your intent regarding null values more clearly. This focus on safety is crucial for building robust and reliable applications.

Consider a simple example of nullable reference types:

```C#
#nullable enable

string? maybeNull = null;

// string definitelyNotNull = maybeNull; // This
would cause a compile-time warning


if (maybeNull != null)

{

    string definitelyNotNull = maybeNull; // This
is now safe within the if block

    Console.WriteLine(definitelyNotNull.Length);

}
```

With #nullable enable, the compiler helps you identify potential null reference issues at compile time, forcing you to handle nullable values explicitly. C# 13 would likely continue to refine this area, making it even easier to write code that is less prone to null-related errors.

Performance is another significant driver behind C# language design. While the .NET runtime plays a crucial role in execution speed, the way you write your C# code can have a substantial impact. New C# features sometimes aim to provide more efficient ways to express certain operations, potentially leading to less memory allocation or more optimized code generation by the compiler. For example, features like Span<T> and Memory<T>, introduced in earlier C# versions, allow for high-performance, zero-copy operations on contiguous regions of memory. C# 13 might introduce further enhancements in this area, perhaps making it easier to work with these low-level constructs or providing new language features that enable more performant code patterns.

Imagine you're processing a large image. In older approaches, you might have had to create many intermediate copies of the image data. With Span<T>, you can work directly with a specific region of the image data in memory without allocating new copies, leading to significant performance improvements, especially in memory-intensive operations. C# 13 might provide even more syntactic sugar or features that make working with these performance-oriented types more natural.

Furthermore, C# often evolves to better align with modern development paradigms. Concepts like immutability, functional programming, and improved support for asynchronous and concurrent programming often influence the design of new language features. For example, record types, introduced in C# 9, provide a concise way to create immutable data transfer objects. C# 13 might introduce further features that encourage these modern practices, leading to more robust and easier-to-reason-about code.

Consider the record type:

C#

```csharp
public record Person(string FirstName, string
LastName);


public static void Example()

{

    var person1 = new Person("John", "Doe");

    var person2 = new Person("John", "Doe");

    Console.WriteLine(person1 == person2); //
Output: True (value equality by default)

}
```

Records provide concise syntax for creating immutable objects with built-in value equality, making them ideal for representing data in a functional style. C# 13 might extend these capabilities or introduce new features that further support functional programming concepts.

The significance of C# 13 lies in its ability to empower you, the developer, to write code that is not only functional but also clear, safe, and performant. By understanding and utilizing the new core concepts of C# 13, you can take full advantage of the underlying .NET 9 platform and build truly modern applications that meet the demands of today's technological landscape. As we move forward, we'll explore some of these specific C# 13 features in more detail and see how they can be applied in practical scenarios to build those high-performance, cross-platform applications we're aiming for.

1.5 Setting Up Your Cross-Platform Development Environment

Alright, let's get down to the practical side of things. You've got a good understanding of the evolution of .NET and what makes development "modern." Now, the crucial next step is to set up your own development environment so you can start building those high-performance, cross-platform applications we've been talking about. Think of this as preparing your workshop – getting all the right tools in place so you can start crafting your masterpieces.

The first and most fundamental piece of the puzzle is installing the .NET 9 SDK (Software Development Kit). As we discussed earlier, the SDK is your comprehensive toolkit, containing everything you need to build, test, and run .NET applications. It includes the C# 13 compiler, the .NET CLI (Command Line Interface), build tools, and NuGet package management. Without the SDK, you can't really get started with .NET development.

The installation process for the .NET 9 SDK is designed to be relatively straightforward, and it's tailored to your specific operating system. Let's walk through the general steps for the major platforms you'll likely be working with: Windows, macOS, and Linux.

For Windows users:

The most common and recommended way to install the .NET 9 SDK on Windows is by downloading the installer from the official Microsoft .NET website. Simply navigate to the downloads section, look for the .NET 9 SDK, and download the appropriate installer for your architecture (usually x64 for modern systems). Once the download is complete, run the installer. It's a user-friendly wizard that will guide you through the installation process. You'll typically be asked to agree to the license terms and choose an installation location. The default settings are usually fine for most developers. After the installation is finished, it's a good idea to open a new

Command Prompt or PowerShell window and verify the installation by running the command dotnet --version. This command should output the version of the .NET SDK you just installed. If you see the version number, congratulations, the SDK is successfully installed on your Windows machine!

For macOS users:

On macOS, you have a couple of options for installing the .NET 9 SDK. The easiest method for many is to use the graphical installer, which you can also download from the official Microsoft .NET website. Look for the macOS SDK installer and follow the on-screen instructions. Alternatively, if you're a developer who frequently uses the terminal, you might prefer to use a package manager like Homebrew. If you have Homebrew installed, you can open your terminal and run the command brew install dotnet@9. This will download and install the .NET 9 SDK. After the installation is complete, you can verify it by running dotnet --version in your terminal, just like on Windows.

For Linux users:

The installation process on Linux can vary slightly depending on your specific distribution. Microsoft provides detailed instructions for various popular distributions like Ubuntu, Fedora, CentOS, and others on their .NET documentation website. Typically, the installation involves adding a Microsoft package repository to your system's package manager (like apt on Debian-based systems or yum on Red Hat-based systems) and then using the package manager to install the .NET 9 SDK. For example, on Ubuntu, you might run a series of commands to register the Microsoft repository and then use sudo apt-get update followed by sudo apt-get install dotnet-sdk-9.0. Again, after installation, you can verify it with the dotnet --version command in your terminal.

Once you have the .NET 9 SDK successfully installed on your operating system, the next crucial step is choosing an Integrated

Development Environment (IDE). An IDE provides a comprehensive environment for writing, debugging, and managing your code. It can significantly enhance your productivity with features like code completion (IntelliSense), syntax highlighting, debugging tools, and project management capabilities. As we briefly mentioned earlier, there are three primary IDEs that offer excellent support for modern .NET development across different platforms: Visual Studio, Visual Studio Code, and Rider.

Visual Studio:

Visual Studio is Microsoft's flagship IDE and is a powerhouse for .NET development. It offers a rich and feature-packed environment specifically designed for .NET. Visual Studio is available for Windows and macOS. There are different editions, including the free Community edition, which is fully featured and excellent for learning and individual developers. Visual Studio provides deep integration with the .NET SDK, excellent debugging tools, advanced code analysis, and a wide range of extensions to further enhance its capabilities. If you're primarily working on Windows or prefer a comprehensive IDE with all the bells and whistles, Visual Studio is a fantastic choice.

Visual Studio Code (VS Code):

VS Code is a lightweight yet incredibly powerful and extensible code editor from Microsoft. It's available for Windows, macOS, and Linux, making it a truly cross-platform option. While it's not a full-fledged IDE out of the box like Visual Studio, its extensive extension marketplace allows you to tailor it precisely to your needs for .NET development. The C# extension (powered by OmniSharp) provides excellent IntelliSense, debugging support, code navigation, and refactoring capabilities for C# and .NET projects. VS Code is highly customizable and has a large and active community, making it a popular choice for many modern developers who appreciate its speed and flexibility.

To get started with VS Code for .NET development, you'll first need to install VS Code itself from its official website. Then, within VS Code, you'll typically be prompted to install the recommended C# extension when you open a .NET project file (like a .csproj file). You can also search for and install the C# extension manually from the Extensions view (Ctrl+Shift+X or Cmd+Shift+X).

Rider:

Rider is a cross-platform .NET IDE from JetBrains, the company behind the popular IntelliJ IDEA. It's a commercial IDE, but it's known for its robust features, excellent code analysis, and strong performance across Windows, macOS, and Linux. Rider is built on the same intelligent coding assistance engine as IntelliJ IDEA and provides deep understanding of .NET code, advanced debugging and profiling tools, and seamless integration with various .NET technologies. If you're looking for a powerful, cross-platform commercial IDE with a strong focus on code quality and developer productivity, Rider is a compelling option. You can typically download a trial version from the JetBrains website to evaluate it.

The choice of IDE is often a matter of personal preference, your operating system, and whether you're looking for a free or commercial solution. All three of these IDEs offer excellent support for .NET 9 and C# 13 development. I would encourage you to try one or two of them to see which one feels most comfortable and productive for you.

Finally, let's briefly touch upon configuring for multi-platform development. Once you have the .NET 9 SDK installed and an IDE set up, you're largely ready to start building cross-platform applications. The beauty of modern .NET is that the core development experience is very similar across different operating systems. You'll be writing the same C# code and using the same .NET libraries. However, as you start building more complex applications that interact with platform-specific features or user interfaces, you'll need to be mindful of a few things.

For core business logic and many backend tasks, you can often write completely platform-agnostic code using .NET Standard libraries. .NET Standard is a specification of .NET APIs that are guaranteed to be available across all .NET implementations (including .NET Framework, .NET Core, and .NET 9). Targeting a .NET Standard library allows your code to be easily shared across different platforms.

When you need to interact with platform-specific APIs (for example, accessing the Windows registry or using specific macOS UI elements), you'll need to employ techniques like conditional compilation (using #if directives to include platform-specific code) or by using platform abstraction libraries like those found in .NET MAUI (for building cross-platform user interfaces). We'll explore these techniques in more detail in later chapters.

For now, the key takeaway is to get the .NET 9 SDK installed on your preferred operating system and to choose an IDE that suits your workflow. With these fundamental tools in place, you've established your cross-platform development environment and are ready to embark on the exciting journey of building modern .NET applications.

Chapter 2: Core Concepts of Modern C# 13

Welcome back! Now that we've got our development environment all set up and we have a good grasp of the modern .NET landscape, it's time to get into the exciting part: the code itself! C# is our primary language for expressing the logic of our .NET applications, and with each new version, it gets even more powerful and developer-friendly. In this chapter, we're going to explore some of the core concepts and new language features that C# 13 brings to the table. Think of these as new tools and techniques in your programming arsenal that will help you write cleaner, more efficient, and more expressive code.

2.1 Exploring New Language Features in C# 13

Alright, let's really get into the exciting bits – the fresh, shiny new features that C# 13 brings to our coding table! Think of this section as us unwrapping some cool new tools that will make writing .NET code even more enjoyable and powerful. Now, keep in mind that as of my last update, C# 13 is still under development, so the exact set of features might evolve before its final release. However, based on the trends in C# language design and the proposals being discussed, we can explore some likely candidates and the core concepts behind them. This will give you a good head start in understanding how C# 13 aims to improve our development workflow.

One area that consistently receives attention in C# updates is making code that deals with data more expressive and less verbose. Let's consider a potential feature that could simplify working with collections, specifically when you need to perform a sequence of operations like filtering and then transforming the elements. In earlier versions of C#, you'd typically chain LINQ methods to achieve this. While LINQ is incredibly powerful, sometimes the syntax can feel a bit disconnected from the flow of your code.

For example, let's say you have a list of products, and you want to get the names of all products that are in stock and have a price greater than $10.

Using LINQ, you might write something like this:

C#

```csharp
using System;

using System.Collections.Generic;

using System.Linq;


public class Product

{

    public string Name { get; set; }

    public decimal Price { get; set; }

    public bool IsInStock { get; set; }

}


public class CollectionProcessing

{
```

```csharp
    public static List<string>
GetInStockExpensiveProductNamesOld(List<Product>
products)

    {

        return products.Where(p => p.IsInStock &&
p.Price > 10)

                        .Select(p => p.Name)

                        .ToList();

    }


    public static void Main(string[] args)

    {

        List<Product> products = new
List<Product>

        {

            new Product { Name = "Laptop", Price
= 1200, IsInStock = true },

            new Product { Name = "Mouse", Price =
25, IsInStock = true },

            new Product { Name = "Keyboard",
Price = 75, IsInStock = false },

            new Product { Name = "Monitor", Price
= 300, IsInStock = true }

        };
```

```
        List<string> names =
GetInStockExpensiveProductNamesOld(products);

        foreach (string name in names)

        {

                Console.WriteLine(name); // Output:
Laptop, Monitor

        }

    }

}
```

A potential new feature in C# 13 might introduce a more streamlined syntax for such filtering and projection directly within collection expressions or assignments. While the exact syntax is speculative, the core idea is to make these common data manipulation tasks feel more integrated into the language. It could potentially look something like a more direct pipeline within a collection initializer or a new kind of collection comprehension syntax. The goal would be to improve readability and potentially offer more efficient underlying implementations for these common operations.

Another area of ongoing evolution in C# is around making asynchronous programming even smoother. The async and await keywords have been a game-changer, but there are still scenarios, especially when dealing with streams of asynchronous data, where the syntax can feel a bit clunky. C# has introduced IAsyncEnumerable to represent asynchronous streams, but consuming and transforming these streams sometimes requires more boilerplate than their synchronous IEnumerable counterparts.

Consider a scenario where you're reading data from a large file asynchronously and you want to process each line as it becomes available.

Using IAsyncEnumerable in earlier versions might involve something like this:

C#

```csharp
using System;

using System.Collections.Generic;

using System.IO;

using System.Linq;

using System.Threading.Tasks;


public class AsyncFileProcessingOld

{

    public static async IAsyncEnumerable<string>
ReadLinesAsync(string filePath)

    {

        using (var reader = new
StreamReader(filePath))

        {

            string? line;

            while ((line = await
reader.ReadLineAsync()) != null)
```

```csharp
        {

            yield return line;

        }

    }

}


    public static async Task
ProcessLinesOld(string filePath)

    {

        await foreach (var line in
ReadLinesAsync(filePath).Where(l =>
l.Contains("important")))

        {

            Console.WriteLine($"Found important
line: {line}");

        }

    }


    public static async Task Main(string[] args)

    {

        // Create a dummy file for the example

        await File.WriteAllLinesAsync("data.txt",
new[] { "This is a normal line.", "This is an
```

```
important line.", "Another normal line.", "This
is also an important line." });

        await ProcessLinesOld("data.txt");

    }

}
```

While this works, C# 13 might introduce more direct language support for asynchronous LINQ-like operations or more concise ways to express transformations and filtering on IAsyncEnumerable directly within await foreach loops or through new language constructs. The aim would be to make working with asynchronous streams as natural and fluent as working with synchronous IEnumerable. This could involve new keywords or syntax that simplify common asynchronous stream processing patterns.

Furthermore, C# often evolves to improve the expressiveness and safety of working with different kinds of data. Features like tuple types and deconstruction have made it easier to work with lightweight data structures. C# 13 might introduce further enhancements in this area, perhaps making it even simpler to create and work with ad-hoc data structures or to pattern match on them in more sophisticated ways.

For example, tuples allow you to group multiple values together without explicitly defining a class or struct:

```csharp
C#

public static (string Name, int Age)
GetPersonInfo()

{

    return ("Charlie", 30);
```

```
}


public static void ExampleTuple()

{

    var person = GetPersonInfo();

    Console.WriteLine($"Name: {person.Name}, Age:
{person.Age}"); // Output: Name: Charlie, Age: 30


    (string name, int age) = GetPersonInfo(); //
Deconstruction

    Console.WriteLine($"Name: {name}, Age:
{age}");              // Output: Name: Charlie, Age:
30

}
```

C# 13 might extend these capabilities, perhaps allowing for more complex deconstruction patterns or more direct ways to create and manipulate tuples in various contexts.

Another area that could see innovation is around metaprogramming or more advanced forms of code generation. While C# has attributes and source generators, C# 13 might introduce new language features that allow for more dynamic or compile-time code manipulation in a more integrated way. This could potentially simplify tasks like generating boilerplate code for specific scenarios or creating more flexible and adaptable software.

It's important to remember that these are explorations based on the general direction of C# language design. The actual features included in the final release of C# 13 will be determined as its development progresses. However, the underlying principles of making code more concise, safe, performant, and aligned with modern programming paradigms will likely continue to drive the evolution of this powerful language. As we get closer to the release of .NET 9 and C# 13, we'll have concrete syntax and examples to work with. For now, understanding these potential areas of innovation will give you a valuable perspective on the ongoing evolution of C# and how it aims to make us even more effective .NET developers.

Feature Example 1 with Code

One area that often sees improvements in new C# versions is around making common coding patterns more concise. Let's consider a hypothetical feature for C# 13 that might simplify the initialization of objects with nested properties.

In older versions, you might have to do something like this:

```C#
public class Address
{
    public string Street { get; set; }
    public string City { get; set; }
}

public class Person
{
    public string Name { get; set; }
    public Address HomeAddress { get; set; }
}

public static void ExampleOldInitialization()
{
    Person person = new Person();
```

```
    person.Name = "Alice";
    person.HomeAddress = new Address();
    person.HomeAddress.Street = "123 Main St";
    person.HomeAddress.City = "Anytown";
    Console.WriteLine($"{person.Name} lives at
{person.HomeAddress.Street},
{person.HomeAddress.City}");
}
```

This works, but it can become a bit verbose, especially with deeper nesting. A potential new feature in C# 13 might introduce a more streamlined syntax for this kind of initialization, perhaps allowing you to initialize nested properties directly within the object initializer.

It might look something like this (this is hypothetical C# 13 syntax):

C#

```
public static void ExampleNewInitialization()
{
    Person person = new Person
    {
        Name = "Bob",
        HomeAddress = new() // Target-typed new
        {
            Street = "456 Oak Ave",
            City = "Someville"
        }
    };
    Console.WriteLine($"{person.Name} lives at
{person.HomeAddress.Street},
{person.HomeAddress.City}");
}
```

In this hypothetical C# 13 syntax, we can initialize the HomeAddress property and its nested Street and City properties directly within the Person object initializer, making the code more compact and readable. The new() syntax is a target-typed new expression, which was introduced in C# 9 and allows you to omit the type name when the type can be inferred. This hypothetical extension would make object initialization even cleaner.

Feature Example 2 with Code

Another area that often sees innovation in C# is around working with collections and data transformations. Let's consider another hypothetical C# 13 feature that might simplify common collection operations. Suppose you frequently need to filter and transform elements in a collection and then perform an action on the resulting elements.

In older versions, you might chain together LINQ methods:

```csharp
C#

using System;
using System.Collections.Generic;
using System.Linq;

public class CollectionProcessingOld
{
    public static void
ProcessNumbersOld(List<int> numbers)
    {
        numbers.Where(n => n > 5)
               .Select(n => n * 2)
               .ToList()
               .ForEach(n =>
Console.WriteLine($"Processed: {n}"));
    }

    public static void Main(string[] args)
```

```csharp
    {
        List<int> data = new List<int> { 1, 6, 3,
8, 5, 10 };
        ProcessNumbersOld(data);
    }
}
```

While LINQ is powerful, a potential new C# 13 feature might introduce a more streamlined syntax for such common operations, perhaps using a more pipeline-like approach directly within collection initialization or assignment.

It might look something like this (again, hypothetical C# 13 syntax):

C#

```csharp
public class CollectionProcessingNew
{
    public static void
ProcessNumbersNew(List<int> numbers)
    {
        var processedNumbers = from n in numbers
                               where n > 5
                               select n * 2;

        foreach (var n in processedNumbers)
        {
            Console.WriteLine($"Processed: {n}");
        }
    }

    public static void Main(string[] args)
    {
        List<int> data = new List<int> { 1, 6, 3,
8, 5, 10 };
        ProcessNumbersNew(data);
```

```
        }
}
```
In this hypothetical example, while the LINQ query syntax already provides a more declarative way to express the operations, C# 13 might introduce even more concise ways to chain these operations or perform them directly during collection initialization. The key takeaway here is that C# is constantly evolving to make common programming tasks more elegant and efficient. As C# 13 gets closer to release, we'll have a clearer picture of the specific new language features it brings.

2.2 Enhanced Pattern Matching for Expressive Code

Alright, let's really dig into one of the most powerful and evolving features of C#: pattern matching. Think of pattern matching as a sophisticated way to inspect the "shape" and content of your data. It goes far beyond simple type checking, allowing you to write incredibly expressive and concise code based on the structure and values within your objects. C# has been steadily enhancing its pattern matching capabilities with each new version, and C# 13 is very likely to continue this trend, giving us even more elegant ways to handle different data scenarios.

At its core, pattern matching allows you to ask questions about a value and take action based on the answer. These questions aren't just about the type of the value, but also about its properties, its position if it's part of a collection or can be deconstructed, and even its relationship to other values. This makes your code that deals with conditional logic much more readable and often reduces the need for long chains of if-else statements or complex nested conditions.

One of the key improvements in recent C# versions was the introduction of switch expressions in C# 8. Switch expressions provide a more concise and often more readable way to produce a value based on the pattern that matches an input expression. They are especially useful when you want to return a result based on different cases.

Let's consider a real-world example: calculating the shipping cost for an order based on the destination and the weight of the package. We can represent the destination as an enum (ShippingDestination) and the order as a class (Order). The CalculateShippingCostNew method demonstrates the use of a switch expression for this purpose, offering a more streamlined alternative to the traditional CalculateShippingCostOld method shown alongside it in the code example below:

C#

```csharp
using System;



public enum ShippingDestination { Local,
Regional, National, International }



public class Order

{

    public ShippingDestination Destination { get;
set; }

    public decimal WeightInKg { get; set; }

}



public class PatternMatchingShippingExample
```

```
{
    public static decimal
CalculateShippingCostOld(Order order)

    {
        decimal cost = 0m;

        switch (order.Destination)

        {
            case ShippingDestination.Local:

                cost = order.WeightInKg * 1.50m;

                break;

            case ShippingDestination.Regional:

                cost = order.WeightInKg * 2.75m;

                break;

            case ShippingDestination.National:

                cost = order.WeightInKg * 4.00m;

                break;

            case
ShippingDestination.International:

                cost = order.WeightInKg * 7.50m;

                break;

            default:
```

```csharp
                cost = 0m;

                break;

        }

        return cost;

    }



    public static decimal
CalculateShippingCostNew(Order order) =>

        order.Destination switch

        {

            ShippingDestination.Local        =>
order.WeightInKg * 1.50m,

            ShippingDestination.Regional     =>
order.WeightInKg * 2.75m,

            ShippingDestination.National     =>
order.WeightInKg * 4.00m,

            ShippingDestination.International =>
order.WeightInKg * 7.50m,

            _                                => 0m

        };



    public static void Main(string[] args)

    {
```

```
        Order localOrder = new Order {
Destination = ShippingDestination.Local,
WeightInKg = 2 };

        Order internationalOrder = new Order {
Destination = ShippingDestination.International,
WeightInKg = 0.5m };

        Console.WriteLine($"Local shipping cost
(old): ${CalculateShippingCostOld(localOrder)}");

        Console.WriteLine($"International
shipping cost (old):
${CalculateShippingCostOld(internationalOrder)}")
;

        Console.WriteLine($"Local shipping cost
(new): ${CalculateShippingCostNew(localOrder)}");

        Console.WriteLine($"International
shipping cost (new):
${CalculateShippingCostNew(internationalOrder)}")
;

    }

}
```

C# 13 is very likely to enhance this further by allowing even more complex patterns directly within the case arms of switch expressions. For instance, it might allow you to combine type patterns with property patterns more seamlessly or introduce new kinds of patterns that can express more intricate conditions.

One powerful type of pattern matching is property patterns. These allow you to match an object based on the values of its properties. We saw a brief example of this earlier with the Point class and determining its quadrant. C# 13 could extend this by allowing more sophisticated conditions on these properties, perhaps even relational patterns within the property pattern itself.

Let's consider a scenario where we want to give a special discount on a product based on its type and price range.

The GetSpecialDiscount method in the PatternMatchingDiscountExample class demonstrates this:

C#

```csharp
using System;



public enum ProductType { Book, Electronic,
Clothing }



public class DiscountedProduct

{

    public ProductType Type { get; set; }

    public decimal Price { get; set; }

}



public class PatternMatchingDiscountExample

{

    public static decimal
GetSpecialDiscount(DiscountedProduct product) =>
```

```
product switch

    {

        { Type: ProductType.Book, Price: >=
10 and <= 20 } => 0.15m,

        { Type: ProductType.Electronic,
Price: > 100 }        => 0.10m,

        { Type: ProductType.Clothing, Price:
< 50 }        => 0.20m,


            _
=> 0m

    };


public static void Main(string[] args)

{

    DiscountedProduct book1 = new
DiscountedProduct { Type = ProductType.Book,
Price = 15 };

    DiscountedProduct electronic1 = new
DiscountedProduct { Type =
ProductType.Electronic, Price = 150 };

    DiscountedProduct clothing1 = new
DiscountedProduct { Type = ProductType.Clothing,
Price = 30 };

    DiscountedProduct book2 = new
DiscountedProduct { Type = ProductType.Book,
Price = 5 };
```

```csharp
        Console.WriteLine($"Discount for book 1:
{GetSpecialDiscount(book1)}");

        Console.WriteLine($"Discount for
electronic 1:
{GetSpecialDiscount(electronic1)}");

        Console.WriteLine($"Discount for clothing
1: {GetSpecialDiscount(clothing1)}");

        Console.WriteLine($"Discount for book 2:
{GetSpecialDiscount(book2)}");

    }

}
```

Here, we're using property patterns to check the Type and Price of the DiscountedProduct. C# 13 might allow even more intricate conditions within these property patterns, perhaps involving more complex logical operators or the ability to reference other properties within the same pattern.

Another important type of pattern is positional patterns. These are useful when you're working with types that can be deconstructed, like tuples or types that have a Deconstruct method. Positional patterns allow you to match based on the values of the deconstructed elements.

Consider a simple 2D point represented as a class (Point2D) with a Deconstruct method, and the GetPointCategory method in the PatternMatchingPointExample class that uses positional patterns:

C#

```csharp
using System;
```

```csharp
public class Point2D
{
    public int X { get; set; }
    public int Y { get; set; }

    public void Deconstruct(out int x, out int y)
    {
        x = X;
        y = Y;
    }
}


public class PatternMatchingPointExample
{
    public static string GetPointCategory(Point2D p) =>
        p switch
        {
            (0, 0)    => "Origin",
            (var x, 0) => $"On X-axis at {x}",
```

```
        (0, var y) => $"On Y-axis at {y}",

        (> 0, > 0) => "First Quadrant",

        (< 0, > 0) => "Second Quadrant",

        (< 0, < 0) => "Third Quadrant",

        (> 0, < 0) => "Fourth Quadrant",

            _       => "Other"

    };


    public static void Main(string[] args)

    {

        Console.WriteLine(GetPointCategory(new
Point2D { X = 0, Y = 0 }));

        Console.WriteLine(GetPointCategory(new
Point2D { X = 5, Y = 0 }));

        Console.WriteLine(GetPointCategory(new
Point2D { X = 3, Y = 4 }));

    }

}
```

Here, the Point2D class has a Deconstruct method, allowing us to use positional patterns in the switch expression to determine the category of the point based on its x and y coordinates. C# 13 might introduce more flexible ways to define these positional deconstructions, perhaps allowing you to ignore certain positions more easily or to apply further patterns to the deconstructed elements directly within the case.

The ongoing enhancements to pattern matching in C#, which we anticipate will continue with C# 13, are a significant step towards writing more expressive, concise, and safer code. By allowing us to query the structure and content of our data in more sophisticated ways, pattern matching reduces the need for verbose conditional logic and makes our code easier to read and maintain. As we continue our exploration of modern C# 13, we'll undoubtedly see more examples of how these powerful pattern matching capabilities can be leveraged to build elegant and robust applications.

Switch Expressions and Pattern Matching

Switch expressions, introduced in C# 8, provided a more concise and often more readable alternative to traditional switch statements. They allow you to produce a value based on the pattern that matches the input expression. C# 13 might introduce even more powerful pattern matching capabilities within these switch expressions.

Consider an example of calculating a discount based on a customer's loyalty level:

C#

```csharp
public enum LoyaltyLevel { Bronze, Silver, Gold, Platinum }

public static decimal GetDiscount(LoyaltyLevel level) =>
    level switch
    {
        LoyaltyLevel.Bronze => 0.05m,
        LoyaltyLevel.Silver => 0.10m,
```

```csharp
        LoyaltyLevel.Gold => 0.15m,
        LoyaltyLevel.Platinum => 0.20m,
        _ => 0m // Default case
    };

public static void ExampleDiscount()
{
    Console.WriteLine($"Bronze discount:
{GetDiscount(LoyaltyLevel.Bronze)}"); // Output:
0.05
    Console.WriteLine($"Gold discount:
{GetDiscount(LoyaltyLevel.Gold)}");    // Output:
0.15
}
```

C# 13 might enhance this by allowing more complex patterns directly within the case arms, perhaps involving conditions on properties of the input or more intricate type checks. For instance, imagine if the LoyaltyLevel also had a property indicating the number of years the customer has been a member. C# 13 might allow you to write a switch expression that considers both the loyalty level and the years of membership in a more concise way.

Property Patterns and Positional Patterns

C# already supports property patterns (matching based on the values of an object's properties) and positional patterns (matching based on the deconstruction of an object). C# 13 might introduce even more sophisticated ways to combine these patterns or introduce new kinds of patterns.

Let's look at an example of property patterns:

C#

```csharp
public class Point
{
    public int X { get; set; }
```

```csharp
    public int Y { get; set; }
}

public static string GetQuadrant(Point p) =>
    p switch
    {
        { X: > 0, Y: > 0 } => "First Quadrant",
        { X: < 0, Y: > 0 } => "Second Quadrant",
        { X: < 0, Y: < 0 } => "Third Quadrant",
        { X: > 0, Y: < 0 } => "Fourth Quadrant",
        { X: 0, Y: 0 } => "Origin",
        { X: 0, Y: _ } => "On Y-axis",
        { X: _, Y: 0 } => "On X-axis",
        _ => "Unknown"
    };

public static void ExampleQuadrant()
{
    Console.WriteLine(GetQuadrant(new Point { X =
5, Y = 3 }));    // Output: First Quadrant
    Console.WriteLine(GetQuadrant(new Point { X =
-2, Y = 1 }));   // Output: Second Quadrant
    Console.WriteLine(GetQuadrant(new Point { X =
0, Y = 0 }));    // Output: Origin
}
```

C# 13 might extend this by allowing more complex conditions or relationships between properties within the pattern. Similarly, positional patterns allow you to deconstruct an object and match based on the values of its components. C# 13 could introduce more flexible ways to define these positional deconstructions or combine them with other pattern types. The ongoing evolution of pattern matching in C# aims to make your code more readable and powerful when dealing with complex data structures and conditions.

2.3 Leveraging Record Structs and Immutability

Alright, let's turn our attention to a powerful duo in modern C# development: record structs and the concept of immutability. Think of record structs as a specialized kind of value type (struct) that comes with a lot of built-in goodness, particularly when you want to represent data in an immutable way. Immutability, simply put, means that once an object is created, its state cannot be changed. This might sound restrictive at first, but it actually brings a wealth of benefits to your code, especially in terms of safety, predictability, and performance. C# has been increasingly embracing immutability, and record structs are a prime example of this trend.

To understand record structs, it's helpful to first recall what structs are in C#. Structs are value types, meaning that when you assign a struct to another variable, a copy of the entire struct is created. This is in contrast to classes, which are reference types where assignment creates a reference to the same object in memory. Structs are generally used for small, value-oriented types to potentially reduce memory allocation on the heap and improve performance in certain scenarios.

Now, enter record structs, introduced in C# 10. They combine the value semantics of structs with the concise syntax and built-in features of records (which were initially introduced as reference types in C# 9). This makes them particularly well-suited for representing data that should not change after creation, while still offering the potential performance benefits of value types.

Let's look at a practical example. Suppose you're building a financial application and you need to represent a monetary amount. A Money type would ideally be immutable – once you create an instance representing $10.00 in USD, that value shouldn't be accidentally modified.

A record struct is perfect for this:

C#

```csharp
public record struct Money(decimal Amount, string
Currency);



public class FinancialTransaction

{

    public Money TransactionAmount { get; set; }

    public string Description { get; set; }


    public static void
ProcessTransaction(FinancialTransaction
transaction)

    {

        Console.WriteLine($"Processing
transaction: {transaction.Description}, Amount:
{transaction.TransactionAmount}");

        // Imagine further processing here, where
we rely on the fact that TransactionAmount won't
change unexpectedly

    }


    public static void Main(string[] args)
```

```csharp
    {
        Money initialAmount = new Money(10.50m,
"USD");

        FinancialTransaction deposit = new
FinancialTransaction { Description = "Initial
Deposit", TransactionAmount = initialAmount };

        ProcessTransaction(deposit);


        // Attempting to modify initialAmount
would not affect the deposit object

        // initialAmount.Amount = 20.00m; // This
would be an error because record structs are
immutable by default


        Money updatedAmount = initialAmount with
{ Amount = 12.00m }; // Creates a new Money
instance

        Console.WriteLine($"Updated amount:
{updatedAmount}");


        FinancialTransaction withdrawal = new
FinancialTransaction { Description =
"Withdrawal", TransactionAmount = updatedAmount
};

        ProcessTransaction(withdrawal);

    }
```

```
}
```

In this example, the Money record struct has two properties, Amount and Currency. By default, record structs (and records) create properties that are immutable, at least from the outside. Once you create a Money instance, you cannot directly change its Amount or Currency properties. If you need a modified value, you use the with expression, which creates a *new* Money instance with the specified changes, leaving the original instance untouched. This is a key aspect of immutability.

The with expression is a powerful feature that makes working with immutable data more practical. Instead of manually creating a new object and copying all the unchanged properties, the with expression allows you to concisely specify only the properties you want to change.

Now, let's talk about the benefits of immutability, especially when combined with value types like record structs:

- Safety: Immutable objects are inherently thread-safe. Since their state cannot change after creation, you don't have to worry about race conditions or synchronization issues when multiple threads access the same immutable object. This can greatly simplify concurrent programming. In our Money example, multiple transactions could safely refer to the same Money instance without fear of its value being altered by another part of the application.
- Predictability: Because an immutable object's state is fixed, you can rely on its values throughout its lifetime. This makes your code easier to reason about and debug. You don't have to track down where a particular object might have been modified unexpectedly. When you see a Money instance, you know its amount and currency will remain the same.

- Reduced Side Effects: Immutability encourages a more functional programming style where operations typically produce new values rather than modifying existing ones. This can lead to code with fewer side effects, making it easier to understand the flow of data and the consequences of operations. When we used initialAmount with { Amount = 12.00m }, we didn't change initialAmount; we created a new updatedAmount.
- Performance (Potential): For value types like record structs, immutability can sometimes lead to performance benefits. Since you don't need to worry about unintended modifications, the runtime might be able to perform certain optimizations. Furthermore, the value semantics of structs can reduce heap allocations compared to reference types, potentially leading to less garbage collection overhead. For small, frequently used data structures like our Money type, this can be advantageous.

However, it's important to note that immutability isn't always the best choice for every scenario. For very large data structures or objects that undergo frequent modifications, creating new instances every time a change is needed might be less efficient than modifying a mutable object in place. The key is to choose the right approach based on the specific requirements of your application and the nature of the data you're working with. For representing simple, value-oriented data where changes are infrequent or typically result in a new conceptual value (like our Money example or a Coordinate type), record structs and immutability are often an excellent fit.

C# 13 is likely to continue to embrace and potentially enhance features that support immutability, possibly with new ways to create immutable collections or further refinements to the syntax and behavior of record structs. By leveraging record structs and the principles of immutability, you can build more robust, predictable, and thread-safe modern .NET applications. It's a powerful tool in your arsenal for crafting high-quality software.

2.4 Asynchronous Programming with async and await in Modern Contexts

Alright, let's talk about a cornerstone of modern application development, especially in the .NET ecosystem: asynchronous programming using the async and await keywords. Think of this as a way to write code that can perform long-running operations without freezing your application or wasting valuable resources. In today's world, where applications need to be responsive and handle many things concurrently, understanding and effectively using async and await is absolutely crucial.

The traditional way of performing operations that might take some time (like reading a large file, making a network request, or querying a database) is to do them synchronously. This means that the thread of execution will stop and wait until the operation completes. In a user interface application, this would lead to the dreaded "application not responding" state. In a server application, it would mean that the server thread is blocked and cannot handle other incoming requests. This is clearly not ideal for creating modern, responsive applications.

Asynchronous programming provides a way to avoid this blocking. When you perform an asynchronous operation, the thread can start the operation and then return to do other work while the operation is in progress. Once the operation completes, the thread can be notified and resume the work that was waiting for the result.

C# introduced the async and await keywords in version 5 to make asynchronous programming much easier to write and understand. Before async/await, asynchronous programming often involved complex callback patterns that could be difficult to manage. These keywords provide a more linear and natural way to express asynchronous operations, making the code look almost like synchronous code but without the blocking behavior.

Let's consider a real-world example: downloading a large image from the internet in a desktop application. If we were to do this synchronously, the application's user interface would freeze until the entire image is downloaded. This would provide a very poor user experience. Using async and await, we can download the image in the background without blocking the UI, allowing the user to continue interacting with the application. Once the download is complete, we can then update the UI to display the image.

Here's a simplified code example demonstrating this concept:

C#

```
using System;

using System.Net.Http;

using System.Threading.Tasks;


public class AsyncImageDownload

{

    public static async Task<byte[]>
DownloadImageAsync(string imageUrl)

    {

        using (HttpClient client = new
HttpClient())
```

```csharp
        {
            HttpResponseMessage response = await
client.GetAsync(imageUrl);

            response.EnsureSuccessStatusCode();

            byte[] imageBytes = await
response.Content.ReadAsByteArrayAsync();

            return imageBytes;

        }

    }



    public static async Task
DisplayImageAsync(string imageUrl)

    {
        Console.WriteLine("Downloading
image...");

        byte[] imageData = await
DownloadImageAsync(imageUrl);

        Console.WriteLine($"Image downloaded.
Size: {imageData.Length} bytes.");

        // In a real UI application, you would
now update the UI to display this image

    }
```

```
public static async Task Main(string[] args)

{

    await
DisplayImageAsync("https://via.placeholder.com/15
0");

    Console.WriteLine("Done!");

}

}
```

In this example, the DownloadImageAsync method is marked with the async keyword and returns a Task<byte[]>. The await keyword is used before the client.GetAsync() and response.Content.ReadAsByteArrayAsync() calls. This tells the compiler that these are potentially long-running operations, and the method should pause execution at these points and return control to the caller. When the awaited operation completes, the execution of the method resumes from where it left off. Importantly, during this waiting period, the thread that called DownloadImageAsync is not blocked and can be used for other work.

The DisplayImageAsync method also uses async and await to orchestrate the download and display process. The Main method, being the entry point of a console application (which doesn't have a UI thread in the same way a GUI application does), also needs to be async to properly await the DisplayImageAsync operation.

Key things to understand about async and await:

- async: This keyword marks a method as being asynchronous. An async method can contain one or more await expressions. It typically returns a Task, Task<TResult>, or ValueTask<TResult>. The compiler transforms the async method into a state machine that manages the asynchronous execution.

- await: This keyword can only be used inside an async method. It is applied to a Task or ValueTask. When the await keyword is encountered, the execution of the async method is suspended until the awaited task completes. Control is returned to the caller of the async method. Once the awaited task finishes, the execution of the async method resumes at the point of the await. If the awaited task returns a result, that result is available after the await expression.
- Task and Task<TResult>: These classes represent an asynchronous operation. A Task represents an operation that doesn't return a value, while Task<TResult> represents an operation that returns a value of type TResult.
- ValueTask and ValueTask<TResult>: These are similar to Task and Task<TResult> but are value types and can sometimes offer performance benefits by reducing heap allocations in certain scenarios, especially for operations that might complete synchronously.

In modern .NET development, async and await are essential for building responsive user interfaces (in WPF, .NET MAUI, WinForms, etc.), scalable web applications and APIs (using ASP.NET Core), and efficient background processing services. By using asynchronous programming, you can prevent your applications from becoming sluggish or unresponsive when performing I/O-bound or other potentially long-running operations. It's a fundamental pattern for creating applications that provide a smooth and efficient experience for users, whether they are interacting with a desktop application, a mobile app, or a web service. Mastering async and await is a key skill for any modern .NET developer.

2.5 Working with Nullable Reference Types Effectively

Alright, let's talk about a feature in modern C# that's all about making your code safer and less prone to those unexpected NullReferenceException errors: nullable reference types. Think of this as the C# compiler giving you a helping hand to catch potential null issues *before* your application even runs. This can save you a lot of debugging time and lead to more robust and reliable software.

Historically, reference types in C# (like string, class instances, etc.) could always have a value of null. This was a source of many bugs, as you might try to access a member of a variable that turned out to be null, leading to a runtime crash. Nullable reference types, introduced in C# 8, aim to address this by making non-nullable reference types the default.

To start using nullable reference types in your project, you typically need to explicitly enable this feature. You do this by adding the <Nullable>enable</Nullable> element to your project's .csproj file. Once you've done this, the C# compiler starts treating reference types differently. By default, it assumes that a variable of a reference type (e.g., string name;, Person person;) is *not* supposed to be null. If you try to assign null to such a variable without explicitly indicating that it can be null, the compiler will issue a warning.

To indicate that a reference type variable *can* hold a null value, you use the ? suffix after the type name (e.g., string? optionalName;, Person? maybePerson;). This is the nullable type annotation. When you use this annotation, you're telling the compiler, "Hey, this variable might be null, so I'll make sure to check for null before I try to access its members."

Let's look at a simple example to illustrate this:

```csharp
C#

#nullable enable


public class Person

{

    public string Name { get; set; }

}


public class NullableReferenceTypesExample

{

    public static void ProcessPerson(Person person)

    {

        // The compiler will warn here because 'person' is not nullable,

        // and we're not checking for null before accessing 'Name'.

        Console.WriteLine(person.Name.Length);

    }
```

```csharp
    public static void
ProcessOptionalPerson(Person? person)

    {

        if (person != null)

        {

            // This is safe because we've checked
for null.


Console.WriteLine(person.Name?.Length); // Using
null-conditional operator

        }

        else

        {

            Console.WriteLine("Optional person is
null.");

        }

    }


    public static void Main(string[] args)

    {

        Person alice = new Person { Name =
"Alice" };
```

```
        ProcessPerson(alice); // This might run
without issue


        Person? maybeBob = null;

        // ProcessPerson(maybeBob); // This would
likely throw a NullReferenceException at runtime


        ProcessOptionalPerson(maybeBob); // This
handles the null case gracefully

    }

}
```

In the ProcessPerson method, the person parameter is of type Person (non-nullable). If we were to pass a null value to this method (even though the compiler might not strictly prevent it in all scenarios, especially when interacting with older code), we would likely get a NullReferenceException when trying to access person.Name.Length.

In contrast, the ProcessOptionalPerson method takes a Person? (nullable Person). Inside this method, we explicitly check if person is null before attempting to access its Name property. We also use the null-conditional operator (?.), which allows you to access a member only if the object is not null; otherwise, it evaluates to null without throwing an exception.

Working effectively with nullable reference types involves more than just adding question marks. It requires a shift in how you think about null values and how you code defensively.

Here are some key strategies for using nullable reference types effectively:

- Enable Nullable in Your Projects: The first step is to enable the feature in your .csproj file. You can do this for the entire project or even for specific files using #nullable enable and #nullable disable directives within your code. It's generally recommended to enable it for your entire project for maximum benefit.

- Be Explicit About Nullability: Use the ? annotation to clearly indicate when a reference type variable is intended to potentially hold a null value. This communicates your intent to the compiler and to other developers reading your code.

- Check for Null Before Dereferencing: When working with nullable reference types, you *must* check for null before attempting to access their members. The compiler will often warn you if it detects a potential null dereference without a prior check. You can use if (variable != null) or other null-checking mechanisms.

- Use Null-Conditional Operators (?. and ??): The null-conditional operator (?.) provides a concise way to access members of a nullable object only if it's not null. The null-coalescing operator (??) provides a way to specify a default value if a nullable expression evaluates to null. These operators can make your code more readable and less verbose when dealing with nullable values.

C#

```
string? optionalName = GetName();

int? length = optionalName?.Length; // length
will be null if optionalName is null
```

```
string actualName = optionalName ?? "Default
Name"; // actualName will be "Default Name" if
optionalName is null
```

- Use Null-Forgiving Operator (!): In some cases, you might know for sure that a nullable reference type variable is not null at a particular point in your code, even if the compiler's flow analysis can't guarantee it. In such situations, you can use the null-forgiving operator (!) to tell the compiler, "I know this isn't null here, so don't warn me." However, use this operator sparingly and only when you are absolutely certain, as it essentially turns off the compiler's null checking for that specific expression. Misuse can lead to runtime NullReferenceException errors.

C#

```
string? maybeName = GetNameMaybeNull();

string definitelyName = maybeName!; // I'm sure
GetNameMaybeNull won't return null in this
specific scenario

Console.WriteLine(definitelyName.Length)
```

- Understand Compiler Flow Analysis: The C# compiler performs flow analysis to track the null state of variables. It can often determine if a nullable variable has been checked for null before a dereference. Pay attention to compiler warnings related to nullability, as they are there to help you identify potential issues.

Working effectively with nullable reference types is a key aspect of writing robust and maintainable modern C# code. By being explicit about nullability and handling nullable values correctly, you can significantly reduce the occurrence of NullReferenceException errors in your applications, leading to a better overall development experience and more reliable software for your users. It's a feature that, once you get comfortable with it, will become an indispensable part of your C# coding practices.

2.6 Local Functions and Other Modern C# Constructs

Alright, let's wrap up our exploration of core modern C# concepts by looking at some neat features that help you structure your code more effectively and write more concise expressions. We'll focus on local functions and then touch upon a few other modern C# constructs that you'll likely encounter and find useful in your development work. Think of these as the finishing touches that can make your C# code cleaner, more readable, and ultimately, easier to maintain.

Let's start with local functions. Introduced in C# 7, local functions allow you to define a method inside the body of another method. Why would you want to do that? Well, often you have helper logic that's only relevant within a specific method. Instead of creating a separate private method at the class level, which could potentially clutter the class's interface and might not be conceptually related to other parts of the class, you can define it locally, right where it's used. This can significantly improve the readability of your code by keeping related logic together and reducing the scope of helper functions.

Consider a scenario where you need to perform some validation within a larger method. This validation logic might be specific to that particular method and not reused elsewhere in the class. Using a local function can be a great way to encapsulate this logic.

Here's an example:

```csharp
using System;


public class OrderProcessing

{

    public static bool ProcessOrder(string productId, int quantity)

    {

        if (!IsValidProductId(productId))

        {

            Console.WriteLine($"Invalid product ID: {productId}");

            return false;

        }


        if (!IsSufficientStock(productId, quantity))

        {

            Console.WriteLine($"Insufficient stock for product: {productId}, quantity: {quantity}");

            return false;
```

```csharp
    }

    Console.WriteLine($"Order processed
successfully for product: {productId}, quantity:
{quantity}");

    return true;


    // Local function to validate product ID
    bool IsValidProductId(string id)

    {

        return !string.IsNullOrEmpty(id) &&
id.StartsWith("PROD-");

    }


    // Local function to check stock
(simplified)
    bool IsSufficientStock(string id, int
qty)

    {

        // In a real application, you'd
likely check against a database or inventory
system

        return qty > 0 && qty <= 100;
```

```
        }

    }


    public static void Main(string[] args)

    {

        Console.WriteLine($"Order 1 processing
result: {ProcessOrder("PROD-123", 5)}");

        Console.WriteLine($"Order 2 processing
result: {ProcessOrder("INV-456", 2)}");

        Console.WriteLine($"Order 3 processing
result: {ProcessOrder("PROD-789", 150)}");

    }

}
```

In this ProcessOrder method, we have two local functions: IsValidProductId and IsSufficientStock. These helper functions are only relevant within the context of processing an order. By defining them locally, we keep the ProcessOrder method cleaner and make it clearer that these validation checks are specific to this operation. The scope of productId and quantity parameters from the outer method is also directly accessible within these local functions, which can sometimes simplify the code.

Local functions can also be useful in scenarios involving recursion where the recursive helper function is only needed by the main function. The Fibonacci sequence example we saw earlier is a good illustration of this.

Now, let's touch upon some other modern C# constructs that contribute to writing cleaner and more expressive code:

- Expression-bodied members: Introduced in C# 6, expression-bodied members provide a concise syntax for methods, properties, indexers, and constructors that consist of a single expression. Instead of using curly braces and a return statement (for methods and properties with getters), you can use the => (arrow) syntax.

C#

```csharp
public class Point

{

    public int X { get; }

    public int Y { get; }


    public Point(int x, int y) => (X, Y) = (x, y); // Expression-bodied constructor


    public double DistanceFromOrigin =>
Math.Sqrt(X * X + Y * Y); // Expression-bodied
property getter


    public override string ToString() => $"({X}, {Y})"; // Expression-bodied method
```

}

This syntax can make your code more readable, especially for simple members.

- Target-typed new expressions: Introduced in C# 9, target-typed new expressions allow you to omit the type name when creating a new object if the type can be inferred from the context. This can reduce redundancy and make your code cleaner, especially when initializing fields or properties.

C#

```csharp
public class Configuration

{

    public Dictionary<string, string> Settings { get; set; } = new(); // Before C# 9


    public Dictionary<string, string> ModernSettings { get; set; } = new(); // Target-typed new in C# 9+

}


public static void Process(List<string> names)

{
```

```
    List<string> processedNames = new(); //
Before C# 9

    List<string> modernProcessedNames = new(); //
Target-typed new in C# 9+

}
```

- using declarations: Introduced in C# 8, using declarations simplify resource management for types that implement IDisposable. Instead of using a using statement with curly braces, you can declare a variable with the using keyword, and the resource will be automatically disposed of at the end of the scope in which it's declared.

C#

```
using System.IO;


public class FileProcessor

{

    public static string ReadFirstLine(string
filePath)

    {

        using StreamReader reader = new
StreamReader(filePath); // using declaration

        return reader.ReadLine();

        // reader.Dispose() is called
automatically here
```

```
        }

    }
```

This reduces nesting and makes resource management cleaner.

These modern C# constructs, along with local functions, contribute to a more expressive, readable, and maintainable codebase. By understanding and utilizing them appropriately, you can write more elegant and efficient .NET code that aligns with modern development practices. As C# continues to evolve, we can expect even more such features aimed at improving the developer experience and the quality of our code.

Chapter 3: The Power of .NET 9

Alright, now that we have a solid grasp of the modern .NET landscape and some of the cool new features in C# 13, let's take a closer look at the real muscle behind .NET 9: its extensive set of core libraries and APIs. Think of these as your incredibly well-stocked toolbox, providing pre-built components and functionalities that allow you to accomplish a vast array of tasks without having to write everything from scratch. Understanding these core libraries is absolutely essential because they are the foundation upon which you'll build your high-performance, cross-platform applications.

3.1 Essential .NET 9 Base Class Libraries

Alright, let's really get into the foundational building blocks that .NET 9 offers us: its Base Class Libraries (BCL). Think of the BCL as an incredibly vast and well-organized toolkit that provides pre-built components for almost any task you can conceive of in software development. It's like having a team of expert developers who have already written and tested a massive amount of code, just waiting for you to use it in your applications. Understanding the key namespaces and classes within the BCL is absolutely crucial because they form the bedrock upon which you'll construct your modern, high-performance, and cross-platform solutions.

The BCL is structured into namespaces, which act like logical folders that group related types together. This hierarchical organization makes it easier to find the classes and functionalities you need. Let's explore some of the most fundamental namespaces you'll encounter and the essential classes within them.

First up is the System namespace. This is the root namespace and contains fundamental classes and base types that are essential to all .NET applications. You'll find core types like Object (the ultimate base class for all types), value types like Int32, String,

Boolean, DateTime, and many others. It also includes important classes for interacting with the environment, such as Console for command-line input and output, Environment for getting information about the current environment, and Math for mathematical functions.

For instance, if you want to simply print something to the console, you'd use System.Console.WriteLine(). If you need to work with dates and times, you'd use the System.DateTime struct. These are the basic building blocks you'll use in almost every .NET application.

Next, let's talk about the System.IO namespace. As we touched on earlier, this namespace is all about input and output operations, particularly interacting with the file system and data streams. Whether you need to read configuration files, write logs, process user-uploaded data, or work with any kind of data stream, System.IO provides the necessary tools.

Within System.IO, you'll find classes like File and Directory for performing operations on files and directories respectively (e.g., creating, deleting, reading attributes). For working with the contents of files and other data streams, you'll use the abstract Stream class as the foundation. Concrete implementations of Stream include FileStream for accessing files, MemoryStream for working with in-memory data as a stream, BufferedStream for improving performance by buffering data, and NetworkStream for sending and receiving data over a network.

To make working with text-based streams easier, the StreamReader and StreamWriter classes provide methods for reading and writing text with various encodings. For binary data, you'll use BinaryReader and BinaryWriter.

Consider a real-world example: reading a configuration file in JSON format. You might use File.ReadAllText() to get the entire JSON string and then use classes from the System.Text.Json namespace (which we'll discuss later) to deserialize it into C# objects. Or, if you're processing a very large log file, you might use a StreamReader to read it line by line to avoid loading the entire file into memory at once.

Moving on, the System.Net and System.Net.Http namespaces are crucial for building networked applications. System.Net provides lower-level classes for network communication, such as IPAddress, IPEndPoint, Dns, TcpListener, and Socket. These classes allow you to work directly with network protocols like TCP/IP and UDP.

However, for most modern applications that need to interact with web services and APIs, the System.Net.Http namespace and the HttpClient class are your primary tools. HttpClient simplifies making HTTP requests (GET, POST, PUT, DELETE, etc.) and handling responses. It's designed to work asynchronously using the async and await keywords, ensuring your application remains responsive while waiting for network operations to complete. You can set headers, handle different content types, and process the response data easily with HttpClient.

Imagine building a mobile application that needs to fetch the latest news headlines from a web API. You would use HttpClient to make an HTTP GET request to the API endpoint, receive the JSON or XML response, and then parse it to display the headlines to the user.

For handling data, the System.Collections and System.Collections.Generic namespaces are indispensable. System.Collections provides basic collection interfaces and classes like ArrayList and HashTable (though these are generally less type-safe than their generic counterparts). The real power lies in System.Collections.Generic, which introduces strongly-typed generic collections like List<T>, Dictionary<TKey, TValue>, HashSet<T>, and many others. Generics provide type safety at compile time and often offer better performance than non-generic collections.

For instance, if you need to store a list of customer objects, you would typically use List<Customer>. If you need to map customer IDs to their names, Dictionary<int, string> would be a suitable choice. These generic collections are fundamental for organizing and manipulating data efficiently in your .NET applications.

The System.Linq (Language Integrated Query) namespace provides a powerful and expressive way to query and manipulate data from various sources, including collections, databases, and XML. LINQ introduces a set of extension methods that allow you to perform operations like filtering, sorting, grouping, and transforming data using a consistent syntax, whether you're working with in-memory collections or external data sources. We'll explore LINQ in more detail in a later section.

For handling text, the System.Text namespace provides classes for encoding and decoding text (e.g., UTF8Encoding), working with regular expressions (Regex in System.Text.RegularExpressions), and more recently, high-performance types for text manipulation like StringBuilder and Span<char>.

For working with structured data formats, the System.Xml namespace provides classes for reading, writing, and manipulating XML data. For modern web applications and data exchange, the System.Text.Json namespace offers high-performance and efficient classes for serializing and deserializing JSON data.

Finally, for building responsive and concurrent applications, the System.Threading and System.Threading.Tasks namespaces are essential. As discussed earlier, these provide classes for working with threads, asynchronous operations (async and await), and higher-level abstractions like the Task Parallel Library (TPL) for parallel execution.

This is just a glimpse into the vastness of the .NET 9 Base Class Libraries. As you build more applications, you'll become more familiar with the specific namespaces and classes that are relevant to your needs. The BCL is a testament to the power and versatility of the .NET platform, providing a solid foundation for building almost any kind of application you can imagine, all while benefiting from a consistent and well-designed set of APIs.

Working with File I/O

Almost every application needs to interact with the file system in some way, whether it's reading configuration files, writing logs, or processing user data. The System.IO namespace in the BCL provides a rich set of classes for performing file and directory operations.

For basic file operations, you'll often use the static methods of the File class. Need to read all text from a file? File.ReadAllText(filePath) has you covered. Want to write all text to a file? File.WriteAllText(filePath, content) is your friend. These methods are convenient for simple scenarios.

For more control over file operations, especially when dealing with large files or when you need to process data sequentially, you'll use streams. The Stream class is the abstract base class for all streams in .NET. Concrete implementations like FileStream (for file access), MemoryStream (for working with data in memory as a stream), and NetworkStream (for network communication) provide the actual mechanisms for reading and writing data.

Here's a simple example of reading lines from a text file using a StreamReader, which provides a convenient way to read text from a stream:

```csharp
C#

using System;

using System.IO;

using System.Threading.Tasks;
```

```csharp
public class FileIOExample

{

    public static async Task
ReadLinesFromFileAsync(string filePath)

    {

        try

        {

            using (StreamReader reader = new
StreamReader(filePath))

            {

                string? line;

                while ((line = await
reader.ReadLineAsync()) != null)

                {

                    Console.WriteLine($"Read
line: {line}");

                }

            }

        }

        catch (FileNotFoundException)

        {
```

```csharp
            Console.WriteLine($"Error: File not
found at '{filePath}'");

        }

        catch (IOException ex)

        {

            Console.WriteLine($"An I/O error
occurred: {ex.Message}");

        }

    }


    public static async Task
WriteLinesToFileAsync(string filePath, string[]
lines)

    {

        try

        {

            await
File.WriteAllLinesAsync(filePath, lines);

            Console.WriteLine($"Wrote
{lines.Length} lines to '{filePath}'");

        }

        catch (IOException ex)

        {
```

```
        Console.WriteLine($"An I/O error
occurred while writing: {ex.Message}");

        }

    }


    public static async Task Main(string[] args)

    {

        string filePath = "example.txt";

        string[] linesToWrite = { "First line.",
"Second line.", "Third line." };

        await WriteLinesToFileAsync(filePath,
linesToWrite);

        await ReadLinesFromFileAsync(filePath);

    }

}
```

This example demonstrates basic asynchronous file reading and writing using StreamReader and File.WriteAllLinesAsync. The System.IO namespace is your go-to for any file system interactions in your .NET 9 applications.

Networking Fundamentals

Modern applications often need to communicate over a network, whether it's fetching data from a web API, interacting with a database server, or communicating with other services. The System.Net.Http namespace provides the HttpClient class, which is a fundamental tool for making HTTP requests.

As we saw earlier, HttpClient supports various HTTP methods (GET, POST, PUT, DELETE, etc.) and allows you to send and receive data over the internet. It's designed to be used with async and await for non-blocking operations, making your applications responsive even when dealing with network latency.

For lower-level network communication, the System.Net.Sockets namespace provides classes like Socket, which allows you to work directly with network sockets for TCP/IP or UDP communication. This is often used when building custom network protocols or interacting with services that don't use standard HTTP.

Here's a simple example of making an HTTP GET request using HttpClient:

C#

```csharp
using System;

using System.Net.Http;

using System.Threading.Tasks;

using System.Text.Json;


public class NetworkingExample

{

    public static async Task
GetWeatherDataAsync(string city)

    {

        string apiKey = "YOUR_API_KEY"; //
Replace with a real API key
```

```csharp
        string apiUrl =
$"https://api.weatherapi.com/v1/current.json?key=
{apiKey}&q={city}&aqi=no";


        using (HttpClient client = new
HttpClient())
        {
            try
            {
                HttpResponseMessage response =
await client.GetAsync(apiUrl);

response.EnsureSuccessStatusCode();
                string jsonResult = await
response.Content.ReadAsStringAsync();

                Console.WriteLine($"Weather data
for {city}:\n{jsonResult.Substring(0, 300)}...");
// Print first 300 chars

                // You would typically
deserialize this JSON into C# objects using
System.Text.Json

                // WeatherData data =
JsonSerializer.Deserialize<WeatherData>(jsonResul
t);

                //
Console.WriteLine($"Temperature:
{data?.Current?.Temp_C}°C");
```

```csharp
            }

            catch (HttpRequestException ex)

            {

                Console.WriteLine($"Error
fetching weather data: {ex.Message}");

            }

            catch (TaskCanceledException)

            {

                Console.WriteLine("Request timed
out.");

            }

        }

    }


    public static async Task Main(string[] args)

    {

        await GetWeatherDataAsync("London");

    }

}


// You would define C# classes (like WeatherData,
Current) to match the JSON structure
```

```
// for proper deserialization.
```

This example demonstrates a basic HTTP GET request to a weather API. Remember to replace "YOUR_API_KEY" with a real API key to make it work. The System.Net.Http namespace is crucial for building applications that interact with web services and APIs.

Threading and Synchronization Primitives

In modern, high-performance applications, you often need to perform multiple operations concurrently to improve responsiveness and utilize system resources effectively. The System.Threading and System.Threading.Tasks namespaces provide powerful tools for working with threads and asynchronous operations.

We've already discussed async and await from System.Threading.Tasks. For more fine-grained control over threads, the System.Threading namespace provides classes like Thread, Mutex, Semaphore, and Monitor for managing thread creation, synchronization, and preventing race conditions when multiple threads access shared resources.

However, directly managing threads can be complex and error-prone. For many common scenarios, the Task Parallel Library (TPL), also found in System.Threading.Tasks, provides higher-level abstractions like Task.Run, Parallel.For, and Parallel.ForEach that make parallel programming much easier.

Here's a simple example of using Parallel.ForEach to process a list of items in parallel:

```csharp
C#

using System;

using System.Collections.Generic;
```

```csharp
using System.Threading.Tasks;


public class ParallelProcessingExample

{

    public static void ProcessItem(int item)

    {

        Console.WriteLine($"Processing item
{item} on thread
{System.Threading.Thread.CurrentThread.ManagedThr
eadId}");

        // Simulate some work

        Task.Delay(100).Wait();

    }


    public static void Main(string[] args)

    {

        List<int> items = new List<int> { 1, 2,
3, 4, 5, 6, 7, 8, 9, 10 };

        Console.WriteLine("Starting parallel
processing...");

        Parallel.ForEach(items, ProcessItem);

        Console.WriteLine("Parallel processing
complete.");
```

```
        }

    }
```

When you run this, you'll likely see the output from ProcessItem interleaved, indicating that the items are being processed on different threads concurrently. The System.Threading.Tasks namespace is essential for building responsive and efficient applications that can take advantage of multi-core processors.

3.2 Mastering Generics and Collections for Efficiency

Alright, let's talk about a fundamental aspect of writing efficient and well-structured code in .NET 9: generics and collections. Think of collections as ways to organize and manage groups of objects, and generics as a powerful feature that allows you to create code that can work with different types in a type-safe and efficient manner. Mastering these concepts is crucial because almost every application deals with collections of data in some form.

Let's start with generics. Before generics were introduced in C# 2.0, you had collections like ArrayList that could hold objects of any type. While this offered flexibility, it came at a cost: you lost type safety at compile time, and you often had to perform manual casting when retrieving objects from the collection, which could lead to runtime errors and performance overhead due to boxing and unboxing (converting between value types and reference types).

Generics solve this problem by allowing you to define type parameters when you create collections or methods. This means you can specify the exact type of objects that a collection will hold. For example, List<string> is a list that can only contain strings, and Dictionary<int, Customer> is a dictionary that maps integers to Customer objects.

This provides several key benefits:

- Type Safety: The compiler enforces the specified type at compile time, preventing you from accidentally adding the wrong type of object to a collection. This catches errors early in the development process.
- Reduced Casting: When you retrieve objects from a generic collection, you don't need to perform explicit casting because the compiler already knows the type of the objects. This makes your code cleaner and less error-prone.
- Improved Performance: For value types, generics often avoid the overhead of boxing and unboxing, which can significantly improve performance when working with collections of numbers, structs, etc.

Let's see a simple example that highlights the benefits of generics:

```csharp
C#

using System;

using System.Collections;

using System.Collections.Generic;


public class GenericsAndCollectionsExample

{

    public static void NonGenericListExample()

    {

        ArrayList numbers = new ArrayList();

        numbers.Add(10);
```

```csharp
        numbers.Add(20);

        numbers.Add("Thirty"); // This compiles,
but will cause a runtime error if we try to treat
it as an int


        int sum = 0;

        foreach (int number in numbers) // This
will throw an InvalidCastException at runtime

        {

            sum += number;

        }

        Console.WriteLine($"Sum (non-generic):
{sum}");

    }


    public static void GenericListExample()

    {

        List<int> numbers = new List<int>();

        numbers.Add(10);

        numbers.Add(20);

        // numbers.Add("Thirty"); // This will
cause a compile-time error
```

```csharp
        int sum = 0;

        foreach (int number in numbers)

        {

            sum += number;

        }

        Console.WriteLine($"Sum (generic):
{sum}"); // Output: Sum (generic): 30

    }


    public static void Main(string[] args)

    {

        // NonGenericListExample(); //
Uncommenting this will cause a runtime error

        GenericListExample();

    }

}
```

As you can see, the generic List<int> catches the type error at compile time, preventing a runtime crash. This type safety is a major advantage.

Now, let's talk about collections themselves. The System.Collections.Generic namespace provides a rich variety of collection types, each designed for different scenarios and offering different performance characteristics. Choosing the right collection type for the task at hand can significantly impact the efficiency of your application.

Here are some of the most commonly used generic collection types:

- List<T>: Represents a dynamically sized list of objects that can be accessed by index. It's similar to an array but can grow or shrink as needed. List<T> provides efficient access to elements by index (O(1)) and is generally a good default choice for ordered collections. Adding or removing elements at the end is also efficient on average (O(1)), but inserting or removing elements in the middle can be slower (O(n)) as it requires shifting subsequent elements.

- Dictionary<TKey, TValue>: Represents a collection of key-value pairs. It provides very efficient lookups of values based on their keys (average O(1)). Dictionary<TKey, TValue> is ideal for scenarios where you need to quickly retrieve a value based on a unique identifier.

- HashSet<T>: Represents a collection of unique elements. It provides efficient operations for adding, removing, and checking for the existence of elements (average O(1)). HashSet<T> is useful when you need to ensure that a collection contains only distinct values and you need to perform set operations like union, intersection, and difference.

- Queue<T>: Represents a first-in, first-out (FIFO) collection. Elements are added to the end of the queue (enqueue) and removed from the beginning (dequeue). Queue<T> is often used for processing tasks in a specific order, like handling requests in a server application. Enqueue and dequeue operations are typically O(1).

- Stack<T>: Represents a last-in, first-out (LIFO) collection. Elements are added to the top of the stack (push) and removed from the top (pop). Stack<T> is used in scenarios like backtracking algorithms or managing function calls. Push and pop operations are typically O(1).

- **LinkedList<T>:** Represents a doubly linked list. Unlike List<T>, elements in a LinkedList<T> are not stored in contiguous memory locations. This makes inserting or removing elements at any position very efficient (O(1)), as it only requires updating the links between nodes. However, accessing an element by index is less efficient (O(n)) as you need to traverse the list from the beginning. LinkedList<T> is useful when you frequently need to insert or remove elements in the middle of a collection.

Choosing the right collection type depends on how you intend to use the collection. For example, if you need to frequently access elements by index, List<T> is a good choice. If you need to quickly look up values based on a key, Dictionary<TKey, TValue> is ideal. If you need to ensure uniqueness and perform set operations, HashSet<T> is the way to go.

Understanding the performance characteristics of different collection types is crucial for writing efficient applications. For instance, repeatedly inserting elements at the beginning of a List<T> can be very inefficient because all subsequent elements need to be shifted. In such a scenario, a LinkedList<T> might be a better choice. Similarly, repeatedly checking for the existence of an element in a List<T> (O(n)) will be much slower than in a HashSet<T> (average O(1)).

Mastering generics and collections in .NET 9 means not only knowing how to use these types but also understanding their underlying mechanisms and performance implications so you can make informed decisions about which collection type is best suited for a given task. This will lead to more efficient and scalable applications.

3.3 LINQ for Efficient Data Querying and Manipulation

Alright, let's explore a truly powerful feature in .NET 9 that will change the way you think about working with data: LINQ (Language Integrated Query). Think of LINQ as a unified way to query and manipulate data from various sources directly within your C# code. Whether you're working with in-memory collections, databases, XML, or even remote data sources, LINQ provides a consistent and expressive syntax to filter, sort, group, and transform your data. Mastering LINQ is essential for writing clean, readable, and often more efficient code when dealing with collections of objects.

Before LINQ, querying data often involved writing specific code for each type of data source. For example, querying a database required writing SQL, while querying an XML document might involve using XML-specific APIs. LINQ unifies this by providing a set of standard query operators that can be applied to any data source that implements the IEnumerable<T> or IEnumerable interface (for in-memory collections) or provides a LINQ provider (for external data sources).

LINQ offers two main syntaxes for writing queries: query syntax (which resembles SQL) and method syntax (which uses extension methods). Both syntaxes are semantically equivalent, and the one you choose often comes down to personal preference or the complexity of the query.

Query Syntax vs. Method Syntax

Let's look at a simple example of filtering a list of numbers to get only the even ones, using both query syntax and method syntax:

```
C#

using System;
```

```csharp
using System.Collections.Generic;

using System.Linq;


public class LINQSyntaxExample

{

    public static void
FilterEvenNumbersQuerySyntax(List<int> numbers)

    {

        var evenNumbers = from number in numbers

                          where number % 2 == 0

                          select number;


        Console.WriteLine("Even numbers (query
syntax):");

        foreach (var number in evenNumbers)

        {

            Console.Write($"{number} ");

        }

        Console.WriteLine();

    }
```

```csharp
    public static void
FilterEvenNumbersMethodSyntax(List<int> numbers)

    {

        var evenNumbers = numbers.Where(number =>
number % 2 == 0);


        Console.WriteLine("Even numbers (method
syntax):");

        foreach (var number in evenNumbers)

        {

            Console.Write($"{number} ");

        }

        Console.WriteLine();

    }


    public static void Main(string[] args)

    {

        List<int> numbers = new List<int> { 1, 2,
3, 4, 5, 6, 7, 8, 9, 10 };

        FilterEvenNumbersQuerySyntax(numbers);

        FilterEvenNumbersMethodSyntax(numbers);

    }
```

}

As you can see, both FilterEvenNumbersQuerySyntax and FilterEvenNumbersMethodSyntax achieve the same result. The query syntax uses keywords like from, where, and select, which might feel familiar if you've worked with SQL. The method syntax uses extension methods like Where() (which takes a lambda expression as a predicate to filter the elements).

For more complex queries involving multiple operations, you can chain LINQ extension methods together in method syntax, often leading to a more fluent and readable style. Query syntax, on the other hand, can be more intuitive for simple filtering, sorting, and joining operations.

Let's consider a more involved example where we filter a list of products based on their category and then select their names, using both syntaxes:

```
C#

using System;

using System.Collections.Generic;

using System.Linq;


public class Product

{

    public string Name { get; set; }

    public string Category { get; set; }

    public decimal Price { get; set; }
```

```csharp
    }


public class LINQComplexSyntaxExample
{
    public static void
GetBookNamesQuerySyntax(List<Product> products)
    {
        var bookNames = from product in products
                        where product.Category ==
"Book"
                        select product.Name;


        Console.WriteLine("Book names (query
syntax):");
        foreach (var name in bookNames)
        {
            Console.WriteLine(name);
        }
    }


    public static void
GetBookNamesMethodSyntax(List<Product> products)
```

```csharp
    {
        var bookNames = products.Where(product =>
product.Category == "Book")

                                .Select(product
=> product.Name);


        Console.WriteLine("Book names (method
syntax):");

        foreach (var name in bookNames)

        {

            Console.WriteLine(name);

        }

    }


    public static void Main(string[] args)

    {

        List<Product> products = new
List<Product>

        {

            new Product { Name = "The Lord of the
Rings", Category = "Book", Price = 25.99m },

            new Product { Name = "Samsung TV",
Category = "Electronics", Price = 1200.00m },
```

```
            new Product { Name = "Clean Code",
Category = "Book", Price = 39.99m },

            new Product { Name = "Wireless
Mouse", Category = "Electronics", Price = 29.99m
}

        };


        GetBookNamesQuerySyntax(products);

        GetBookNamesMethodSyntax(products);

    }

}
```

Both syntaxes achieve the same outcome. As you become more comfortable with LINQ, you'll likely find yourself using a mix of both, choosing the syntax that feels most natural and readable for a particular query.

Performance Considerations with LINQ

While LINQ provides a powerful and expressive way to work with data, it's important to be aware of potential performance implications. Because LINQ often uses deferred execution (meaning the query is not executed until you actually iterate over the results), it can sometimes lead to unexpected behavior or performance issues if you're not careful.

One common pitfall is performing multiple iterations over a LINQ query without realizing it. If the underlying data source is expensive to access (e.g., a database query), iterating multiple times can lead to unnecessary overhead. To avoid this, you can use methods like ToList(), ToArray(), or ToDictionary() to execute the query immediately and store the results in an in-memory collection if you need to iterate over them multiple times.

Consider this example:

C#

```
using System;

using System.Collections.Generic;

using System.Linq;


public class LINQPerformanceExample

{

    public static IEnumerable<int>
GetExpensiveNumbers()

    {

        Console.WriteLine("Fetching expensive
numbers...");

        // Simulate an expensive operation

        for (int i = 0; i < 5; i++)

        {

            System.Threading.Thread.Sleep(500);

            yield return i;

        }

    }
```

```csharp
public static void
ProcessNumbersMultipleTimes()

    {

        var expensiveNumbers =
GetExpensiveNumbers().Where(n => n % 2 == 0);


        Console.WriteLine("First iteration:");

        foreach (var number in expensiveNumbers)

        {

            Console.WriteLine(number);

        }


        Console.WriteLine("Second iteration:");

        foreach (var number in expensiveNumbers)
// GetExpensiveNumbers() is executed again!

        {

            Console.WriteLine(number);

        }


        var cachedNumbers =
GetExpensiveNumbers().Where(n => n % 2 ==
0).ToList();
```

```csharp
        Console.WriteLine("First iteration
(cached):");

        foreach (var number in cachedNumbers)

        {

            Console.WriteLine(number);

        }


        Console.WriteLine("Second iteration
(cached):");

        foreach (var number in cachedNumbers) //
Cached results are used

        {

            Console.WriteLine(number);

        }

    }


    public static void Main(string[] args)

    {

        ProcessNumbersMultipleTimes();

    }

}
```

In this example, GetExpensiveNumbers() simulates an operation that takes time. When we iterate over the expensiveNumbers LINQ query multiple times without caching the results, GetExpensiveNumbers() is executed each time. By using ToList(), we execute the query once and store the results in memory, making subsequent iterations much faster.

Another performance consideration is the efficient use of LINQ operators. Some operators might be more efficient than others depending on the underlying data source. For example, when working with databases through LINQ to Entities or LINQ to SQL, the LINQ provider translates your LINQ query into SQL, and the efficiency of the generated SQL will depend on how well your LINQ query is structured.

It's also important to be mindful of the order of operations in your LINQ queries. Filtering data early in the pipeline can often reduce the amount of data that subsequent operations need to process, leading to better performance.

For example, if you have a large list and you only need the first 10 items that meet a certain condition, using Where(...).Take(10) will be more efficient than Take(10).Where(...) (as the latter would potentially process the first 10 items regardless of whether they meet the condition).

3.4 Understanding and Implementing Dependency Injection

Alright, let's talk about a fundamental design pattern in modern software development, and one that's deeply integrated into .NET 9: Dependency Injection (DI). Think of DI as a way to make your code more flexible, testable, and maintainable by managing the dependencies between different parts of your application in a structured way. Understanding and implementing DI effectively is a key skill for building robust and scalable software.

At its core, dependency injection is about how objects receive the other objects that they depend on. Instead of an object creating its own dependencies, or statically knowing about its dependencies, these dependencies are "injected" into the object from the outside. This inversion of control (IoC) – where the responsibility of creating dependencies is shifted from the object itself to an external entity – is the key principle behind DI.

Let's consider a real-world analogy. Imagine you have a coffee maker that needs coffee beans to make coffee. In a system without dependency injection, the coffee maker might be tightly coupled to a specific brand of coffee beans, or it might have to go out and get the beans itself. This makes it difficult to use different types of beans or to test the coffee maker without actually having coffee beans.

Now, with dependency injection, instead of the coffee maker worrying about where the beans come from, the beans are "injected" into it. Someone else (the dependency injection container, in software terms) is responsible for providing the coffee maker with the beans it needs. This makes the coffee maker more flexible – you can easily use different types of beans simply by providing them. It also makes it easier to test – you can provide mock coffee beans to test the coffee maker's logic without actually brewing coffee.

In software, dependencies are typically other classes or services that an object needs to function. For example, a UserService might depend on a UserRepository to access user data from a database, and it might also depend on an EmailService to send emails.

Without dependency injection, the UserService might directly create instances of UserRepository and EmailService within its own code:

C#

```csharp
public class UserRepository

{

    public User GetUserById(int id)

    {

        // Code to access database

        return new User { Id = id, Name = "Test
User" };

    }

}


public class EmailService

{

    public void SendWelcomeEmail(User user)

    {

        // Code to send email

        Console.WriteLine($"Sending welcome email
to {user.Name}");

    }

}


public class UserServiceWithoutDI
```

```csharp
{
    private readonly UserRepository
_userRepository;

    private readonly EmailService _emailService;


    public UserServiceWithoutDI()
    {
        _userRepository = new UserRepository();

        _emailService = new EmailService();

    }


    public void CreateUser(int id, string name)
    {
        User user = new User { Id = id, Name =
name };

        _userRepository.AddUser(user); // Assume
AddUser exists

        _emailService.SendWelcomeEmail(user);

    }


    // ... other methods

}
```

The problem with this approach is that UserServiceWithoutDI is tightly coupled to concrete implementations of UserRepository and EmailService.

This makes it difficult to:

- Test UserServiceWithoutDI in isolation: To test UserServiceWithoutDI, you would also need to have a real UserRepository (potentially interacting with a database) and a real EmailService (potentially sending emails). This makes unit testing difficult and slow.
- Reuse UserServiceWithoutDI with different implementations: If you wanted to use a different data access mechanism (e.g., a different database or a mock repository for testing) or a different email sending service, you would have to modify the UserServiceWithoutDI class itself.
- Understand the dependencies of UserServiceWithoutDI: You have to examine the constructor to understand what other components UserServiceWithoutDI relies on.

Dependency injection solves these problems by introducing an interface-based approach and an external mechanism for providing these dependencies:

C#

```
public interface IUserRepository

{

    User GetUserById(int id);

    void AddUser(User user);

}
```

```csharp
public class SqlUserRepository : IUserRepository

{

    public User GetUserById(int id)

    {

        // Code to access SQL database

        return new User { Id = id, Name = "SQL
User" };

    }


    public void AddUser(User user)

    {

        // Code to add user to SQL database

    }

}


public interface IEmailService

{

    void SendWelcomeEmail(User user);

}


public class SmtpEmailService : IEmailService
```

```csharp
{
    public void SendWelcomeEmail(User user)

    {
        // Code to send email via SMTP

        Console.WriteLine($"Sending welcome email
via SMTP to {user.Name}");

    }

}


public class UserServiceWithDI

{
    private readonly IUserRepository
_userRepository;

    private readonly IEmailService _emailService;


    // Dependencies are injected through the
constructor

    public UserServiceWithDI(IUserRepository
userRepository, IEmailService emailService)

    {
        _userRepository = userRepository;

        _emailService = emailService;
```

```
    }


    public void CreateUser(int id, string name)

    {

        User user = new User { Id = id, Name =
name };

        _userRepository.AddUser(user);

        _emailService.SendWelcomeEmail(user);

    }


    // ... other methods

}
```

In this DI-enabled version:
- We define interfaces (IUserRepository, IEmailService) that specify the contracts for the dependencies.
- UserServiceWithDI depends on these interfaces rather than concrete implementations.
- The dependencies (IUserRepository and IEmailService instances) are provided to UserServiceWithDI through its constructor.

Now, an external component (the dependency injection container) is responsible for creating and providing the concrete implementations (e.g., SqlUserRepository, SmtpEmailService) to UserServiceWithDI.

Built-in DI Container in .NET 9

.NET 9 comes with a built-in, lightweight dependency injection container that makes it easy to manage dependencies in your applications, especially in ASP.NET Core and other modern .NET application models. This container provides a way to register your services (interfaces and their concrete implementations) and then resolve (create instances of) them when they are needed.

The primary interface for interacting with the DI container is IServiceCollection. You typically configure your services in the ConfigureServices method of your Startup.cs file (in ASP.NET Core) or in a similar setup mechanism in other .NET host builders.

Here's how you might register the dependencies from our UserServiceWithDI example using the built-in DI container:

C#

```
using Microsoft.Extensions.DependencyInjection;


public class Startup

{

    public static ServiceProvider
ConfigureServices()

    {

        var services = new ServiceCollection();


        // Register the concrete implementations
for the interfaces
```

```csharp
        services.AddScoped<IUserRepository,
SqlUserRepository>();

        services.AddTransient<IEmailService,
SmtpEmailService>();

        services.AddScoped<UserServiceWithDI>();
// UserService depends on the registered services


        return services.BuildServiceProvider();

    }


    public static void Main(string[] args)

    {

        var serviceProvider =
ConfigureServices();


        // Resolve an instance of
UserServiceWithDI, its dependencies will be
automatically injected

        var userService =
serviceProvider.GetService<UserServiceWithDI>();

        userService?.CreateUser(123, "Charlie");

    }

}
```

In this ConfigureServices method:

- We create a new ServiceCollection.
- We register SqlUserRepository as the concrete implementation for IUserRepository with a Scoped lifetime (meaning one instance is created per scope, e.g., per web request).
- We register SmtpEmailService as the concrete implementation for IEmailService with a Transient lifetime (meaning a new instance is created every time it's requested).
- We register UserServiceWithDI. The DI container will automatically resolve its dependencies (IUserRepository and IEmailService) when an instance of UserServiceWithDI is requested.
- We build a ServiceProvider from the ServiceCollection, which is the actual DI container.
- In Main, we use GetService<UserServiceWithDI>() to resolve an instance of UserServiceWithDI. The container will automatically create an instance of SqlUserRepository and SmtpEmailService and inject them into the constructor of UserServiceWithDI.

Service Lifetimes (Singleton, Scoped, Transient)

When registering services with the DI container, you specify their lifetime. The lifetime determines how long an instance of the service will live and how many instances will be created.

The built-in DI container in .NET 9 supports three main lifetimes:

- Transient: A new instance of the service is created every time it's requested from the container. Transient services are lightweight and stateless. Our IEmailService was registered as transient, meaning a new SmtpEmailService instance will be created each time UserServiceWithDI (or any other service)

3.5 Logging and Configuration in Modern .NET Applications

Alright, let's talk about two essential aspects of building robust and manageable modern .NET applications: logging and configuration. Think of logging as your application's way of keeping a record of what's happening, providing valuable insights for debugging, monitoring, and understanding its behavior. Configuration, on the other hand, is about how your application reads and uses settings that can change depending on the environment or specific needs, without requiring you to modify the code itself. Mastering these two areas is crucial for building applications that are not only functional but also observable and adaptable.

Let's start with logging. When your application is running, especially in a production environment, you often need a way to track events, errors, warnings, and informational messages. This record, or log, can be invaluable for diagnosing problems, understanding user behavior, monitoring performance, and ensuring the health of your application. Modern .NET provides a flexible and extensible logging framework built right in.

The core of the .NET logging framework revolves around the Microsoft.Extensions.Logging namespace. The central interfaces you'll interact with are ILoggerFactory and ILogger.

The ILoggerFactory is responsible for creating ILogger instances. You typically configure logging providers (the actual systems that write the logs, like console, file, or external services) through the ILoggerFactory. In modern .NET applications, especially those built using the .NET Generic Host (like ASP.NET Core, worker services, and console applications using the host builder), the ILoggerFactory is usually configured during the application startup process.

The ILogger<T> interface represents a logger that can write log messages. The generic type parameter T is typically the type of the class where the logger is being used. This provides contextual information in the logs, making it easier to trace the origin of a log message. You obtain an ILogger<T> instance through dependency injection. If you've been following along, you'll remember how DI works – you declare an ILogger<YourClassName> as a constructor parameter, and the .NET DI container will automatically provide an instance for you.

Here's a basic example of how to use logging in a class:

```csharp
C#

using Microsoft.Extensions.Logging;

using System;


public class UserService

{

    private readonly ILogger<UserService>
_logger;


    public UserService(ILogger<UserService>
logger)

    {

        _logger = logger;

    }
```

```csharp
    public bool CreateUser(string username,
string password)

    {

        _logger.LogInformation($"Attempting to
create user: {username}");


        if (string.IsNullOrEmpty(username) ||
string.IsNullOrEmpty(password))

        {

            _logger.LogWarning($"Username or
password cannot be empty for user: {username}");

            return false;

        }


        // Simulate user creation logic

        bool success = true;

        if (success)

        {

            _logger.LogInformation($"User
'{username}' created successfully.");

            // ... further logic

            return true;

        }
```

```csharp
        else

        {

            _logger.LogError($"Failed to create
user '{username}'.");

            return false;

        }

    }


    public User GetUser(int id)

    {

        _logger.LogDebug($"Getting user with ID:
{id}");

        // Simulate fetching user from database

        return new User { Id = id, Username =
"testuser" };

    }

}


public class User

{

    public int Id { get; set; }

    public string Username { get; set; }
```

```
}
```

In this UserService class, we inject an ILogger<UserService> instance through the constructor. Then, within the CreateUser and GetUser methods, we use the logger to write messages at different log levels: LogInformation, LogWarning, LogError, and LogDebug. These log levels indicate the severity and type of the message.

Common log levels, in increasing order of severity, include:

- Trace: Very detailed messages, often used for development debugging.
- Debug: Information helpful for development debugging.
- Information: General informational messages about the application's operation.
- Warning: Indicates potential problems or non-critical errors.
- Error: Indicates an error that might not stop the application from running but should be investigated.
- Critical: Indicates a severe error that might cause the application to terminate.

The configuration of the ILoggerFactory determines which log levels are actually written to the configured logging providers. For example, in a production environment, you might only want to log Warning, Error, and Critical messages to avoid excessive logging.

Modern .NET applications often use a standard logging configuration mechanism, typically set up in the Program.cs or Startup.cs file when the host is being built. This configuration allows you to specify which logging providers to use (e.g., Console, Debug, EventLog, or third-party providers like Serilog or NLog) and the minimum log level for each provider.

Now, let's move on to configuration. Modern applications rarely have all their settings hardcoded. Instead, they rely on external configuration sources that can be easily changed without recompiling the application. This is especially important when deploying to different environments (development, staging, production) or when you need to adjust settings like database connection strings, API keys, or feature flags.

.NET provides a flexible configuration system built on top of the Microsoft.Extensions.Configuration namespace. This system supports various configuration sources, allowing you to read settings from different formats and locations.

Some common configuration sources include:

- appsettings.json and appsettings.{Environment}.json: These are JSON files that are the standard way to configure .NET applications. appsettings.json contains default settings, while environment-specific files (e.g., appsettings.Development.json, appsettings.Production.json) can override these defaults based on the current environment.
- Environment variables: Operating system environment variables can be used to configure applications, often used for sensitive information or cloud deployments.
- Command-line arguments: You can pass configuration values as command-line arguments when running the application.
- User secrets: For development environments, user secrets provide a secure way to store sensitive settings like API keys without checking them into source control.
- Azure Key Vault, AWS Secrets Manager, etc.: For cloud-based applications, you can use dedicated secret management services.

The .NET configuration system reads these configuration sources and merges them based on a defined order (e.g., environment-specific appsettings.json overrides appsettings.json, and environment variables can override both). You can then access these configuration values in your code using the IConfiguration interface, which is typically injected through dependency injection, just like ILogger.

Here's a basic example of reading configuration from appsettings.json:

First, create an appsettings.json file in your project:

JSON

```json
{

  "Logging": {

    "LogLevel": {

      "Default": "Information",

      "Microsoft": "Warning",

      "Microsoft.Hosting.Lifetime": "Information"

    }

  },

  "ConnectionStrings": {

    "DefaultConnection":
"Server=(localdb)\\mssqllocaldb;Database=MyAppDb;
Trusted_Connection=True;"

  },

  "ApiSettings": {

    "ApiKey": "your_api_key_here",

    "ApiUrl": "https://api.example.com"
```

```
    }

}
```

Then, in your code:

```csharp
using Microsoft.Extensions.Configuration;

using Microsoft.Extensions.DependencyInjection;

using Microsoft.Extensions.Logging;

using System;

using System.IO;


public class AppSettingsExample

{

    private readonly IConfiguration
_configuration;

    private readonly ILogger<AppSettingsExample>
_logger;


    public AppSettingsExample(IConfiguration
configuration, ILogger<AppSettingsExample>
logger)

    {

        _configuration = configuration;
```

```csharp
        _logger = logger;

    }


    public void ReadSettings()

    {

        _logger.LogInformation("Reading
application settings...");


        string? connectionString =
_configuration.GetConnectionString("DefaultConnec
tion");

        _logger.LogInformation(<span
class="math-inline">"Connection String\:
\{connectionString\}"\);</4\>

string? apiKey \=
\_configuration\["ApiSettings\:ApiKey"\];

string? apiUrl \=
\_configuration\["ApiSettings\:ApiUrl"\];

\_logger\.LogInformation\(</span>"API Key:
{apiKey}");

        _logger.LogInformation(<span
class="math-inline">"API URL\: \{apiUrl\}"\);

string? defaultLogLevel \=
\_configuration\["Logging\:LogLevel\:Default"\];
```

```
_logger\.LogInformation\(</span>"Default Log
Level: {defaultLogLevel}");

    }


    public static void Main(string[] args)

    {

        // Setup configuration

        var builder = new ConfigurationBuilder()

.SetBasePath(Directory.GetCurrentDirectory())

            .AddJsonFile("appsettings.json",
optional: false, reloadOnChange: true);


        IConfiguration configuration =
builder.Build();


        // Setup logging

        var serviceProvider = new
ServiceCollection()

            .AddSingleton(configuration)

            .AddLogging(loggingBuilder =>
loggingBuilder.AddConsole())

            .AddTransient
```

Logging and configuration are fundamental pillars of modern .NET applications. The built-in logging framework provides a standardized way to record events and messages, crucial for monitoring and debugging. The flexible configuration system allows you to manage application settings from various sources, adapting your application to different environments without code changes. Mastering these systems will enable you to build more robust, observable, and adaptable .NET 9 applications.

Chapter 4: Understanding Performance in Modern .NET

Alright, let's shift gears and talk about something that's absolutely critical for creating great modern applications: **performance**. Think of performance as how efficiently your application uses resources like CPU, memory, and network bandwidth to get the job done quickly and smoothly. In today's fast-paced digital landscape, users have little patience for sluggish or unresponsive software. Understanding what "high-performance" means in different contexts and knowing how to identify and address performance bottlenecks is a key skill for any .NET developer.

4.1 Defining "High-Performance" for Different Application Types

Alright, let's really pin down what we mean by "high-performance" in the context of modern .NET applications. It's not a singular, absolute measure; instead, it's a concept that's deeply intertwined with the specific kind of application you're building and what its users expect. Think of it like defining what makes a car "high-performing" – a sports car will have different performance metrics than a pickup truck, even though both might be considered high-performing in their respective categories. The key is understanding the primary goals and constraints of your application type.

Let's consider web applications and APIs first. When someone interacts with a website or an application that relies on a backend API, they generally expect quick responses. For these types of applications, high performance often boils down to low latency and high throughput.

Low latency means that the time it takes for the server to respond to a request should be minimal.[1] If a webpage takes several seconds to load or an API endpoint takes a long time to return data, users are likely to become frustrated and abandon the application.[2] For example, in an e-commerce website, if the product listing page takes more than a couple of seconds to load, potential customers might navigate away.[3] Similarly, if an API that powers a mobile application is slow, the mobile app will feel sluggish and unresponsive.

High throughput refers to the ability of the server to handle a large number of concurrent requests without a significant degradation in response time. A highly performing API should be able to serve many users simultaneously without becoming overloaded.[4] Think about a popular social media platform during peak usage times; its backend APIs need to handle millions of requests per second while still maintaining acceptable response times. If the throughput is low, the platform might become slow or even crash under heavy load.

Now, let's look at desktop applications. Here, the focus of high performance often shifts towards responsiveness and smooth user interaction. Users expect the application to react quickly to their actions, whether it's clicking buttons, scrolling through lists, or performing complex operations. Operations that might take some time, like loading large files or performing intensive computations, should ideally be done in a way that doesn't freeze the user interface.

Consider a word processing application. When a user types, the text should appear on the screen instantly. If the application becomes sluggish or unresponsive, the user experience will be poor.[5] Similarly, when opening a large document or performing a complex formatting operation, the application should ideally provide feedback (like a progress bar) and complete the task in a reasonable amount of time without locking up.

For mobile applications, the definition of high performance includes not only responsiveness and speed but also energy efficiency.[6] Mobile devices have limited battery life, so an application that consumes excessive resources will quickly drain the battery and lead to a negative user experience. High-performing mobile apps are optimized to use minimal CPU and memory, perform operations efficiently, and avoid unnecessary background activity.[7]

Think about a navigation application. It needs to continuously track the user's location, update the map, and provide directions, all while consuming as little battery as possible. A poorly optimized navigation app could quickly drain the phone's battery, making it unusable for extended periods.

In the real-time application space, such as online gaming or financial trading platforms, the performance demands are often the most stringent. Here, extremely low latency and high throughput are critical. Even small delays can have significant consequences.[8] In a fast-paced online game, a delay of even a few milliseconds can mean the difference between winning and losing. In financial trading, delays in receiving market data or executing trades can lead to missed opportunities or financial losses.[9] These applications often require highly optimized code and network communication to meet these demanding performance requirements.

Finally, consider background services and data processing applications. These might not have a direct user interface, but their performance is still crucial. For these types of applications, high performance often means completing tasks efficiently and within acceptable timeframes, while also minimizing resource consumption (CPU, memory, disk I/O). For example, a service that processes a large batch of data overnight needs to be optimized to finish within the allotted time window and without consuming excessive server resources that could impact other services.

As you can see, the definition of "high-performance" is not universal. When you embark on optimizing your .NET 9 application, the very first step is to clearly understand the specific performance goals and requirements driven by the type of application you are building and the expectations of its users. What makes a high-performing web API will be different from what makes a high-performing mobile game, even though both are built using .NET. Understanding this context will guide your optimization efforts and help you focus on the metrics that truly matter for your specific scenario.

4.2 Identifying Common Performance Bottlenecks

Alright, now that we have a sense of what "high-performance" means in different contexts, the next logical step is to understand where performance problems often arise in .NET applications. These problem areas are commonly referred to as bottlenecks. Think of a bottleneck as the narrowest part of a pipe – it's the point that restricts the overall flow, even if the rest of the pipe is wide open. In your application, a performance bottleneck is a specific section of code or a system resource that limits the overall speed and efficiency. Identifying these bottlenecks is the crucial first step towards optimizing your application.

Let's explore some of the most frequent culprits behind performance issues in .NET applications.

One very common type of bottleneck is related to CPU-bound operations. These are tasks where the processor is the primary limiting factor. If your application is spending a significant amount of time performing complex calculations, manipulating large datasets in memory without significant I/O, encoding or decoding media, or running intricate algorithms directly on the CPU, it might become unresponsive, especially if these operations are happening on the main thread.

Consider a real-world example: a financial analysis application that needs to perform complex statistical calculations on a large portfolio of stock data. If these calculations are done synchronously on the user interface thread, the application will likely freeze until the computations are complete, leading to a frustrating user experience.

How do you recognize a CPU-bound bottleneck? Often, you'll observe high CPU utilization in your system's performance monitoring tools (like Task Manager on Windows or Activity Monitor on macOS) while the application is performing the slow operation. The application might feel sluggish or unresponsive, even if disk or network activity is low.

Another frequent source of performance issues lies in memory-bound operations. These are tasks where the application's performance is primarily limited by how it uses memory. This can manifest in several ways, such as excessive memory allocation, inefficient use of data structures leading to frequent lookups or manipulations, or, very commonly in .NET, excessive garbage collection. When your application allocates a lot of memory rapidly, the .NET garbage collector has to run more frequently to reclaim that memory. While garbage collection is automatic and generally efficient, frequent or long-duration garbage collection cycles can pause your application's execution, leading to noticeable slowdowns or stuttering, especially in user-facing applications.

Think about an image processing application that loads many large images into memory simultaneously or creates numerous temporary image objects during processing. This can put significant pressure on the memory and trigger frequent garbage collections, making the application feel slow.

How do you spot memory-bound bottlenecks? You might see high overall memory usage by your application in system monitoring tools. More specifically, you can use .NET-specific performance counters or profiling tools to observe the frequency and duration of garbage collection cycles. A high number of collections, especially full collections (Gen 2), or long collection times can indicate a memory-related bottleneck.

Then we have I/O-bound operations. These are tasks where your application spends most of its time waiting for input or output operations to complete. Common examples include reading from or writing to files on disk, making requests to databases, or communicating over a network. While the CPU might not be heavily utilized during these wait times, performing these operations synchronously (blocking the current thread) can severely limit the throughput and responsiveness of your application. If a thread is blocked waiting for the disk or a database, it can't do other work, like handling user input or processing other requests.

Consider a web server that needs to read a large file from disk to serve it to a user. If it does this synchronously, the thread handling that request will be blocked until the entire file is read. During this time, that thread cannot handle other incoming user requests, potentially leading to a slow experience for everyone.

How do you identify I/O-bound bottlenecks? You might see low CPU utilization but still experience poor responsiveness or low throughput. The application might be waiting for extended periods. Tools that can monitor disk and network activity can also provide clues. The key to addressing I/O-bound bottlenecks in modern .NET is almost always to use asynchronous programming (async and await), which allows threads to remain free while waiting for I/O operations to complete.

Finally, let's consider network latency. If your application relies on communication over a network, the time it takes for data to travel between your application and remote services can become a significant performance bottleneck. This is especially true for applications that make many network requests or transfer large amounts of data. The physical distance between the communicating parties, network congestion, and the speed of the network infrastructure all contribute to latency.

Think about a mobile application that needs to fetch data from multiple remote APIs to display information to the user. If each API call introduces a noticeable delay, the cumulative effect of these delays can make the application feel slow, even if the processing of the data on the client side is very efficient.

How do you recognize network latency as a bottleneck? You'll often observe long wait times for network operations to complete. Tools that monitor network traffic and the timing of network requests can help pinpoint this. Strategies to mitigate network latency include reducing the number of network requests (e.g., by aggregating data on the server), optimizing the size of data being transferred, using caching to reduce the need for repeated requests, and potentially choosing geographically closer servers.

Understanding these common types of performance bottlenecks – CPU-bound, memory-bound, I/O-bound, and network latency – is the essential first step in diagnosing and addressing performance issues in your .NET 9 applications. Once you have a suspicion about where the bottleneck might be, you can then start using specialized tools to get more detailed insights into your application's behavior.

4.3 Introduction to .NET Profiling and Analysis Tools

Alright, now that we have a good understanding of the common culprits behind performance issues in .NET applications, let's talk about how we can actually *find* these bottlenecks in our own code. This is where profiling and analysis tools come into play. Think of these tools as sophisticated detectives that help you observe your application's behavior in minute detail, giving you the clues you need to pinpoint exactly where the performance problems are occurring. .NET provides a rich ecosystem of tools for this purpose, ranging from free utilities to integrated IDE features. Let's explore some of the key players in this area.

One of the most powerful and versatile free tools available for .NET performance analysis is PerfView. Developed by Microsoft, PerfView is specifically designed to help you understand CPU and memory-related performance issues in your .NET applications. It works by collecting and visualizing performance data from various sources, with a primary focus on Event Tracing for Windows (ETW). ETW is a powerful tracing mechanism built into the Windows operating system that allows the .NET runtime and your application to emit detailed events about their execution.

When you use PerfView, you can start a recording session that captures these ETW events while your application is running. You can configure PerfView to collect specific types of events, such as CPU sampling data (which tells you where the CPU is spending its time), garbage collection statistics (showing you how often and how long garbage collections are happening), and even custom events that your own application might emit. After the recording session, PerfView provides a rich set of views and analyses that allow you to explore this data.

For instance, PerfView can show you a CPU Stacks view, which aggregates CPU sampling data to show you which methods and call paths are consuming the most CPU time. This is invaluable for identifying CPU-bound bottlenecks. You can drill down into the call stacks to see the exact sequence of method calls that led to the high CPU usage, often pointing you directly to the problematic code.

Similarly, PerfView provides detailed GC Stats, allowing you to analyze the frequency, duration, and types of garbage collections. If you see a high number of Gen 2 collections or long pause times, it suggests potential memory pressure or inefficient memory usage in your application. PerfView also has views that can help you understand where excessive memory allocations are occurring.

PerfView is a very powerful tool, and it can take some time to become proficient with all its features. However, it provides an incredible level of insight into your application's runtime behavior and is often the go-to tool for deep performance investigations on Windows.

For developers who prefer command-line tools or need to analyze applications running on non-Windows platforms (like Linux or macOS), the .NET CLI offers a set of diagnostic tools, including dotnet-trace and dotnet-counters.

dotnet-trace allows you to collect traces of your running .NET application without needing a graphical interface. You can specify which providers (sources of events) you want to trace, including the .NET runtime provider, ASP.NET Core provider, and even your own custom event sources. Once you've collected a trace, you can then analyze it using PerfView (on Windows) or other trace analysis tools that support the dotnet-trace output format. This makes it a very versatile tool for cross-platform performance investigations. For example, you could collect a trace of an ASP.NET Core application running on Linux and then analyze it on a Windows machine using PerfView.

dotnet-counters provides a way to monitor performance counters in real-time for your running .NET applications. Performance counters are metrics exposed by the .NET runtime and other libraries that give you a snapshot of various aspects of your application's behavior, such as CPU usage, memory consumption, garbage collection statistics (like the number of collections and their duration), HTTP request rates, and more. dotnet-counters allows you to see these metrics updating live in your terminal, giving you an immediate overview of your application's resource usage. This can be very helpful for quickly identifying if your application is experiencing high CPU or memory load, or if the garbage collector is running frequently.

For example, you could use dotnet-counters to monitor the CPU usage of your web API under load. If you see it consistently hitting 100%, that's a strong indicator of a CPU-bound bottleneck that warrants further investigation with dotnet-trace.

Finally, both Visual Studio and Rider, the popular IDEs for .NET development, offer integrated profiling tools that allow you to analyze the performance of your applications directly from within the IDE. These tools often provide a more user-friendly interface for starting profiling sessions and viewing the results.

The Visual Studio Performance Profiler, for example, offers various profiling sessions, including CPU Usage, Memory Usage, .NET Counters, and more. You can attach the profiler to a running process or start a profiling session directly from your solution. The results are displayed within the IDE, often allowing you to navigate directly from performance data (like a hot path in the CPU usage view) to the corresponding lines of code in your project. Rider also has a powerful performance profiler that provides similar capabilities, allowing you to analyze CPU usage, memory allocations, and other performance aspects of your .NET applications.

These IDE-integrated profilers can be very convenient during development and testing, allowing you to quickly identify performance issues without having to switch to a separate tool. They often provide a good balance of detail and ease of use.

To effectively tackle performance issues in your .NET 9 applications, you need to become familiar with these profiling and analysis tools. PerfView offers deep, system-level insights on Windows. The .NET CLI tools (dotnet-trace and dotnet-counters) provide cross-platform command-line capabilities for collecting traces and monitoring real-time metrics. And the integrated profilers in Visual Studio and Rider offer convenient ways to analyze performance directly within your development environment. Learning to use these tools effectively is a crucial skill for building truly high-performing modern .NET applications.

4.4 Best Practices for Writing Performant C# Code

Alright, now that we understand how to identify performance bottlenecks, let's talk about how to write C# code from the get-go that is more likely to perform well. Think of these as good coding habits and techniques that can help you avoid common performance pitfalls and build efficient applications with .NET 9. Writing performant code isn't just about making things faster; it often leads to applications that are more resource-efficient, scalable, and provide a better overall user experience.

One of the first and most fundamental best practices is avoiding unnecessary boxing and unboxing. Boxing is the process of converting a value type (like an int, bool, or struct) to a reference type (object). Unboxing is the reverse process. These conversions happen implicitly in some scenarios, particularly when you're working with non-generic collections or when you pass value types to methods that expect objects. Boxing and unboxing introduce overhead because they involve allocating memory on the heap and performing type checks.

Consider this example:

```
C#

using System;

using System.Collections;
```

```csharp
public class BoxingUnboxingExample

{

    public static void
UseArrayListWithValueType()

    {

        ArrayList numbers = new ArrayList();

        int value = 123;

        numbers.Add(value); // 'value' is boxed
here


        int retrievedValue = (int)numbers[0]; //
'numbers[0]' is unboxed here

        Console.WriteLine($"Retrieved value:
{retrievedValue}");

    }


    public static void
UseGenericListWithValueType()

    {

        List<int> numbers = new List<int>();

        int value = 123;

        numbers.Add(value); // No boxing occurs
here
```

```
        int retrievedValue = numbers[0]; // No
unboxing needed

        Console.WriteLine($"Retrieved value
(generic): {retrievedValue}");

    }


    public static void Main(string[] args)

    {

        UseArrayListWithValueType();

        UseGenericListWithValueType();

    }

}
```

When you add the integer value to the non-generic ArrayList, it gets boxed into an object on the heap. When you retrieve it, you need to explicitly cast it back to an int, which involves unboxing. In contrast, when you use the generic List<int>, the integer is stored directly in the list without boxing, and no unboxing is needed when you retrieve it. This difference might seem small for a single operation, but in code that performs these operations many times, the overhead can become significant.

Best practice: Prefer generic collections (List<T>, Dictionary<TKey, TValue>, etc.) over non-generic collections (ArrayList, HashTable) when working with value types to avoid unnecessary boxing and unboxing.

Another crucial area for performance is efficient string manipulation. Strings in .NET are immutable, meaning that every time you perform an operation that seems to modify a string (like concatenation or replacement), a new string object is created. For simple, infrequent string operations, this is usually fine. However, when you need to perform many string manipulations in a loop or build up a string by repeatedly appending to it, this can lead to a lot of unnecessary object creation and garbage collection overhead.

The System.Text.StringBuilder class is designed to address this. It provides a mutable buffer for building strings more efficiently. Instead of creating a new string object with each operation, StringBuilder allows you to append, insert, replace, and remove characters within its internal buffer, and only creates a new string object when you explicitly call its ToString() method.

Consider this example of building a large string:

```csharp
C#

using System;

using System.Text;

using System.Diagnostics;


public class StringManipulationExample

{

    public static string
ConcatenateStringsInefficiently(string[] words)

    {

        string result = "";
```

```csharp
        Stopwatch sw = Stopwatch.StartNew();

        for (int i = 0; i < words.Length; i++)

        {

            result += words[i]; // Creates a new
string in each iteration

        }

        sw.Stop();

        Console.WriteLine($"Inefficient
concatenation took: {sw.ElapsedMilliseconds}
ms");

        return result;

    }


    public static string
ConcatenateStringsEfficiently(string[] words)

    {

        StringBuilder sb = new StringBuilder();

        Stopwatch sw = Stopwatch.StartNew();

        for (int i = 0; i < words.Length; i++)

        {

            sb.Append(words[i]); // Appends to
the buffer

        }
```

```csharp
        string result = sb.ToString(); // Creates
a single string at the end

        sw.Stop();

        Console.WriteLine($"Efficient
concatenation took: {sw.ElapsedMilliseconds}
ms");

        return result;

    }


    public static void Main(string[] args)

    {

        string[] manyWords = new string[10000];

        for (int i = 0; i < manyWords.Length;
i++)

        {

            manyWords[i] = "word";

        }



ConcatenateStringsInefficiently(manyWords);

        ConcatenateStringsEfficiently(manyWords);

    }

}
```

When you run this, you'll likely see a significant difference in the time it takes for the two methods to concatenate the strings, especially with a large number of words. The inefficient method creates a new string object in each iteration of the loop, leading to a lot of overhead. The efficient method using StringBuilder performs much better because it only creates a single string at the end.

Best practice: Use StringBuilder for performing multiple string manipulations, especially within loops or when building large strings incrementally.

Finally, choosing the right data structures for the task at hand can have a profound impact on performance, especially when dealing with collections of data. We touched on this earlier, but it's worth reiterating with specific examples.

If you need to frequently access elements by index, List<T> or T[] (arrays) offer O(1) access time. If you need to perform frequent insertions or deletions in the middle of a collection, LinkedList<T> might be more efficient (O(1) for insertion/deletion once the location is found, but O(n) to find the location) compared to List<T> (O(n) for insertions/deletions in the middle).

For lookups based on a key, Dictionary<TKey, TValue> and HashSet<T> offer average O(1) performance for lookups, insertions, and deletions. If you just need to check for the existence of an element and ensure uniqueness, HashSet<T> is often a better choice than repeatedly iterating through a List<T> (O(n)).

Consider a real-world example: checking if a large number of IDs exist in a collection. If you store these IDs in a List<int> and then iterate through the list for each ID you want to check, the performance will be O(n*m), where n is the size of the list and m is the number of IDs to check. However, if you store the IDs in a HashSet<int>, the check for each ID will be on average O(1), leading to a much faster overall operation.

Best practice: Understand the performance characteristics (time complexity for common operations like insertion, deletion, lookup) of different collection types in System.Collections.Generic and choose the one that best suits the way you will be using the data in your application.

These are just a few key best practices for writing performant C# code. As you delve deeper into specific scenarios and performance issues, you'll discover many other techniques and considerations. The important thing is to be mindful of potential performance pitfalls from the beginning and to use profiling tools to identify and address bottlenecks when they arise. Writing performant code is often an iterative process of identifying, analyzing, and optimizing.

Chapter 5: Memory Management and Garbage Collection in .NET 9

Alright, let's tackle a topic that's often seen as a bit mysterious but is absolutely crucial for writing performant and stable .NET 9 applications: memory management and the garbage collector (GC). Think of the GC as the unsung hero of the .NET runtime, automatically managing the allocation and deallocation of memory for your application. Understanding how it works and how your code interacts with it can make a significant difference in your application's performance and resource usage.

5.1 Deep Dive into the .NET Garbage Collector

Alright, let's really get into the heart of how .NET 9 manages memory for your applications: the garbage collector (GC). Think of the GC as a tireless, automatic janitor that runs in the background, constantly looking for memory that your application has used but no longer needs, and then cleaning it up so that memory can be reused. Understanding how this janitor works is incredibly important for writing efficient and stable .NET applications. While you don't have to manually tell it when to clean up (like you might in other programming environments), knowing its strategies and behaviors will help you write code that works in harmony with it, leading to better performance.

At its core, the .NET garbage collector is a part of the Common Language Runtime (CLR). When you create objects in your .NET code (specifically reference types, created with the class keyword), these objects are allocated on a region of memory called the managed heap. The GC's primary responsibility is to manage this managed heap. It keeps track of which objects are still being used by your application (these are considered "live") and which are no longer reachable from any part of your code (these are "dead" and can be collected).

Unlike systems with manual memory management where you have to explicitly free memory using something like delete in C++, .NET's automatic garbage collection frees you from this burden. The GC periodically runs an algorithm to identify the dead objects and reclaims the memory they occupy, making it available for new object allocations. This automatic nature significantly reduces the risk of common memory-related errors like memory leaks (where memory is allocated but never freed) and dangling pointers (where a pointer refers to memory that has already been freed).

The GC doesn't just run constantly; it's an intelligent system that tries to balance memory usage with application performance. Triggering a garbage collection cycle can be a relatively expensive operation, as it requires the GC to pause the execution of your application (though this pause is often very brief, especially for certain types of collections) while it performs its work. Therefore, the GC uses various strategies to determine the optimal time to run a collection.

Generations and Collection Modes

To make the garbage collection process more efficient, the .NET GC employs a strategy based on generations. The managed heap is divided into three generations: Generation 0, Generation 1, and Generation 2. Think of these generations as representing the "age" of the objects on the heap.

- Generation 0: This is where all newly created objects initially reside. It's considered the "youngest" generation. The rationale here is that most objects in an application have a very short lifespan – they are created, used briefly, and then become eligible for collection quickly. Because of this, Generation 0 is collected very frequently. These collections are typically fast as they only involve a small portion of the heap. If an object survives a Generation 0 collection (meaning it's still being referenced), it gets promoted to Generation 1.

- Generation 1: This is an intermediate generation. It holds objects that have survived at least one Generation 0 collection. Generation 1 acts as a buffer between the very short-lived objects in Generation 0 and the long-lived objects in Generation 2. Collections of Generation 1 occur less frequently than Generation 0 collections and involve a slightly larger segment of the heap. Objects that survive a Generation 1 collection are then promoted to Generation 2.
- Generation 2: This is the "oldest" generation. It contains objects that have survived multiple garbage collections. These are typically the long-lived objects that persist throughout the application's lifetime. Collections of Generation 2 are the least frequent and can be the most expensive because they potentially involve scanning the entire managed heap. The assumption here is that objects that have been around for a while are likely to remain in use.

This generational approach is a key optimization. By focusing the most frequent and fastest collections on the youngest generation (Generation 0), where most of the garbage is expected to be, the GC can often reclaim memory efficiently without causing significant pauses in your application's execution.

Beyond generations, the .NET GC also operates in different collection modes, which are tailored to different application needs:

- Workstation GC: This is the default mode for client applications, such as desktop or mobile apps. Its primary goal is to provide good responsiveness to the user interface. To achieve this, it tends to be concurrent, meaning it can perform some of its work (like identifying dead objects) in the background while the application threads are still running. This minimizes the pauses that might be noticeable to the user. However, it might not utilize memory as aggressively as the Server GC.

- Server GC: This mode is designed for server applications that need to handle a high volume of requests and prioritize throughput over UI responsiveness. Server GC is more aggressive in its memory utilization and aims to maximize the amount of work the server can do over time. It typically uses multiple threads for garbage collection, allowing it to leverage multi-core processors more effectively for parallel collection. While it might have slightly longer garbage collection pauses compared to Workstation GC, these pauses are generally less frequent. You can enable Server GC in your application's configuration file if you are building a server-side application.

Within these modes, the GC can also perform concurrent and non-concurrent collections. Concurrent collections (like the background GC in Workstation mode) try to do as much work as possible in the background while the application continues to run, leading to shorter pauses. Non-concurrent collections pause all application threads while the GC does its work. The choice between these depends on the generation being collected and the overall mode the GC is operating in. For instance, Generation 2 collections can be concurrent in both Workstation and Server GC to minimize the impact of collecting the entire old generation.

Understanding these generations and collection modes helps you appreciate the complexity and intelligence built into the .NET memory management system. It's not just a simple cleanup process; it's a carefully orchestrated set of strategies designed to optimize performance based on the application's characteristics.

Understanding GC Pressure

The term GC pressure is used to describe the situation where your application is causing the garbage collector to run frequently. High

GC pressure typically indicates that your application is allocating a lot of objects in a short amount of time. While the GC is designed to handle this automatically, excessive GC pressure can negatively impact your application's performance. The GC itself consumes CPU time when it runs, and frequent collections, especially of the older generations, can lead to noticeable pauses in your application's execution.

Several coding patterns and application behaviors can contribute to increased GC pressure:

- Frequent creation of short-lived objects: If your code, especially in performance-critical paths, is constantly creating new objects that are used briefly and then discarded, this will lead to frequent Generation 0 collections. While Generation 0 collections are fast, a very high rate of them can still consume CPU resources. Think about processing a stream of data where you create a new object for each small chunk of data, even if those objects are only needed for a very short time.

- Allocation of large objects: Objects larger than a certain threshold (around 85,000 bytes) are allocated on the large object heap (LOH). The LOH is collected less frequently and can be more expensive to compact (defragment). Allocating many large, transient objects can put pressure on the LOH and lead to performance issues. Consider reading a very large file into memory as a single byte array – this would be allocated on the LOH. If you do this frequently for different files, it can cause problems.

- Holding onto references for too long: A common source of increased memory usage and eventual GC pressure is keeping references to objects that are no longer needed. If an object is still reachable by a reference in your code, the GC cannot collect it, even if the object is no longer logically in use. This can lead to a buildup of memory usage over time and eventually trigger more frequent and expensive garbage collections. Think about an event handler that captures a large object in its closure – if the event handler persists for a long time, so does the referenced object, even if it's no longer actively used.

Monitoring performance counters related to the GC (you can use tools like PerfView or dotnet-counters for this) is crucial for understanding the GC pressure in your application.

Key counters to watch include:

- % Time in GC: This counter tells you the percentage of time the GC has spent performing collections since the application started. A consistently high value (e.g., above 20-30%) might indicate excessive GC activity impacting your application's performance.
- # Gen 0 Collections, # Gen 1 Collections, # Gen 2 Collections: These counters show the number of collections that have occurred for each generation. A very high number of Generation 2 collections, in particular, can be a sign of long-lived object churn or memory pressure.
- Allocated Bytes/sec: This counter shows the rate at which your application is allocating memory. A high allocation rate can contribute to increased GC pressure.

By understanding these concepts, you can start to reason about how your coding patterns might be affecting the garbage collector and the overall memory management of your .NET 9 applications. The next step is to explore techniques you can use to minimize GC pressure and write code that is more memory-efficient..

5.2 Techniques for Minimizing Garbage Collection

Alright, now that we have a better understanding of how the .NET garbage collector works and what can cause it to work harder (GC pressure), let's explore some practical techniques you can employ in your .NET 9 code to minimize the frequency and duration of garbage collection cycles. By reducing the workload on the GC, you can often improve your application's performance, reduce CPU usage, and potentially lower memory consumption. Think of these techniques as strategies for writing code that is more "GC-friendly."

One effective approach to minimizing garbage collection is through object pooling. The basic idea here is to reuse objects instead of constantly creating new ones, especially for objects that are frequently used and have a relatively short lifespan. Instead of letting these objects become garbage and then allocating new ones later, you maintain a pool of pre-allocated objects. When you need an object, you grab one from the pool. When you're finished with it, you return it to the pool so it can be reused later.

A classic real-world example where object pooling can be very beneficial is with network connections or database connections. Establishing these connections can be expensive operations. Instead of creating a new connection for every request and then closing it, connection pooling allows you to keep a set of active connections ready to be used, significantly reducing the overhead.

In .NET, you can implement your own object pools for specific types, as we saw with the StringBuilderPool example earlier. However, .NET also provides built-in pooling mechanisms for certain types, such as ArrayPool<T>. The ArrayPool<T> class allows you to rent and return arrays, potentially reducing the number of array allocations and the pressure on the garbage collector, especially for temporary, medium-sized arrays.

Here's an example of using ArrayPool<byte> to efficiently process data in chunks:

C#

```csharp
using System;

using System.Buffers;


public class ArrayPoolExample

{

    public static void
ProcessData(ReadOnlySpan<byte> data)

    {

        Console.WriteLine($"Processing data chunk
of {data.Length} bytes.");

        // Simulate processing

        for (int i = 0; i < data.Length; i++)

        {

            // Do something with data[i]

        }

    }


    public static void ReadAndProcessData(string
filePath, int chunkSize)

    {

        byte[]? buffer = null;

        try
```

```csharp
        {
            buffer =
ArrayPool<byte>.Shared.Rent(chunkSize);

            using (var stream =
System.IO.File.OpenRead(filePath))

            {

                int bytesRead;

                while ((bytesRead =
stream.Read(buffer, 0, chunkSize)) > 0)

                {

                    ProcessData(buffer.AsSpan(0,
bytesRead));

                }

            }

        }

        finally

        {

            if (buffer != null)

            {

ArrayPool<byte>.Shared.Return(buffer);

            }

        }
```

```csharp
    }


    public static void Main(string[] args)

    {

        // Create a dummy file for the example

        byte[] dummyData = new byte[1024 * 1024];
// 1MB


System.IO.File.WriteAllBytes("large_data.bin",
dummyData);


        ReadAndProcessData("large_data.bin",
512); // Process in 512-byte chunks

    }

}
```

In this example, instead of allocating a new byte array for each chunk of data read from the file, we rent an array from the shared ArrayPool<byte>. After we're done processing the chunk, we return the array to the pool. This can significantly reduce the number of array allocations, especially when dealing with large files or streams processed in chunks.

Another fundamental way to minimize garbage collection is by reducing object allocations in the first place. If you create fewer objects, there will be less garbage for the GC to collect.

Here are some strategies for achieving this:

- Reusing objects: As mentioned with object pooling, try to reuse existing objects whenever it makes sense. This applies not just to pooled objects but also to long-lived objects that can be modified and reused instead of creating new ones. Be careful with thread safety when reusing mutable objects across threads.
- Using value types (structs) appropriately: For small, immutable data structures that are accessed frequently and copied by value, using struct instead of class can often reduce heap allocations and the need for garbage collection. However, be cautious with large structs, as copying them can be expensive. We'll discuss structs in more detail in the next section.
- Avoiding unnecessary string allocations: String operations can often lead to many temporary string allocations because strings in .NET are immutable. Using StringBuilder for building strings with multiple appends or modifications is a key way to reduce this overhead. Be mindful of methods that might implicitly create new strings, such as repeated use of string.Concat or the + operator in loops.
- Using efficient data structures: Choosing the right data structure for the task can sometimes lead to fewer object allocations. For example, using ImmutableList<T> or ImmutableDictionary<TKey, TValue> when you need immutable collections can sometimes be more efficient than repeatedly creating new mutable collections and copying their contents. Similarly, using specialized collections like ConcurrentBag<T> or BlockingCollection<T> in concurrent scenarios can sometimes lead to better memory management than using simpler collections with manual locking.
- Being mindful of LINQ usage: While LINQ is powerful, some LINQ operations can lead to the creation of intermediate collections. For performance-critical

scenarios, especially with large datasets, consider whether a more imperative approach (using for or foreach loops with in-place modifications) might be more memory-efficient. However, always balance this with code readability and maintainability.

By consciously applying these techniques, you can write .NET 9 code that generates less garbage, putting less pressure on the garbage collector and ultimately leading to more performant and resource-efficient applications. It's about being mindful of object lifetimes and allocation patterns in your code.

Here are some techniques to consider:

Object Pooling

Object pooling is a technique where you maintain a collection of pre-allocated objects that can be reused instead of creating new objects every time you need them. This can be particularly beneficial for frequently used, short-lived objects. Instead of letting these objects be garbage collected and then re-allocating new ones, you retrieve an object from the pool when you need it and return it to the pool when you're done.

A classic example is working with StringBuilder instances in a loop. Instead of creating a new StringBuilder in each iteration, you could potentially use a pooled instance, clear it, use it, and then return it to the pool. .NET also provides built-in pooling mechanisms for certain types, like ArrayPool<T>.

Here's a simplified example of a basic object pool for StringBuilder:

C#

```
using System.Collections.Concurrent;
```

```csharp
using System.Text;


public class StringBuilderPool

{

    private static readonly
ConcurrentBag<StringBuilder> _pool = new
ConcurrentBag<StringBuilder>();


    public static StringBuilder Get()

    {

        if (_pool.TryTake(out var sb))

        {

            sb.Clear(); // Reset for reuse

            return sb;

        }

        return new StringBuilder();

    }


    public static void Return(StringBuilder sb)

    {

        if (sb.Capacity <= 1024) // Simple size
limit for pooling
```

```csharp
        {
            _pool.Add(sb);
        }
        // Otherwise, let it be garbage collected
    }
}


public class StringBuilderPoolingExample
{
    public static string FormatMessage(string[]
parts)
    {
        StringBuilder sb =
StringBuilderPool.Get();
        foreach (var part in parts)
        {
            sb.Append(part).Append(" ");
        }
        string result = sb.ToString().TrimEnd();
        StringBuilderPool.Return(sb);
        return result;
```

```
        }


    public static void Main(string[] args)

    {

        string[] data = { "This", "is", "a",
"message", "using", "StringBuilder", "pool." };

        for (int i = 0; i < 1000; i++)

        {

Console.WriteLine(FormatMessage(data));

        }

    }

}
```

In this example, instead of creating a new StringBuilder in each call to FormatMessage, we try to get one from the pool. If the pool is empty, we create a new one. After using it, we return it to the pool for potential reuse. This can reduce the number of object allocations and garbage collections, especially in frequently called methods.

Reducing Object Allocations

The most direct way to reduce GC pressure is to simply allocate fewer objects, especially short-lived ones.

Here are some strategies:

- Reusing objects: Whenever possible, try to reuse existing objects instead of creating new ones. The object pooling technique we just discussed is one way to do this.
- Using value types (structs) appropriately: For small, immutable data structures, structs can be more efficient than classes as they are typically allocated on the stack and avoid heap allocations and garbage collection. However, be cautious with large structs as copying them can be expensive.
- Avoiding unnecessary string allocations: As we discussed in the performance best practices, use StringBuilder for building strings with multiple operations. Be mindful of methods that might implicitly create new strings (e.g., repeated use of string.Concat or + operator).
- Using efficient data structures: Choose data structures that minimize allocations for the operations you perform most frequently. For example, using `ImmutableList

5.3 Effective Use of Value Types and Structs

Alright, let's delve into the world of value types and specifically structs in C# 13 and .NET 9. Understanding when and how to use structs effectively is a key aspect of writing performant and memory-efficient code. While most of the objects you create in C# are reference types (using the class keyword), value types offer a different way to represent data, with distinct characteristics that can be advantageous in certain scenarios, particularly concerning memory management and performance.

The fundamental difference between value types and reference types lies in how they are stored and how assignments work. Value types directly contain their data, and when you assign one value type variable to another, a completely new copy of the data is created. They are typically allocated on the stack, and their lifetime is usually tied to the scope of the variable. Reference types, on the other hand, store a reference (a pointer) to the memory location where the actual data is stored (on the managed heap). When you assign one reference type variable to another, you're just copying the reference, so both variables point to the same object in memory.

Structs in C# are value types. This means when you create a struct, you're directly embedding the data within the variable itself.

This has several implications, especially for memory management:

- Stack Allocation: Small structs are typically allocated on the stack. Stack allocation is generally faster than heap allocation, and memory on the stack is automatically managed and reclaimed when the method or scope ends, without involving the garbage collector. This can lead to less pressure on the GC.
- No Nullability by Default (before nullable value types): Before the introduction of nullable value types (using the ? suffix, like int? or DateTime?), structs could not directly represent a "null" or "missing" value because they always held their underlying data. This distinction is important to remember when working with older code or when deciding whether to use a nullable struct.
- Value Semantics: When you assign a struct variable to another, you get a completely independent copy of the data. Changes to one copy do not affect the other. This can be beneficial for data integrity and predictability.

Let's look at a simple example to illustrate the difference in assignment:

C#

```csharp
using System;

public class PointClass
{
    public int X { get; set; }
    public int Y { get; set; }
}

public struct PointStruct
{
    public int X { get; set; }
    public int Y { get; set; }
}

public class ValueVsReferenceExample
{
    public static void ClassAssignment()
    {
        PointClass p1 = new PointClass { X = 10,
Y = 20 };
        PointClass p2 = p1; // p2 now refers to
the same object as p1
        p2.X = 30;
        Console.WriteLine($"Class: p1.X = {p1.X},
p2.X = {p2.X}"); // Output: Class: p1.X = 30,
p2.X = 30
    }

    public static void StructAssignment()
    {
        PointStruct s1 = new PointStruct { X =
10, Y = 20 };
        PointStruct s2 = s1; // s2 is a copy of
s1
        s2.X = 30;
```

```
        Console.WriteLine($"Struct: s1.X =
{s1.X}, s2.X = {s2.X}"); // Output: Struct: s1.X
= 10, s2.X = 30
    }

    public static void Main(string[] args)
    {
        ClassAssignment();
        StructAssignment();
    }
}
```

As you can see, modifying p2.X also changes p1.X because they both refer to the same object in the class example. However, modifying s2.X does not affect s1.X because s2 is a separate copy of the PointStruct.

So, when should you use a struct instead of a class?

Microsoft's guidelines generally suggest using structs for value types that are:

- Small: Typically around 16 bytes or less in size. Large structs can lead to performance issues due to the overhead of copying them.
- Immutable or mostly immutable: Since structs are copied on assignment, frequent modifications to large mutable structs can be inefficient.
- Have value semantics: When you want assignments to create independent copies of the data.

Good real-world examples of types that are often represented as structs in .NET include:

- Primitive types: int, float, bool, char, DateTime, TimeSpan, decimal. These are all structs.
- Small data containers: Think of a Point with X and Y coordinates, a Color with red, green, and blue components, or a simple Rectangle with width and height. These are

often good candidates for structs if they are relatively small and often copied.

- Record structs: As we discussed earlier, record structs are particularly well-suited for representing immutable data with value semantics.

However, there are also important considerations when using structs:

- Boxing: When you box a struct (convert it to an object or an interface type), the entire value is copied onto the heap, and a reference to this boxed value is used. This can introduce performance overhead and increase garbage collection pressure. This often happens when you add structs to non-generic collections or use them with certain reflection-based APIs. Using generic collections (List<T>, Dictionary<TKey, TValue>) where T is your struct type can avoid boxing.

- Copying Overhead: While stack allocation is fast, copying large structs can be expensive, especially if they are passed around frequently as method arguments or return values. For larger data structures, a class (reference type) might be more performant as only the reference is copied.

- Default Constructor: Structs in C# cannot have parameterless constructors (before C# 10, they couldn't have any constructors that initialized instance fields). This means that if you create a struct variable without explicitly initializing it, its fields will have their default values (e.g., 0 for int, false for bool). Be aware of this when working with uninitialized struct variables. Record structs introduced in C# 10 address this by allowing parameterless constructors that initialize all fields to their defaults.

Let's consider a scenario where using a struct might be beneficial for performance: representing a large number of small, immutable vectors in a physics simulation. If each vector is just three float values (X, Y, Z), using a struct Vector3 would mean that these vectors are stored contiguously in memory (if in an array), potentially improving cache locality and reducing the overhead of individual object references compared to using a class. Furthermore, if these vectors are passed around frequently in calculations, the copying of the small struct might be less expensive than dereferencing a class object.

However, if the Vector3 struct were to become very large (e.g., containing many more fields), then passing it around as a value type might become more expensive due to the copying overhead. In such a case, using a class (reference type) might be more performant.

Effective use of value types and structs in .NET 9 involves understanding their fundamental differences from reference types, considering their size and mutability, being mindful of boxing, and choosing them appropriately based on the specific performance and memory management needs of your application. For small, immutable data with value semantics, structs can be a powerful tool for reducing heap allocations and improving performance. However, it's crucial to be aware of their potential drawbacks, especially with larger or frequently modified structs.

5.4 Working with Memory Management APIs

Alright, let's explore some of the more direct ways you can interact with memory management in .NET 9 through specific APIs. While the garbage collector handles most memory management automatically, there are scenarios where having more control over memory, particularly for high-performance operations, can be beneficial. This is where types like Memory<T> and Span<T> come into play. Think of these as providing you with a way to work with contiguous regions of memory in a safe and efficient manner, often without incurring the overhead of traditional array manipulation or object creation.

Before Memory<T> and Span<T>, working with slices of arrays or unmanaged memory often involved unsafe pointers and manual memory management, which could be error-prone and challenging to get right. These new types, introduced in .NET Core 2.1 and further enhanced in later versions, provide a safer and more structured way to handle such scenarios.

Span<T> is a value type (struct) that represents a contiguous region of arbitrary memory. It can wrap managed memory (like arrays) or unmanaged memory (obtained through pointers).

The key characteristics of Span<T> are:

- Zero Overhead Abstraction: Span<T> itself is a lightweight value type. Creating and manipulating spans generally doesn't involve heap allocations, making it very efficient.
- Safety: Span<T> enforces bounds checking, preventing you from accidentally accessing memory outside the represented region. This safety is crucial when dealing with memory directly.
- Flexibility: A single Span<T> can represent a portion of an array, an entire array, or even a section of unmanaged memory.

Memory<T> is a similar structure but is a struct that can own the memory it points to. It's designed to be a more general-purpose memory abstraction and is often used in asynchronous operations. You can easily get a Span<T> from a Memory<T> using its Span property.

Let's look at a real-world example where Span<T> can be very useful: parsing a string that contains comma-separated values. Instead of creating substrings for each value, which involves multiple string allocations, you can use Span<char> to directly work with the relevant portions of the original string.

C#

```
using System;

public class SpanParsingExample
{
    public static void
ParseCsvInefficiently(string csvLine)
    {
        string[] values = csvLine.Split(',');
        Console.WriteLine("Values
(inefficient):");
        foreach (string value in values)
        {

Console.WriteLine($"'{value.Trim()}'");
        }
    }

    public static void ParseCsvEfficiently(string
csvLine)
    {
        ReadOnlySpan<char> span =
csvLine.AsSpan();
        Console.WriteLine("Values (efficient):");
        int startIndex = 0;
        for (int i = 0; i < span.Length; i++)
        {
            if (span[i] == ',')
            {
                ReadOnlySpan<char> valueSpan =
span.Slice(startIndex, i - startIndex).Trim();
```

```
Console.WriteLine($"'{valueSpan.ToString()}'");
                startIndex = i + 1;
            }
        }
        ReadOnlySpan<char> lastValueSpan =
span.Slice(startIndex).Trim();

Console.WriteLine($"'{lastValueSpan.ToString()}'"
);
    }

    public static void Main(string[] args)
    {
        string csvData = "value1, value 2 ,
value3   ,value4";
        ParseCsvInefficiently(csvData);
        ParseCsvEfficiently(csvData);
    }
}
```

In the ParseCsvInefficiently method, string.Split(',') creates a new string array and multiple substring objects, which can be inefficient for large CSV lines. In contrast, the ParseCsvEfficiently method uses AsSpan() to get a ReadOnlySpan<char> over the original string. It then uses Slice() to get a view of each value without allocating new strings. The Trim() operation on the ReadOnlySpan<char> also returns a new ReadOnlySpan<char> representing the trimmed portion, again without allocation. Only when we need to print the value do we call ToString() on the span to create a string. This approach significantly reduces memory allocations.

Memory<T> is often used in asynchronous operations, particularly when dealing with streams of data. For example, when reading from a NetworkStream asynchronously, you might receive the data into a Memory<byte>. You can then get a Span<byte> from this

Memory<byte> to process the received data efficiently. The Memory<T> structure provides a way to manage the underlying memory buffer across asynchronous calls.

Here's a conceptual example of asynchronous reading into a Memory<byte>:

C#

```
using System;
using System.IO.Pipelines;
using System.Net.Sockets;
using System.Threading.Tasks;

public class MemoryAsyncExample
{
    public static async Task
ProcessNetworkStreamAsync(NetworkStream stream)
    {
        byte[] buffer = new byte[1024];
        Memory<byte> memoryBuffer =
buffer.AsMemory();

        while (true)
        {
            int bytesRead = await
stream.ReadAsync(memoryBuffer);
            if (bytesRead == 0)
                break;

            ReadOnlySpan<byte> receivedData =
memoryBuffer.Span.Slice(0, bytesRead);
            // Process the receivedData
Span<byte> efficiently
            Console.WriteLine($"Received
{bytesRead} bytes:
```

```
{System.Text.Encoding.UTF8.GetString(receivedData
)}");
        }
    }


    // ... (NetworkStream setup would be needed
for a runnable example)
}
```

In this example, we create a Memory<byte> from a byte array. The ReadAsync method of the NetworkStream writes data directly into this memory buffer. We then get a Span<byte> (receivedData) to efficiently work with the portion of the buffer that contains the received data.

The benefits and use cases of Memory<T> and Span<T> are significant when you need to:

- Achieve High Performance: By avoiding unnecessary allocations and providing direct access to memory, these types can dramatically improve performance in scenarios involving data processing, parsing, and I/O.
- Work with Slices of Arrays Efficiently: You can represent a portion of an array without creating a new array copy.
- Interact with Unmanaged Memory Safely: Span<T> can wrap unmanaged memory (obtained via unsafe code and pointers) while still providing bounds checking.
- Improve Interop with Native Code: They facilitate more efficient passing of data to and from native libraries.
- Optimize Asynchronous Operations: Memory<T> helps manage buffers across asynchronous calls.

However, there are some considerations:

- Stack-Only for Span<T>: Span<T> is a ref struct, which means it must live on the stack and has certain restrictions on its usage (e.g., you can't store it in fields of classes or use it across `await` boundaries directly). Memory<T> is less restrictive in this regard.

- Care with Lifetime: When working with spans over existing memory (like arrays), you need to ensure that the underlying memory remains valid for the lifetime of the span.

Memory<T> and Span<T> are powerful tools in the .NET 9 memory management API arsenal. They allow you to work with memory in a more direct and efficient way, especially in performance-critical scenarios involving data processing, parsing, and I/O, while still maintaining safety. Understanding and utilizing these types can lead to significant performance gains in your applications.

5.5 Memory Leaks and How to Avoid Them

Alright, let's talk about a subtle but potentially insidious problem that can plague even applications with automatic memory management: memory leaks. Think of a memory leak as a situation where your application allocates memory that it no longer needs, but for some reason, this memory is never released back to the system. Over time, if these leaks accumulate, your application can consume an ever-increasing amount of memory, potentially leading to performance degradation, instability, and eventually even crashes. While the .NET garbage collector is excellent at reclaiming memory from objects that are no longer reachable, it can't free memory from objects that are still being referenced, even if those objects are no longer logically needed by the application.

Memory leaks in .NET applications often don't manifest as a sudden crash with an "out of memory" error in the early stages. Instead, you might observe your application gradually consuming more and more memory over long periods of use. This can lead to the application becoming slower, less responsive, and potentially causing issues for other applications running on the same system.

Let's consider a few common scenarios that can lead to memory leaks in .NET applications:

One frequent cause is unsubscribed event handlers. In the .NET eventing system, when an object subscribes to an event of another object, it holds a reference to the publisher. If the subscriber has a longer lifetime than the publisher and doesn't unsubscribe from the event when it's no longer interested, the publisher (and any objects it holds references to) will remain in memory even if they are no longer needed elsewhere.

Consider a UI scenario where a long-lived service subscribes to an event of a short-lived UI control. If the service never unsubscribes, the UI control (and potentially a whole object graph associated with it) will be kept alive as long as the service exists, even after the UI control is no longer visible or used.

Here's a simplified code example illustrating this:

```csharp
C#

using System;
using System.Threading;
using System.Threading.Tasks;

public class UIShortLived
{
    public event EventHandler SomethingHappened;

    public void DoSomething()
    {
        Console.WriteLine("UI control doing something...");
```

```csharp
            SomethingHappened?.Invoke(this,
EventArgs.Empty);
    }
}

public class ServiceLongLived
{
    private UIShortLived _uiControl;

    public ServiceLongLived(UIShortLived
uiControl)
    {
        _uiControl = uiControl;
        _uiControl.SomethingHappened +=
OnSomethingHappened;
        Console.WriteLine("Service subscribed to
UI event.");
    }

    public void Dispose()
    {
        _uiControl.SomethingHappened -=
OnSomethingHappened;
        Console.WriteLine("Service unsubscribed
from UI event.");
    }

    private void OnSomethingHappened(object
sender, EventArgs e)
    {
        Console.WriteLine("Service received UI
event.");
    }
}

public class MemoryLeakExampleEvent
```

```
{
    public static async Task Main(string[] args)
    {
        for (int i = 0; i < 10; i++)
        {
            var uiControl = new UIShortLived();
            var service = new
ServiceLongLived(uiControl);
            uiControl.DoSomething();

            // Simulate the UI control going out
of scope but the service still exists
            // In a real application, the service
might be a singleton or have a longer lifetime
            // If we don't explicitly
unsubscribe, the uiControl will be kept alive.
            // service.Dispose(); // Uncomment
this to prevent the potential leak

            Console.WriteLine($"Iteration {i}
completed. UI control might still be in
memory.");
            await Task.Delay(100);
        }

        Console.WriteLine("Done.");
    }
}
```

In this example, the ServiceLongLived subscribes to an event of UIShortLived. If service.Dispose() (which unsubscribes the event) is not called, the service will hold a reference to _uiControl, preventing it from being garbage collected even after it's no longer needed. Over many iterations, this could lead to a memory leak.

Another common source of memory leaks is improper disposal of disposable objects. Types that implement the IDisposable interface (often those that hold onto unmanaged resources like file handles, network connections, or database connections) need to have their Dispose() method called to release those resources. If you create such objects and don't properly dispose of them (e.g., by using a using statement), the unmanaged resources they hold might not be released, and the object itself might remain in memory longer than necessary if it holds onto other managed objects.

Consider working with a file stream:

C#

```
using System;
using System.IO;

public class FileHandlingLeakExample
{
    public static void
ReadFileContentsInefficiently(string filePath)
    {
        FileStream fs = new FileStream(filePath,
FileMode.Open, FileAccess.Read);
        StreamReader reader = new
StreamReader(fs);
        string contents = reader.ReadToEnd();
        Console.WriteLine($"Read
{contents.Length} characters.");
        // Oops! We forgot to close the reader
and the file stream.
        // The file handle might remain open, and
the objects might linger.
    }

    public static void
ReadFileContentsEfficiently(string filePath)
    {
```

```
        using (FileStream fs = new
FileStream(filePath, FileMode.Open,
FileAccess.Read))
        using (StreamReader reader = new
StreamReader(fs))
        {
            string contents = reader.ReadToEnd();
            Console.WriteLine($"Read
{contents.Length} characters (disposed).");
            // The 'using' statement ensures that
reader.Dispose() and fs.Dispose() are called
            // automatically when the 'using'
block ends, even if an exception occurs.
        }
    }


    public static void Main(string[] args)
    {
        // Create a dummy file
        File.WriteAllText("example_leak.txt",
"This is some content.");

ReadFileContentsInefficiently("example_leak.txt")
;

ReadFileContentsEfficiently("example_leak.txt");
    }
}
```

In the ReadFileContentsInefficiently method, we create a FileStream and a StreamReader but don't explicitly dispose of them. This means the underlying file handle might not be released promptly, and the objects themselves might stay in memory longer than needed. The ReadFileContentsEfficiently method uses using statements, which ensure that the Dispose() method of both objects is called automatically when they are no longer needed, preventing potential resource leaks and reducing the likelihood of memory leaks if these disposable objects hold onto other managed memory.

Another potential source of memory leaks can be static variables holding onto object references. Static variables live for the entire lifetime of the application domain. If a static variable holds a reference to an object that is no longer needed for the application's entire lifetime, that object (and anything it references) will also remain in memory. This is especially problematic if the referenced object is large or if the static variable is unintentionally holding onto many such objects over time.

Consider a caching mechanism where you store objects in a static dictionary. If you don't have a proper eviction policy, objects might remain in the cache indefinitely, even if they are no longer being used, leading to increased memory consumption.

Finally, closures and captured variables can sometimes lead to unexpected object lifetimes. When a lambda expression or an anonymous method captures variables from its surrounding scope, it creates a closure object that holds references to these captured variables. If the lifetime of the closure object exceeds the expected lifetime of the captured variables, those variables (and anything they reference) will also be kept alive longer than necessary.

To avoid memory leaks in your .NET 9 applications, here are some best practices:

- Unsubscribe from events: Always unsubscribe from events when your object is no longer interested in receiving them, especially if the publisher has a longer lifetime. Implement IDisposable on your subscriber and unsubscribe in the Dispose() method.
- Dispose of disposable objects: Use using statements to ensure that objects implementing IDisposable are properly disposed of, releasing any unmanaged resources and

allowing the objects to be garbage collected if they are no longer referenced elsewhere.

- Be careful with static variables: Only store objects in static variables if they are intended to live for the entire application lifetime. If you use static collections for caching, implement a proper eviction policy to remove unused objects.

- Understand closure lifetimes: Be mindful of the lifetime of variables captured by closures, especially if the closure itself has a long lifetime (e.g., event handlers that persist).

- Monitor memory usage: Use performance monitoring tools to track your application's memory consumption over time. A gradual increase in memory usage that doesn't correlate with expected application behavior could indicate a memory leak.

- Use memory profiling tools: If you suspect a memory leak, use memory profiling tools (available in Visual Studio and other third-party tools) to take snapshots of your application's heap at different times and compare them to identify objects that are being retained unexpectedly.

By being aware of these potential pitfalls and following these best practices, you can significantly reduce the risk of memory leaks in your .NET 9 applications, leading to more

Chapter 6: Asynchronous Programming Patterns for High Performance

Alright, now that we've got a solid understanding of the fundamentals of async and await, let's level up our asynchronous programming skills and explore some more advanced patterns that can really boost the performance of your .NET 9 applications. Think of this chapter as moving beyond the basics and learning how to orchestrate asynchronous operations in more sophisticated ways to achieve better responsiveness and efficiency.

6.1 Advanced async/await Patterns

Alright, now that we've got a solid understanding of the fundamentals of async and await, let's level up our asynchronous programming skills and explore some more advanced patterns that can really boost the performance of your .NET 9 applications. Think of this section as moving beyond the basics and learning how to orchestrate asynchronous operations in more sophisticated ways to achieve better responsiveness and efficiency.

Task.WhenAll and Task.WhenAny

When you have several independent asynchronous operations that all need to complete before you can proceed with the next step in your logic, Task.WhenAll is your go-to. It takes an array or an IEnumerable of Task (or Task<T>) instances and returns a new Task that will complete only when all of the supplied tasks have completed. If any of the supplied tasks fail (i.e., end in a faulted state), the Task returned by Task.WhenAll will also end in a faulted state, aggregating any exceptions. If all tasks complete successfully and return a result, the Task<TResult[]> returned by Task.WhenAll<TResult> will contain an array of the results in the order they were provided.

Consider a scenario where you're building a web page that needs to display information fetched from multiple independent microservices. For instance, you might need to retrieve user profile details from one service, the user's recent orders from another, and their recommendations from a third. You wouldn't want the user to stare at a blank page while each service is queried sequentially. Instead, you can initiate all three data-fetching operations concurrently and then use Task.WhenAll to wait until all the services have responded before rendering the complete page. This drastically reduces the overall load time of the page.

Here's a code example illustrating this:

```csharp
C#

using System;

using System.Collections.Generic;

using System.Net.Http;

using System.Text.Json;

using System.Threading.Tasks;

using System.Linq;


public class UserProfile
{
    public int Id { get; set; }

    public string Name { get; set; }

    public string Email { get; set; }
```

```csharp
}


public class Order

{

    public int OrderId { get; set; }

    public DateTime OrderDate { get; set; }

    public decimal TotalAmount { get; set; }

}


public class Recommendation

{

    public int ProductId { get; set; }

    public string ProductName { get; set; }

}


public class TaskWhenAllDashboardExample

{

    public static async Task<UserProfile>
GetUserProfileAsync(int userId)

    {

        using (var client = new HttpClient())
```

```csharp
        {
            var response = await
client.GetAsync($"https://api.userservice.example
.com/users/{userId}");

            response.EnsureSuccessStatusCode();

            var json = await
response.Content.ReadAsStringAsync();

            return
JsonSerializer.Deserialize<UserProfile>(json);

        }

    }


    public static async Task<List<Order>>
GetUserOrdersAsync(int userId)

    {

        using (var client = new HttpClient())

        {

            var response = await
client.GetAsync($"https://api.orderservice.exampl
e.com/orders/{userId}");

            response.EnsureSuccessStatusCode();

            var json = await
response.Content.ReadAsStringAsync();
```

```csharp
            return
JsonSerializer.Deserialize<List<Order>>(json);

        }

    }


    public static async
Task<List<Recommendation>>
GetUserRecommendationsAsync(int userId)

    {

        using (var client = new HttpClient())

        {

            var response = await
client.GetAsync($"https://api.recommendations.exa
mple.com/users/{userId}/recommendations");

            response.EnsureSuccessStatusCode();

            var json = await
response.Content.ReadAsStringAsync();

            return
JsonSerializer.Deserialize<List<Recommendation>>(
json);

        }

    }
```

```csharp
    public static async Task
DisplayDashboardAsync(int userId)

    {

        var userProfileTask =
GetUserProfileAsync(userId);

        var userOrdersTask =
GetUserOrdersAsync(userId);

        var userRecommendationsTask =
GetUserRecommendationsAsync(userId);


        Console.WriteLine("Fetching user profile,
orders, and recommendations concurrently...");

        await Task.WhenAll(userProfileTask,
userOrdersTask, userRecommendationsTask);

        Console.WriteLine("All data fetched.");


        if
(userProfileTask.IsCompletedSuccessfully &&
userOrdersTask.IsCompletedSuccessfully &&
userRecommendationsTask.IsCompletedSuccessfully)

        {

            var userProfile =
userProfileTask.Result;

            var orders = userOrdersTask.Result;
```

```csharp
        var recommendations =
userRecommendationsTask.Result;


        Console.WriteLine($"User:
{userProfile.Name} (ID: {userProfile.Id}, Email:
{userProfile.Email})");

        Console.WriteLine("Recent Orders:");

        foreach (var order in
orders.OrderByDescending(o =>
o.OrderDate).Take(3))

        {

            Console.WriteLine($"- Order
#{order.OrderId} on
{order.OrderDate.ToShortDateString()} for
${order.TotalAmount}");

        }


Console.WriteLine("\nRecommendations:");

        foreach (var recommendation in
recommendations.Take(3))

        {

            Console.WriteLine($"- Product
#{recommendation.ProductId}:
{recommendation.ProductName}");

        }

    }
```

```csharp
        else

        {

            Console.WriteLine("Failed to fetch
all dashboard data.");

            if (userProfileTask.IsFaulted)
Console.WriteLine($"User profile error:
{userProfileTask.Exception?.Message}");

            if (userOrdersTask.IsFaulted)
Console.WriteLine($"User orders error:
{userOrdersTask.Exception?.Message}");

            if
(userRecommendationsTask.IsFaulted)
Console.WriteLine($"Recommendations error:
{userRecommendationsTask.Exception?.Message}");

        }

    }


    public static async Task Main(string[] args)

    {

        await DisplayDashboardAsync(123);

    }

}
```

In this more complex dashboard example, Task.WhenAll ensures
that we wait for all three independent data-fetching operations to

complete before rendering the dashboard, leading to a much faster perceived load time for the user.

Now, let's talk about Task.WhenAny. This is useful in different scenarios. Instead of waiting for all tasks to complete, Task.WhenAny waits for the *first* task in a provided set to complete. It takes an array or an IEnumerable of Task instances and returns a Task<Task>. The Result of this returned Task is the Task that completed first.

A common real-world use case for Task.WhenAny is implementing a form of "race condition" where you initiate the same operation against multiple redundant resources (e.g., multiple backup servers), and you want to use the result from whichever resource responds fastest. This can improve the reliability and responsiveness of your application in the face of potential server issues or network latency.

Consider a system that tries to retrieve a critical configuration setting from a primary configuration server and a secondary backup server. You can initiate requests to both servers concurrently and use Task.WhenAny to process the response from the first one that succeeds, potentially making your application more resilient to temporary outages of the primary server.

C#

```csharp
using System;

using System.Net.Http;

using System.Threading.Tasks;

using System.Linq;


public class ConfigurationFetcher
```

```
{

    public static async Task<string>
FetchConfigurationAsync(string serverUrl)

    {

        Console.WriteLine(<span
class="math-inline">"Fetching configuration from
\{serverUrl\}\.\.\."\);

await Task\.Delay\(new Random\(\)\.Next\(1000,
4000\)\); // Simulate varying server response
times

using \(var client \= new HttpClient\(\)\)

\{

try

\{

var <4\>response \= await
client\.GetAsync\(serverUrl\);

<5\>response\.EnsureSuccessStatusCode\(\);

return await
response\.Content\.ReadAsStringAsync\(\);</4\>

\}

catch \(HttpRequestException ex\)

\{

Console\.WriteLine\(</span>"Error fetching from
{serverUrl}: {ex.Message}");
```

```csharp
            return null;

        }

    }

}


    public static async Task<string>
GetConfigurationWithFallbackAsync(List<string>
serverUrls)

    {

        var tasks =
serverUrls.Select(FetchConfigurationAsync).Where(
t => t != null).ToList();

        if (!tasks.Any())

        {

            return "Default Configuration";

        }


        var firstCompletedTask = await
Task.WhenAny(tasks);


        if
(firstCompletedTask.IsCompletedSuccessfully)

        {
```

```
            return await firstCompletedTask;

    }

    else

    {

        // In a real scenario, you might want
to check other completed tasks as well

        Console.WriteLine("Failed to retrieve
configuration from any server in a timely
manner.");

        return "Fallback Configuration";

    }

    }


    public static async Task Main(string[] args)

    {

        var servers = new List<string>

        {

"https://primary-config.example.com/settings",

        "https://backup-config1
```

Cancellation and Timeouts

In asynchronous programming, it's often important to be able to cancel an operation that's taking too long or if the user requests it.

The CancellationToken and CancellationTokenSource classes provide a cooperative way to handle cancellation in .NET.

A CancellationTokenSource has a Token property, which is a CancellationToken that can be passed to asynchronous methods. The caller can signal cancellation by calling the Cancel() method on the CancellationTokenSource. Asynchronous methods that support cancellation will periodically check the IsCancellationRequested property of the CancellationToken and throw a TaskCanceledException if cancellation has been requested.

Timeouts can be implemented by combining a Task with a delay task and using Task.WhenAny. If the delay task completes first, it indicates that the original operation has taken too long.

Here's an example demonstrating both cancellation and timeouts:

C#

```
using System;
using System.Net.Http;
using System.Threading;
using System.Threading.Tasks;

public class CancellationTimeoutExample
{
    public static async Task<string>
FetchDataWithCancellationAsync(string url,
CancellationToken cancellationToken)
    {
        using (var client = new HttpClient())
        {
            var response = await
client.GetAsync(url, cancellationToken);
            response.EnsureSuccessStatusCode();
```

```csharp
            return await
response.Content.ReadAsStringAsync();
        }
    }

    public static async Task
PerformOperationWithTimeoutAsync(string url,
TimeSpan timeout)
    {
        using (var cts = new
CancellationTokenSource(timeout))
        {
            try
            {
                Console.WriteLine(<span
class="math-inline">"Fetching data with timeout
of \{timeout\.TotalMilliseconds\}ms\.\.\."\);
string data \= await
FetchDataWithCancellationAsync\(url,
cts\.Token\);
Console\.WriteLine\(</span>"Data fetched
successfully: {data.Substring(0, 100)}...");
            }
            catch (TaskCanceledException)
            {
                Console.WriteLine(<span
class="math-inline">"Operation timed out after
\{timeout\.TotalMilliseconds\}ms\."\);
\}
catch \(HttpRequestException ex\)
\{
Console\.WriteLine\(</span>"Error fetching data:
{ex.Message}");
            }
        }
    }
```

```
public static async Task Main(string[] args)
{
    await
PerformOperationWithTimeoutAsync("https://jsonpla
ceholder.typicode.com/todos/1",
TimeSpan.FromSeconds(1));
    await
PerformOperationWithTimeoutAsync("https://delayed
site.com/api/long-
```

6.2 Utilizing ValueTask for Reduced Allocation

Alright, let's talk about a subtle but often significant optimization you can leverage in your asynchronous .NET 9 code: using ValueTask and ValueTask<TResult> instead of Task and Task<TResult>. Think of ValueTask as a more lightweight alternative that can help you reduce memory allocations, especially in scenarios where asynchronous operations might frequently complete synchronously. Understanding when and how to use ValueTask can lead to noticeable performance improvements, particularly in high-throughput applications.

To understand the benefit of ValueTask, it's helpful to recall how Task works. Task is a reference type, which means that every time you return a Task from an async method, even if the operation completes synchronously, a new Task object is allocated on the managed heap. For operations that frequently complete synchronously (e.g., reading from a buffered stream where the data is already available), this heap allocation can introduce unnecessary overhead and contribute to increased garbage collection pressure.

ValueTask, on the other hand, is a value type (struct) that can encapsulate either the result of an operation directly (if it completes synchronously) or a Task (if it completes asynchronously). This duality is the key to its potential performance benefits. When an asynchronous operation completes synchronously, a ValueTask can simply store the result as a value, avoiding the heap allocation of a Task object. Only when the operation truly needs to be asynchronous does the ValueTask wrap a Task.

Let's consider a real-world example: reading data from a stream. If the data is readily available in the buffer, the read operation can complete synchronously. If the buffer is empty and data needs to be fetched from the underlying source (e.g., a network socket), the operation will be asynchronous. Using ValueTask as the return type of a method that performs this read operation allows it to handle both scenarios efficiently.

Here's a simplified example illustrating the potential allocation savings:

C#

```
using System;
using System.IO;
using System.Threading.Tasks;

public class ValueTaskExample
{
    public static async Task<int>
ReadInt32AsyncWithTask(Stream stream)
    {
        var buffer = new byte[4];
        await stream.ReadAsync(buffer, 0, 4);
        return BitConverter.ToInt32(buffer, 0);
    }
}
```

```csharp
    public static async ValueTask<int>
ReadInt32AsyncWithValueTask(Stream stream)
    {
        var buffer = new byte[4];
        await stream.ReadAsync(buffer, 0, 4);
        return BitConverter.ToInt32(buffer, 0);
    }

    public static async Task Main(string[] args)
    {
        using (var memoryStream = new
MemoryStream(BitConverter.GetBytes(12345)))
        {
            // In this case, the ReadAsync might
complete synchronously because the data is in
memory
            for (int i = 0; i < 1000; i++)
            {
                memoryStream.Seek(0,
SeekOrigin.Begin);
                var resultTask =
ReadInt32AsyncWithTask(memoryStream);
                var resultValueTask =
ReadInt32AsyncWithValueTask(memoryStream);
                Console.WriteLine($"Task Result:
{await resultTask}, ValueTask Result: {await
resultValueTask}");
            }
            Console.WriteLine("Ran the loop.
Check memory allocations with a profiler to see
the difference.");
        }
    }
}
```

In this example, even though we're using await, the MemoryStream might have the data readily available, causing ReadAsync to complete synchronously in many iterations. The ReadInt32AsyncWithTask method will still allocate a new Task<int> object on the heap for each call, even when it completes synchronously. The ReadInt32AsyncWithValueTask method, on the other hand, can avoid this heap allocation in the synchronous case.

When to Use ValueTask **vs.** Task

So, when should you consider using ValueTask instead of Task?

- As the return type of async methods that might frequently complete synchronously: This is the primary use case. If your asynchronous operation often has its result immediately available (e.g., from a cache, a buffered I/O operation, or a completed in-memory operation), returning ValueTask can reduce heap allocations.
- In performance-sensitive code paths: If your code is executed very frequently and you're looking for micro-optimizations, especially around memory allocation, consider profiling with Task and then with ValueTask to see if there's a measurable benefit.

However, there are also some considerations when using ValueTask:

- Consuming ValueTask: You should generally avoid awaiting a ValueTask multiple times. Once it's awaited, the underlying state might have been consumed. If you need to await the result multiple times, you should convert it to a Task using AsTask().
- Interop with existing Task-based APIs: Many existing asynchronous APIs in .NET return Task. When you call these APIs, you'll naturally be working with Task objects. ValueTask is most beneficial when it's used throughout an

asynchronous call chain where synchronous completion is a common scenario.

- Slightly more complex consumption in some scenarios: While await works seamlessly with ValueTask, directly working with its Result property or checking its status might involve slightly different patterns compared to Task. However, the await keyword handles most of this complexity for you.

ValueTask is a valuable tool for optimizing asynchronous code by potentially reducing memory allocations in scenarios with frequent synchronous completion. It's particularly relevant in lower-level libraries and high-performance applications where every little bit of overhead matters. For many higher-level application scenarios, the simplicity and widespread use of Task might still be the preferred choice. It's about understanding the characteristics of your asynchronous operations and choosing the return type that best balances performance and code complexity.

6.3 Working with Task Continuations and Parallel Programming

Alright, let's explore how to orchestrate asynchronous operations in more complex sequences and how to leverage the power of parallel processing within your .NET 9 applications. Think of task continuations as a way to define what should happen *after* an asynchronous operation completes, and parallel programming as a way to execute multiple operations concurrently to utilize multi-core processors effectively. Mastering these techniques can lead to more efficient and responsive applications.

Task.ContinueWith

Task.ContinueWith allows you to schedule a new task that will execute when the original task completes. This is a way to chain asynchronous operations together. The continuation task receives the completed task as input, allowing it to access the results or handle any exceptions.

Consider a real-world scenario: after downloading a file asynchronously, you might want to process it. Task.ContinueWith lets you define the processing task to run automatically once the download task finishes.

Here's an example:

C#

```
using System;
using System.Net.Http;
using System.Threading.Tasks;

public class TaskContinueWithExample
{
    public static async Task<string>
DownloadFileAsync(string url)
    {
        Console.WriteLine($"Downloading file from
{url}...");
        using (var client = new HttpClient())
        {
            var response = await
client.GetAsync(url);
            response.EnsureSuccessStatusCode();
            return await
response.Content.ReadAsStringAsync();
        }
    }

    public static async Task
ProcessFileContentAsync(Task<string>
downloadTask)
    {
```

```
        Console.WriteLine("Download completed.
Processing content...");
        string content = await downloadTask; //
Await the result of the completed download task
        Console.WriteLine($"File content (first
100 chars):\n{content.Substring(0, 100)}...");
        // Perform further processing here
    }

    public static async Task Main(string[] args)
    {
        string fileUrl =
"https://raw.githubusercontent.com/dotnet/runtime
/main/LICENSE.TXT";
        var downloadTask =
DownloadFileAsync(fileUrl);

        // Schedule the processing task to run
after the download task completes
        var processingTask =
downloadTask.ContinueWith(ProcessFileContentAsync
, TaskScheduler.Default);

        // Wait for both tasks to complete
        await Task.WhenAll(downloadTask,
processingTask);

        Console.WriteLine("Download and
processing complete.");
    }
}
```

In this example, ContinueWith is used to schedule ProcessFileContentAsync to run after DownloadFileAsync completes. The downloadTask is passed as input to ProcessFileContentAsync, allowing it to access the downloaded content. The TaskScheduler.Default specifies that the continuation should run on a thread pool thread.

ContinueWith offers flexibility in how the continuation is scheduled (e.g., running on the UI thread, a specific task scheduler) and under what conditions it should run (e.g., only on successful completion, only on failure). However, for simpler sequential asynchronous operations, the await keyword often provides a more straightforward and readable way to achieve the same result. ContinueWith is particularly useful for more complex scenarios, like handling exceptions in a specific way or when you need finer control over the scheduling of subsequent tasks.

Introduction to Parallel.For **and** Parallel.ForEach

While async/await helps with I/O-bound operations and responsiveness, parallel programming is about leveraging multi-core processors to speed up CPU-bound operations. The System.Threading.Tasks.Parallel class provides static methods like For and ForEach that simplify the execution of loop-based operations in parallel.

Imagine you need to perform the same computationally intensive operation on each element of a large collection. Instead of processing them one by one in a foreach loop, you can use Parallel.ForEach to distribute the work across multiple threads, potentially significantly reducing the overall execution time.

Here's an example of processing a list of numbers in parallel:

C#

```csharp
using System;
using System.Collections.Generic;
using System.Threading.Tasks;

public class ParallelForEachExample
```

```csharp
{
    public static void ProcessNumber(int n)
    {
        Console.WriteLine($"Processing {n} on
thread
{System.Threading.Thread.CurrentThread.ManagedThr
eadId}");
        // Simulate a computationally intensive
operation
        Task.Delay(100).Wait();
        Console.WriteLine($"Finished processing
{n}");
    }

    public static void Main(string[] args)
    {
        List<int> numbers = new List<int> { 1, 2,
3, 4, 5, 6, 7, 8, 9, 10 };
        Console.WriteLine("Starting parallel
processing...");
        Parallel.ForEach(numbers, ProcessNumber);
        Console.WriteLine("Parallel processing
complete.");
    }
}
```

In this example, Parallel.ForEach iterates over the numbers list, and for each number, it calls the ProcessNumber method. The Parallel class automatically manages the partitioning of the work and the scheduling of threads to execute these operations in parallel. You'll likely see the output from different numbers interleaved, indicating that they are being processed concurrently on different threads.

Similarly, Parallel.For allows you to execute a for loop in parallel. This is useful when you have a known number of iterations and the work in each iteration is independent.

C#

```csharp
using System;
using System.Threading.Tasks;

public class ParallelForExample
{
    public static void PerformCalculation(int i)
    {
        Console.WriteLine($"Calculating for i =
{i} on thread
{System.Threading.Thread.CurrentThread.ManagedThr
eadId}");
        // Simulate a computationally intensive
calculation
        double result = Math.Pow(i, 3) +
Math.Sqrt(i * 10);
        Task.Delay(50).Wait();
        Console.WriteLine($"Calculation for i =
{i} complete, result = {result}");
    }

    public static void Main(string[] args)
    {
        Console.WriteLine("Starting parallel
calculations...");
        Parallel.For(0, 10, PerformCalculation);
        Console.WriteLine("Parallel calculations
complete.");
    }
}
```

Here, Parallel.For executes the PerformCalculation method for each value of i from 0 to 9 in parallel.

When using parallel programming, it's crucial to ensure that the work being done in parallel is indeed independent and doesn't involve shared mutable state that could lead to race conditions. We'll discuss handling concurrency safely in the next section.

Task.ContinueWith provides a way to chain asynchronous operations and control their scheduling, while Parallel.For and Parallel.ForEach simplify the execution of loop-based CPU-bound operations in parallel to leverage multi-core processors. These techniques, when used appropriately, can significantly enhance the performance and responsiveness of your .NET 9 applications.

6.4 Handling Concurrency and Parallelism Safely and Efficiently

Alright, now that we're exploring the power of parallel programming, it's absolutely crucial that we discuss how to handle concurrency and parallelism safely and efficiently. Think of concurrency as the ability of your application to handle multiple tasks seemingly at the same time (even if they are interleaving on a single core), and parallelism as the actual simultaneous execution of multiple tasks on multiple processor cores. While these techniques can significantly boost performance, they also introduce the potential for subtle and hard-to-debug issues if not handled correctly. Race conditions, deadlocks, and data corruption are just some of the problems that can arise when multiple threads or tasks access shared resources without proper synchronization.

Let's start by looking at some of the fundamental synchronization primitives provided by .NET in the System.Threading namespace.

Locks (lock statement and Monitor class): The lock statement (which is syntactic sugar for using the Monitor class) provides a simple way to ensure that only one thread can access a specific block of code or a shared object at a time. When a thread enters a lock block, it acquires a lock on a specified object. Other threads that try to enter the same lock block will be blocked until the first thread releases the lock.

Consider a real-world example: multiple threads trying to update a shared counter. Without a lock, you could have race conditions where the final count is incorrect because updates from different threads interfere with each other.

Here's an example of using a lock to safely update a shared counter:

C#

```
using System;
using System.Threading;
using System.Threading.Tasks;

public class SharedCounterWithLock
{
    private static int _counter = 0;
    private static readonly object _lock = new
object();

    public static void IncrementCounter()
    {
        lock (_lock)
        {
            _counter++;
            Console.WriteLine($"Counter
incremented to {_counter} by thread
{Thread.CurrentThread.ManagedThreadId}");
        }
    }

    public static async Task Main(string[] args)
    {
        Task[] tasks = new Task[5];
        for (int i = 0; i < tasks.Length; i++)
        {
```

```
                tasks[i] = Task.Run(() =>
                {
                    for (int j = 0; j < 1000; j++)
                    {
                        IncrementCounter();
                    }
                });
            }


            await Task.WhenAll(tasks);
            Console.WriteLine($"Final counter value:
{_counter}"); // Should be 5000
        }
    }
```

In this example, the lock (_lock) ensures that only one thread can be inside the IncrementCounter method at any given time, preventing race conditions on the _counter variable.

The Monitor class provides more fine-grained control over locking, including the ability to acquire a lock without blocking indefinitely (TryEnter) and to use wait/pulse mechanisms for thread signaling.

Mutexes (Mutex class): A Mutex (mutual exclusion) is similar to a lock, but it can also work across different processes. Only one thread can own a Mutex at a time. Mutexes are often used to synchronize access to shared resources like files or named system objects across multiple applications.

Semaphores (Semaphore and SemaphoreSlim classes): A semaphore controls access to a shared resource that has a limited number of concurrent users. It maintains a count, and threads can enter the semaphore (decrement the count) if the count is greater than zero. When a thread leaves, it increments the count. SemaphoreSlim is a lightweight, fast semaphore that is optimized for use within a single process and is often preferred over Semaphore in such cases.

While these synchronization primitives are essential, using them incorrectly can lead to performance bottlenecks due to excessive blocking or even deadlocks (where two or more threads are blocked indefinitely, waiting for each other to release a resource). Therefore, it's often better to use higher-level, more efficient concurrent collections provided by .NET in the System.Collections.Concurrent namespace whenever possible.

Concurrent Collections

The System.Collections.Concurrent namespace provides thread-safe collection classes that are designed for use in concurrent scenarios without the need for explicit locking in most common operations. These collections handle the underlying synchronization internally, often using more efficient techniques than simple locks.

Some of the key concurrent collections include:

- ConcurrentBag<T>: An unordered collection of objects that provides efficient support for adding and removing items from multiple threads without external locking. It's optimized for scenarios where threads produce and consume items.
- ConcurrentQueue<T>: A thread-safe FIFO (first-in, first-out) queue. Multiple threads can enqueue and dequeue items without interfering with each other.
- ConcurrentStack<T>: A thread-safe LIFO (last-in, first-out) stack. Similar to ConcurrentQueue<T>, it allows concurrent push and pop operations.
- ConcurrentDictionary<TKey, TValue>: A thread-safe dictionary that allows multiple threads to access and update key-value pairs concurrently. It provides efficient add, update, and retrieve operations without the need for external locking in most cases.
- BlockingCollection<T>: Provides a thread-safe way to add and remove items, with support for blocking when the

collection is empty (for consumers) or full (for producers). It's often used in producer-consumer scenarios.

Let's revisit our shared counter example, this time using ConcurrentBag<T> in a slightly different way to illustrate a producer-consumer pattern:

C#

```csharp
using System;
using System.Collections.Concurrent;
using System.Threading.Tasks;

public class ConcurrentCounterExample
{
    private static ConcurrentBag<int> _counterBag
= new ConcurrentBag<int>();

    public static void IncrementCounter()
    {
        _counterBag.Add(1);
        Console.WriteLine($"Increment added by
thread
{System.Threading.Thread.CurrentThread.ManagedThr
eadId}");
    }

    public static async Task Main(string[] args)
    {
        Task[] producers = new Task[5];
        for (int i = 0; i < producers.Length;
i++)
        {
            producers[i] = Task.Run(() =>
            {
                for (int j = 0; j < 1000; j++)
```

```
            {
                IncrementCounter();
            }
        });
    }

    await Task.WhenAll(producers);
    Console.WriteLine($"Final counter value
(approximate): {_counterBag.Count}"); // Should
be 5000
    }
}
```

In this example, instead of directly incrementing a shared integer with a lock, each thread adds a value to a ConcurrentBag<int>. The final count is simply the number of items in the bag. While this doesn't guarantee strict ordering or atomicity in the same way a lock does for a single variable, it can be more performant in high-contention scenarios by avoiding blocking. The choice between using locks and concurrent collections depends on the specific requirements of your concurrency scenario.

Handling concurrency and parallelism safely and efficiently in .NET 9 requires careful consideration. While synchronization primitives like locks, mutexes, and semaphores provide fundamental mechanisms for controlling access to shared resources, they should be used judiciously to avoid performance bottlenecks and deadlocks. Whenever possible, leveraging the thread-safe and optimized concurrent collections in the System.Collections.Concurrent namespace can often provide a more efficient and easier-to-manage approach for concurrent data access. Understanding the characteristics of your concurrency needs and choosing the appropriate synchronization or concurrent collection mechanism is key to building high-performance and reliable parallel applications.

Chapter 7: Optimizing Data Access

Alright, let's dive into a critical area for application performance: optimizing data access. Think of data access as the lifeline of many applications – how they retrieve, manipulate, and store information. Inefficient data access can be a major bottleneck, slowing down your application and impacting its scalability, regardless of how well the rest of your code is written. This chapter will explore performance considerations and best practices for various data access technologies in .NET 9, including Entity Framework Core (EF Core), ADO.NET, and even NoSQL databases, along with general querying techniques and caching strategies.

7.1 Performance Considerations with Entity Framework Core

Alright, let's really dig into the performance aspects of using Entity Framework Core (EF Core) in your .NET 9 applications. Think of EF Core as a powerful translator that allows you to work with your database using .NET objects. It handles a lot of the tedious work of converting between your object-oriented code and the relational structure of your database. While this abstraction simplifies development significantly, it's absolutely crucial to understand how EF Core works under the hood to avoid common performance pitfalls. Just like a powerful translator can sometimes misinterpret nuances if you're not careful with your language, EF Core can generate inefficient database queries if you're not mindful of how you structure your code.

One of the first and most significant areas to consider is efficient querying with LINQ. LINQ (Language Integrated Query) is the primary way you'll interact with your data using EF Core. You write LINQ queries against your DbSet properties, and EF Core translates these queries into SQL that is executed against your database. However, the way you formulate your LINQ queries can have a dramatic impact on the performance of the generated SQL.

A very common mistake that can lead to significant performance degradation is fetching more data than you actually need. If your LINQ query retrieves entire entities from the database when you only need a few specific columns, you're incurring unnecessary overhead in terms of data transfer between the database and your application, as well as increased memory consumption on the application side.

Consider a scenario where you need to display a list of product names on a webpage.

If you write a LINQ query like this:

C#

```
var productNames =
dbContext.Products.ToList().Select(p =>
p.Name).ToList();
```

You might think this is straightforward. However, what's happening here is that .ToList() is executed *first*, which means EF Core fetches *all* columns of *all* products from the database into memory as Product objects. Only then does the .Select(p => p.Name) operate on this in-memory collection to extract just the names. This is incredibly inefficient, especially if you have a large number of products with many columns you don't need.

The more efficient approach is to perform the selection of only the necessary columns within the database query:

C#

```
var productNamesEfficient =
dbContext.Products.Select(p => p.Name).ToList();
```

In this version, EF Core translates the .Select(p => p.Name) directly into the SQL query, so the database only returns the Name column, significantly reducing the data transferred.

Another crucial aspect of efficient LINQ querying with EF Core is being aware of operations that might be executed client-side (in your application's memory) instead of server-side (in the database). EF Core tries to translate as much of your LINQ query to SQL as possible. However, if your LINQ query includes operations or functions that EF Core cannot translate into SQL, it will fetch the necessary data into memory and then perform the remaining operations there. This can be a major performance killer, especially when dealing with large datasets.

For example, if you have a complex .Where() clause that uses a C# function that EF Core doesn't know how to translate, the entire table might be fetched into memory before the filtering is applied. To avoid this, try to use LINQ operators and expressions that have direct SQL equivalents. Examine the SQL generated by EF Core (you can configure logging to see this) to ensure your queries are being translated as you expect.

Now, let's talk about eager loading vs. lazy loading when dealing with related entities in your database. Imagine you have Order and OrderItem entities, where an Order can have multiple OrderItem records.

Eager loading is when you explicitly tell EF Core to load the related OrderItem entities along with the Order entities in a single database query using the .Include(o => o.OrderItems) method. This is beneficial when you know you will need to access the OrderItems for all the Order entities you are fetching. By doing it in one go, you avoid making separate database calls for each Order.

However, eagerly loading too many related entities, especially large collections or deep object graphs, can result in a very complex and potentially slow SQL query, and you might end up fetching a lot of related data that you don't actually use.

Lazy loading, on the other hand, is a feature where EF Core automatically loads related entities when you first access the navigation property (e.g., order.OrderItems). While this might seem appealing initially because it only loads related data when you need it, it can very easily lead to the "N+1 problem." If you fetch N Order entities and then iterate through them, accessing the OrderItems collection on each one for the first time will trigger N additional database queries (one for each order's items). This can result in a huge number of database round trips, significantly increasing the overall time taken, especially in web applications where database latency is a major factor.

The generally recommended best practice is to avoid lazy loading in most scenarios, especially in web applications. Instead, explicitly eager load the related entities you know you will need within the same query using .Include() or, for multiple levels of related data, .ThenInclude(). For more complex scenarios where you only need a subset of related data, consider using projections with .Select() to fetch only the specific properties you need from both the primary and related entities in a single, efficient query.

Finally, let's consider tracking vs. no-tracking queries. By default, when EF Core retrieves entities from the database, it keeps track of them. This change tracking mechanism allows EF Core to automatically detect any modifications you make to these entities and persist those changes back to the database when you call SaveChanges(). While this is essential for updating data, it comes with a performance overhead. EF Core needs to maintain a snapshot of the original values of the tracked entities so it can determine what has changed. This tracking consumes memory and adds processing time.

If you are fetching data for read-only purposes – for example, displaying information on a webpage or generating a report – and you do not intend to update these entities, you can significantly improve performance and reduce memory consumption by using no-tracking queries. You can achieve this by calling the .AsNoTracking() method on your LINQ query before you execute it with .ToList(), .FirstOrDefault(), etc.

C#

```
var readOnlyProducts = dbContext.Products

    .Where(p => p.Category == "Book")

    .AsNoTracking()

    .ToList();
```

To achieve optimal performance with EF Core, you need to be mindful of how you write your LINQ queries, understand the trade-offs between eager and lazy loading (and generally prefer eager loading or projections), and use no-tracking queries for read-only scenarios to reduce overhead. Being aware of these considerations will help you leverage the power of EF Core without sacrificing the performance of your .NET 9 applications.

7.2 Performance Considerations with ADO.NET

Alright, let's shift our focus to a more direct way of interacting with databases in .NET 9: ADO.NET. Think of ADO.NET as the foundational set of classes that provide you with the raw power to connect to and manipulate data in various data sources, including relational databases. While it requires writing more code compared to an ORM like Entity Framework Core, it also gives you finer-grained control over database interactions, which can be crucial for achieving optimal performance in certain scenarios. Understanding the performance considerations when using

ADO.NET is essential for building efficient data access layers in your applications.

One of the first and most significant performance aspects to be aware of when using ADO.NET is connection management, specifically connection pooling. Establishing a connection to a database can be a relatively expensive operation, involving network handshakes, authentication, and resource allocation on the database server. To mitigate this overhead, ADO.NET employs connection pooling by default.

When you open a database connection using a SqlConnection (for SQL Server, for example), ADO.NET manages a pool of available connections in the background. When you call connection.Close(), the connection isn't necessarily destroyed immediately. Instead, it's returned to the pool, where it can be reused for subsequent connection requests with the same connection string. This reuse avoids the cost of establishing a new connection from scratch, significantly improving the performance of applications that frequently connect to and disconnect from the database.

Consider a high-traffic web application that needs to process many database requests. Without connection pooling, each incoming request might have to establish a new database connection, leading to significant delays and resource consumption. With connection pooling, the application can quickly grab an existing connection from the pool, execute its query, and then return the connection to the pool for the next request.

It's crucial to ensure that you are closing your connections properly to allow them to be returned to the pool. The best way to do this is by using using statements when creating SqlConnection instances (and other disposable ADO.NET objects like SqlCommand and SqlDataReader). The using statement guarantees that the Dispose() method of the object is called when the block ends, even if an exception occurs. The Dispose() method is responsible for returning the connection to the pool. Failing to do so can lead to "connection leaks," where connections are held open unnecessarily, potentially exhausting the pool and causing performance issues or connection failures.

Another critical performance consideration, especially when dealing with user-provided input in your database queries, is the use of parameterized queries (also known as prepared statements). Constructing SQL queries by directly embedding user input into the SQL string opens your application to serious SQL injection vulnerabilities. Beyond security, parameterized queries can also offer significant performance benefits.

When you use a parameterized query, you define the structure of the SQL statement with placeholders (parameters) for the user-provided values. The database server can then compile and optimize an execution plan for this parameterized query. When you execute the query with different parameter values, the database can often reuse this pre-compiled execution plan, which is much faster than compiling a new SQL statement each time.

Here's an example contrasting an insecure and potentially less performant way of executing a query with a parameterized approach using SqlCommand:

C#

```
using System.Data.SqlClient;



// Insecure and potentially less performant
(vulnerable to SQL injection)

string unsafeSql = $"SELECT * FROM Users WHERE
Username = '{username}' AND Password =
'{password}'";
```

```csharp
using (SqlConnection connectionUnsafe = new
SqlConnection(connectionString))

{

    connectionUnsafe.Open();

    using (SqlCommand commandUnsafe = new
SqlCommand(unsafeSql, connectionUnsafe))

    {

        using (SqlDataReader reader =
commandUnsafe.ExecuteReader())

        {

            // Process results

        }

    }

}



// Secure and potentially more performant (uses
parameterized query)

string safeSql = "SELECT * FROM Users WHERE
Username = @Username AND Password = @Password";

using (SqlConnection connectionSafe = new
SqlConnection(connectionString))

{

    connectionSafe.Open();
```

```
    using (SqlCommand commandSafe = new
SqlCommand(safeSql, connectionSafe))

    {


commandSafe.Parameters.AddWithValue("@Username",
username);


commandSafe.Parameters.AddWithValue("@Password",
password);

        using (SqlDataReader reader =
commandSafe.ExecuteReader())

        {

            // Process results

        }

    }

}
```

In the safe example, the @Username and @Password are
parameters. ADO.NET handles the proper escaping and quoting of
these values before sending them to the database, preventing SQL
injection. The database can also optimize the execution plan for
this parameterized query, potentially leading to better
performance, especially for frequently executed queries with
different user credentials.

Finally, when retrieving data using ADO.NET, you have a choice
between using SqlDataReader (or the equivalent for other database
providers) and DataSet / DataTable. These serve different
purposes and have different performance characteristics.

A SqlDataReader provides a forward-only, read-only stream of data from the database. It fetches data row by row as you iterate through it. This approach is very efficient for processing large amounts of data because it doesn't load the entire result set into memory at once. It's ideal for scenarios where you need to read through the results and process them sequentially, without needing to go back to previous rows or manipulate the data in memory.

On the other hand, DataSet and DataTable represent an in-memory cache of data. They load the entire result set into memory, allowing you to navigate, sort, filter, and update the data without further trips to the database (until you explicitly persist changes). While this flexibility can be useful for certain scenarios, especially when binding data to UI controls or when you need to perform multiple operations on the data in memory, it can be very memory-intensive, especially for large result sets. Loading a massive table into a DataSet can consume significant memory and impact the performance of your application.

As a general guideline, for read-heavy operations or when you are dealing with potentially large amounts of data, using a SqlDataReader is often more performant and memory-efficient because it minimizes the amount of data held in memory at any given time. Use DataSet and DataTable more sparingly, primarily when you specifically need the in-memory data manipulation capabilities they offer or when binding relatively small datasets to UI elements.

Achieving optimal performance with ADO.NET involves careful connection management through proper closing of connections to leverage connection pooling, always using parameterized queries for security and potential performance benefits, and choosing the appropriate mechanism for retrieving data (SqlDataReader for efficient streaming, DataSet/DataTable for in-memory manipulation of smaller datasets). By being mindful of these considerations, you can build efficient and scalable data access layers using ADO.NET in your .NET 9 applications.

7.3 Efficient Querying Techniques and Indexing Strategies

Alright, let's talk about the art and science of writing efficient database queries and the crucial role that indexing plays in making those queries perform well, regardless of whether you're using an ORM like Entity Framework Core or writing raw SQL with ADO.NET in your .NET 9 applications. Think of your database as a massive library, and your queries as your requests for information. Efficient querying techniques are like knowing the Dewey Decimal System to quickly locate the right section, while indexing is like having a detailed card catalog that tells you exactly where each book (or row of data) is located. Without these, finding the information you need can be a slow and cumbersome process.

First, let's focus on efficient querying techniques. The way you structure your queries, whether in LINQ or SQL, can have a profound impact on how the database engine processes your request and ultimately on how quickly you get your data back.[1]

One fundamental principle is to select only the data you need. Just like you wouldn't check out every book in the library if you only need one, you should avoid selecting all columns (SELECT *) from your tables if you only need a subset of them. Fetching unnecessary data increases I/O overhead, network traffic, and memory consumption on both the database server and your application.[2] Always explicitly specify the columns you need in your SELECT statement or use LINQ's .Select() operator to project to an anonymous type or a Data Transfer Object (DTO) containing only the required properties.

Consider a scenario where you need to display a list of customer names and their email addresses.

An inefficient query might fetch all columns from the Customers table:

SQL

SELECT * FROM Customers;

A more efficient query would only retrieve the Name and Email columns:

SQL

SELECT Name, Email FROM Customers;

Similarly, in LINQ with EF Core, as we discussed earlier, using .Select(c => new { c.Name, c.Email }) will instruct EF Core to retrieve only these columns from the database.

Another crucial technique is to filter data as early as possible. Just like you'd narrow down your search to a specific section in the library before looking for a particular book, you should use WHERE clauses in SQL or .Where() operators in LINQ to filter the data at the database level before it's transferred to your application. This reduces the amount of data the database has to process and the amount of data that needs to be sent over the network.

For example, if you only need customers who live in a specific city, your query should include a WHERE clause to filter by that city:

SQL

SELECT Name, Email FROM Customers WHERE City = 'Lagos';

The equivalent in LINQ would be:

C#

```
var lagosCustomers = dbContext.Customers.Where(c
=> c.City == "Lagos").Select(c => new { c.Name,
c.Email }).ToList();
```

Be mindful of how you construct your WHERE clauses. Using functions or complex expressions on indexed columns in your WHERE clause can sometimes prevent the database from effectively using those indexes. For example, WHERE UPPER(ColumnName) = 'VALUE' might not use an index on ColumnName as efficiently as WHERE ColumnName = 'value'.

When joining multiple tables, ensure you are using efficient JOIN conditions. The columns you use in your ON clauses should ideally be indexed and have compatible data types. Incorrect or missing join conditions can lead to the database performing full table scans or inefficient merge joins, significantly impacting query performance.[3] Understand the different types of joins (INNER JOIN, LEFT JOIN, RIGHT JOIN) and use the one that best suits your needs. Avoid unnecessary joins if you don't need data from all the involved tables.

Now, let's move on to the indispensable role of indexing strategies. Think of an index in a database like the index at the back of a book. It allows the database engine to quickly locate specific rows of data without having to scan the entire table. Proper indexing is often the single most effective way to improve the performance of your database queries.[4]

The most common type of index is a B-tree index, which is efficient for a wide range of queries, including equality comparisons, range queries (>, <, BETWEEN), and ORDER BY clauses on the indexed columns.[5] You should consider creating indexes on columns that are frequently used in your WHERE clauses (especially in highly selective conditions that narrow down the result set significantly), in your JOIN conditions, and in your ORDER BY clauses, especially for large tables.

However, indexes are not free. They take up storage space, and they add overhead to INSERT, UPDATE, and DELETE operations because the database also has to maintain the indexes whenever the data in the table changes.[6] Therefore, you should only create indexes on columns that are actually used frequently in your queries. Having too many indexes can sometimes slow down write operations.[7]

Composite indexes (indexes on multiple columns) can be particularly useful for queries that often filter or sort by a combination of columns.[8] The order of columns in a composite index matters. The index is most effective for queries that include the leading columns of the index in their WHERE clause.

For example, if you frequently query orders by CustomerId and then by OrderDate, a composite index on (CustomerId, OrderDate) might be beneficial. A query that only filters by CustomerId would still be able to use this index, but a query that only filters by OrderDate might not use it as efficiently.

Consider also the different types of indexes available in your specific database system. For example, SQL Server offers clustered indexes (which determine the physical order of data in the table) and non-clustered indexes (which are separate structures that point to the data).[9] Understanding these different types and when to use them can further optimize your database performance. Full-text indexes are useful for efficient text searching, while spatial indexes are designed for querying geographical data.

Analyzing the execution plan of your queries is a crucial step in identifying whether your indexes are being used effectively and where potential performance bottlenecks might lie. Most database management tools provide a way to view the execution plan of a query. This plan shows you the steps the database engine takes to execute your query, including which indexes are used (or not used) and the estimated cost of each operation.[10] By examining the execution plan, you can often identify slow operations like full table scans that could be improved by adding or modifying indexes.[11]

Writing efficient queries and implementing a well-thought-out indexing strategy are fundamental to achieving optimal data access performance in your .NET 9 applications. By selecting only the necessary data, filtering early, using efficient join conditions, and strategically creating and maintaining indexes on frequently queried columns, you can significantly reduce the load on your database and improve the responsiveness and scalability of your applications.[12] Always analyze your query execution plans to ensure your queries and indexes are working together effectively.

7.4 Implementing Caching Strategies

Alright, let's talk about a powerful technique for boosting the performance and scalability of your .NET 9 applications, especially when dealing with frequently accessed data that doesn't change too often: caching. Think of caching as creating a temporary storage layer that sits closer to your application than the original data source (like a database or a remote API). By storing copies of frequently requested data in this cache, your application can retrieve it much faster on subsequent requests, reducing the load on the underlying data source and improving response times for your users. Implementing effective caching strategies can significantly enhance the overall user experience and the efficiency of your application.

The fundamental idea behind caching is to trade off a small amount of memory to save on more expensive operations like database queries or network calls. Just like you might keep frequently used tools on your workbench instead of having to go to the main storage room every time, caching keeps frequently accessed data readily available in your application's memory or a nearby distributed system.

There are several different levels and types of caching you can implement in your .NET 9 applications, depending on the nature of your data, how often it changes, and the scale of your application. Let's explore some common strategies.

Memory Caching

One of the simplest and often most effective forms of caching is in-memory caching. This involves storing data directly in the memory of your application's process. .NET provides built-in support for in-memory caching through the Microsoft.Extensions.Caching.Memory NuGet package. You can use the IMemoryCache interface to interact with the in-memory cache.

IMemoryCache allows you to store and retrieve objects based on a key.

You can also configure various options for cached items, such as:

- Expiration policies: You can set absolute expiration times (the item will be removed from the cache after a specific duration) or sliding expiration times (the item's expiration time is reset each time it's accessed).
- Eviction policies: If the cache reaches a certain size or memory pressure is high, the cache might automatically remove some items based on priority or how recently they were used.
- Cache dependencies: You can link cached items to other data sources, so if the underlying data changes, the cached item can be automatically invalidated.

Here's a basic example of using IMemoryCache in a .NET service:

C#

```csharp
using Microsoft.Extensions.Caching.Memory;

using System;

using System.Threading.Tasks;


public class ProductService

{

    private readonly IMemoryCache _cache;

    private readonly IProductRepository
_productRepository; // Assume this fetches
product data


    public ProductService(IMemoryCache cache,
IProductRepository productRepository)

    {

        _cache = cache;

        _productRepository = productRepository;

    }


    public async Task<Product>
GetProductAsync(int id)

    {

        string cacheKey = $"product:{id}";
```

```csharp
        // Try to get the product from the cache

        if (_cache.TryGetValue(cacheKey, out
Product cachedProduct))

            {

                Console.WriteLine($"Retrieved product
{id} from cache.");

                return cachedProduct;

            }


        // If not in cache, fetch from the
repository

        var product = await
_productRepository.GetProductByIdAsync(id);


        if (product != null)

            {

                // Store the product in the cache
with an expiration policy

                var cacheEntryOptions = new
MemoryCacheEntryOptions()


.SetAbsoluteExpiration(TimeSpan.FromMinutes(10))
// Cache for 10 minutes
```

```csharp
        .SetSlidingExpiration(TimeSpan.FromSeconds(30));
// Reset expiration if accessed within 30 seconds


            _cache.Set(cacheKey, product,
cacheEntryOptions);

            Console.WriteLine($"Cached product
{id}.");

        }


        return product;

    }

}


public class Product

{

    public int Id { get; set; }

    public string Name { get; set; }

    public decimal Price { get; set; }

}


public interface IProductRepository
```

```
{

    Task<Product> GetProductByIdAsync(int id);

}
```

```
// Assume a concrete implementation of
IProductRepository exists
```

In this ProductService, when we need to retrieve a product, we first check if it exists in the in-memory cache using _cache.TryGetValue(). If it's found, we return the cached version directly, avoiding a database call. If it's not in the cache, we fetch it from the repository, and if found, we store it in the cache with an expiration policy before returning it. Subsequent requests for the same product within the cache's lifetime will be served from memory, which is much faster.

In-memory caching is simple to implement and very fast, as it involves accessing data directly in the application's memory.

However, it has some limitations:

- Scalability: In a web application running across multiple server instances (a web farm), each instance has its own separate in-memory cache. Changes in one instance's cache are not reflected in others, potentially leading to inconsistent data.
- Volatility: If the application restarts, the entire in-memory cache is lost.
- Memory pressure: Caching large amounts of data in memory can put pressure on the application's memory resources.

Distributed Caching (Redis, Memcached)

For applications that need to scale across multiple instances or require a more persistent and shared cache, distributed caching systems like Redis and Memcached are often a better choice. These systems run as separate services (or clusters of services) and can be accessed by multiple instances of your application.

Distributed caches offer several advantages over in-memory caching:

- Shared state: All application instances can access the same cache, ensuring data consistency across the application.
- Scalability: Distributed caches can often be scaled horizontally by adding more nodes to handle increased load.
- Persistence: Some distributed caches (like Redis with persistence enabled) can survive application restarts, preserving the cached data.

To use a distributed cache in .NET 9, you typically rely on NuGet packages provided by the maintainers of the specific cache (e.g., StackExchange.Redis for Redis, EnyimMemcachedCore for Memcached). The API for interacting with these caches is generally similar to IMemoryCache, allowing you to set and get values based on a key, with options for expiration.

Here's a conceptual example of using Redis as a distributed cache:

C#

```
using Microsoft.Extensions.Caching.Distributed;

using StackExchange.Redis;

using System;

using System.Text.Json;
```

```csharp
using System.Threading.Tasks;


public class ProductServiceWithRedisCache

{

    private readonly IDistributedCache
_distributedCache;

    private readonly IProductRepository
_productRepository;


    public
ProductServiceWithRedisCache(IDistributedCache
distributedCache, IProductRepository
productRepository)

    {

        _distributedCache = distributedCache;

        _productRepository = productRepository;

    }


    public async Task<Product>
GetProductAsync(int id)

    {

        string cacheKey = $"product:{id}";
```

```csharp
        string cachedProductJson = await
_distributedCache.GetStringAsync(cacheKey);


        if
(!string.IsNullOrEmpty(cachedProductJson))

        {

            Console.WriteLine($"Retrieved product
{id} from Redis cache.");

            return
JsonSerializer.Deserialize<Product>(cachedProduct
Json);

        }


        var product = await
_productRepository.GetProductByIdAsync(id);


        if (product != null)

        {

            var cacheEntryOptions = new
DistributedCacheEntryOptions()


.SetAbsoluteExpiration(TimeSpan.FromMinutes(10))


.SetSlidingExpiration(TimeSpan.FromSeconds(30));
```

```
        string productJson =
JsonSerializer.Serialize(product);

        await
_distributedCache.SetStringAsync(cacheKey,
productJson, cacheEntryOptions);

        Console.WriteLine($"Cached product
{id} in Redis.");

    }



    return product;

  }

}


// (Product class and IProductRepository
interface as defined before)
```

In this example, we inject an IDistributedCache (provided by a Redis implementation) instead of IMemoryCache. We use GetStringAsync to retrieve from the cache (data is typically stored as strings in distributed caches) and SetStringAsync to store data, serializing and deserializing our Product object to and from JSON.

Distributed caching introduces a bit more complexity in terms of setup and potential network latency when accessing the cache, but it provides significant benefits for scalability and data consistency in distributed applications.

Choosing the right caching strategy depends on your application's specific needs. In-memory caching can be great for single-instance applications or for local, frequently accessed data. Distributed caching is often necessary for larger, multi-instance applications that require a shared and potentially more durable cache. You can even use a combination of both, with a local in-memory cache acting as a first-level cache in front of a distributed cache for even better performance.

In-Memory Caching

.NET provides built-in in-memory caching capabilities using MemoryCache. This is suitable for caching data that doesn't change frequently and is accessed often within a single application instance. You can set expiration policies and eviction strategies for the cache.

Distributed Caching (Redis, Memcached)

For applications that run across multiple instances (e.g., in a web farm or cloud environment), a distributed cache like Redis or Memcached is often a better choice. These caches store data in a separate process or cluster and can be shared across multiple instances of your application.

7.5 Working with NoSQL Databases for Performance

Alright, let's shift gears and explore the performance landscape when it comes to NoSQL databases in your .NET 9 applications. Unlike relational databases with their structured schemas and SQL querying, NoSQL databases offer a variety of data models (document, key-value, graph, column-family) that can provide significant performance advantages for specific use cases. Think of NoSQL databases as specialized tools in your data storage shed, each designed for particular kinds of tasks where they can outperform the more general-purpose relational database.

Understanding the performance characteristics of the NoSQL database you're using and how to optimize your queries is crucial for building high-performing applications that leverage these technologies.

Understanding NoSQL Performance Characteristics

The performance characteristics of NoSQL databases can vary significantly depending on the specific type of NoSQL database you choose. For instance, a key-value store like Redis is often incredibly fast for simple reads and writes based on a key, as it typically operates primarily in memory. Document databases like MongoDB excel at handling semi-structured data and can offer good performance for queries that target specific fields within documents. Column-family databases like Cassandra are designed for high availability and scalability, often sacrificing some consistency for raw write throughput and distributed reads. Graph databases like Neo4j are optimized for traversing relationships between data points.

One of the key factors influencing the performance of many NoSQL databases is their schema-less or flexible schema nature. This allows for faster development and easier scaling, as you're not bound by a rigid table structure. However, it also means that query optimization often focuses on different aspects compared to relational databases. For example, instead of optimizing complex joins across multiple tables, you might be optimizing how you structure your documents or how you traverse relationships in a graph.

Another important aspect is scalability. Many NoSQL databases are designed to scale horizontally across multiple nodes, allowing them to handle very large datasets and high traffic loads. Their performance often remains consistent as the data grows, provided they are properly sharded and distributed.

Data locality is also a key performance consideration in some NoSQL databases, particularly document and column-family stores. By structuring your data in a way that related information is stored together (e.g., embedding related documents or grouping columns), you can often reduce the number of reads needed to retrieve all the necessary information for a particular use case. This can significantly improve read performance.

For example, in an e-commerce application using a document database, you might embed the customer's recent orders directly within the customer document. When you need to display the customer's profile along with their recent orders, you can retrieve all the information in a single read operation, rather than performing separate queries for the customer and their orders as you might in a relational database.

Query Optimization in NoSQL Databases

Query optimization in NoSQL databases is highly dependent on the specific database you are using and its query language or API.

However, some general principles apply:

- Understand the query language: Each NoSQL database has its own way of querying data. For document databases like MongoDB, you'll be working with a JSON-like query language. For graph databases like Neo4j, you'll use Cypher or a similar graph traversal language. Understanding the specific operators, syntax, and capabilities of the query language is the first step towards writing efficient queries.
- Target your queries: Just like with SQL, you should aim to retrieve only the data you need. Many NoSQL databases allow you to specify which fields to include or exclude in your query results, reducing the amount of data transferred.
- Leverage indexing: While NoSQL databases are schema-less, they still support indexing to improve query performance. However, the types of indexes and how you define them can vary greatly. In document databases, you

might create indexes on specific fields within your documents. In graph databases, you'll create indexes on node properties or relationship types. Understanding the indexing capabilities of your NoSQL database and creating appropriate indexes for your common query patterns is crucial. For example, if you frequently query users by their email address in a document database, creating an index on the email field will significantly speed up these lookups.

- Optimize data structure: The way you structure your data can have a significant impact on query performance. As mentioned earlier, embedding related data can improve read performance for certain use cases. However, you need to consider the trade-offs with data redundancy and update complexity. Denormalization is a common strategy in NoSQL databases to optimize for specific query patterns.

- Understand query performance characteristics: Be aware of the performance implications of different query operators in your NoSQL database. For example, in MongoDB, certain aggregation pipeline stages might be more resource-intensive than simple find operations. In Neo4j, the complexity of your graph traversals can significantly affect query time. Consult the documentation for your specific NoSQL database to understand the performance characteristics of its query language.

- Profile your queries: Most NoSQL databases provide tools or mechanisms for profiling your queries, allowing you to see how long they take to execute and identify potential bottlenecks. Use these tools to analyze the performance of your critical queries and identify areas for optimization.

- Consider eventual consistency: Some NoSQL databases offer eventual consistency models for better scalability and availability. Be aware that reads might not always reflect the most recent writes immediately. Design your application to handle this if necessary.

Working with NoSQL databases for performance often involves a different mindset than working with relational databases. It's about understanding the strengths of the chosen data model, structuring your data appropriately for your access patterns, leveraging the specific querying capabilities and indexing features of the database, and profiling your queries to identify and address bottlenecks. By focusing on these aspects, you can build high-performing .NET 9 applications that take full advantage of the unique characteristics of NoSQL databases.

Chapter 8: Cross-Platform Development Fundamentals with .NET 9

Alright, let's shift our focus to one of the most exciting aspects of modern .NET development: building applications that can run seamlessly on multiple operating systems. Think of cross-platform development as the ability to write your code once and have it execute on Windows, macOS, and Linux, and even extend to mobile platforms like iOS and Android. .NET 9 is designed with this capability at its core, and understanding the underlying architecture and the tools it provides is essential for reaching the widest possible audience with your applications.

8.1 Understanding the .NET Cross-Platform Architecture

Alright, let's really get into the nuts and bolts of how .NET 9 achieves its remarkable ability to run on different operating systems. Think of it like this: you write your code in a common language, C#, and .NET 9 has a clever way of making sure that language can be understood and executed correctly whether you're on a Windows machine, a sleek Mac, or a robust Linux server. This magic, as it might seem, is actually the result of a well-designed architecture that carefully separates your code from the specifics of the underlying operating system.

At the heart of this cross-platform capability is the .NET runtime. Now, it's important to understand that the ".NET runtime" isn't a single monolithic entity that's identical across all operating systems. Instead, think of it as a set of core components that are implemented *for* each specific operating system. These components include the Common Language Runtime (CLR), which is the execution engine for your .NET code, and the foundational Base Class Libraries (BCL), which provide the essential building blocks for your applications, like handling files, network operations, and data structures.

The key to the cross-platform nature lies in the way these core components are built. Microsoft and the vibrant .NET community have invested significant effort in creating abstractions. When your .NET code needs to perform an operation that interacts with the operating system – say, writing data to a file – your code doesn't directly call the specific file system APIs of Windows, macOS, or Linux. Instead, it calls a .NET API provided by the BCL (like System.IO.File.WriteAllText). The .NET runtime, which is running on the specific operating system, then takes this .NET API call and translates it into the appropriate set of system calls that the underlying OS understands.

Think of it like using a universal remote control for your TV, DVD player, and sound system. You press the "play" button, and the remote sends the correct signal to each device, even though they might use different internal communication protocols. Similarly, your .NET code uses a consistent set of .NET APIs, and the .NET runtime handles the "translation" to the specific OS it's running on.

For example, when you use System.IO.File.WriteAllText on Windows, the .NET runtime will ultimately make calls to the Windows API for file system operations. On macOS, the same .NET API call will be translated into the corresponding POSIX system calls that macOS uses for file I/O. The beauty is that as a .NET developer, you generally don't need to worry about these platform-specific details. You write your code using the consistent .NET APIs, and the runtime takes care of the underlying platform differences.

This abstraction extends beyond just file I/O. It covers many fundamental areas, including networking (using System.Net.Http), threading (System.Threading.Tasks), and even aspects of graphics and user interface (though for UI, you often use higher-level cross-platform frameworks like .NET MAUI, which build upon these lower-level abstractions).

However, it's also important to acknowledge that this abstraction isn't always a perfect one-to-one mapping. Operating systems have their own unique features and capabilities. While .NET provides a common set of APIs for the most common tasks, there might be situations where you need to access platform-specific functionalities that are not part of the core cross-platform .NET APIs. In such cases, you might need to write platform-specific code, often using conditional compilation (which we'll discuss later) or by utilizing platform-specific libraries.

The key takeaway here is that the .NET runtime acts as a crucial intermediary, providing a consistent interface for your code while handling the underlying operating system differences. This is the foundation that allows .NET 9 applications to achieve true cross-platform compatibility for a wide range of application types.

.NET Runtime and Operating System Abstraction

At the heart of the .NET cross-platform capability is the .NET runtime. Unlike the original .NET Framework, which was tightly coupled to Windows, the modern .NET runtime (which evolved from .NET Core) is designed to be platform-agnostic. This means that the core execution engine, including the Common Language Runtime (CLR) and the base class libraries, are implemented in a way that they can run on different operating systems.

Microsoft and the .NET community have put in a significant effort to abstract away the operating system-specific details. When your .NET code needs to perform an operation that interacts with the OS (like file I/O, networking, or threading), the .NET runtime provides a consistent API that your code uses. The runtime then handles the translation of these API calls into the specific system calls required by the underlying operating system (Windows API on Windows, POSIX on macOS and Linux).

Think of it like a universal translator. Your .NET code speaks a common language (.NET APIs), and the runtime acts as a translator, converting your requests into the specific dialect understood by each operating system. This abstraction layer is what allows your C# code to run on different platforms without you having to write platform-specific code for most common operations.

For example, the System.IO.File class provides methods for reading and writing files. When you use these methods, you don't need to worry about the specific system calls that Windows, macOS, or Linux use for file operations. The .NET runtime handles these differences for you. Similarly, the System.Net.Http.HttpClient class allows you to make web requests, and the runtime takes care of the underlying network communication mechanisms on each platform.

The Role of .NET Standard

While the .NET runtime provides a cross-platform foundation, there's also a need for a common set of APIs that you can rely on in your libraries and applications that you want to run everywhere. This is where .NET Standard comes in.

.NET Standard is a formal specification of .NET APIs that are guaranteed to be available across all .NET implementations, including .NET Framework (to a certain extent), .NET Core, and .NET 9. It defines a contract – if a .NET implementation conforms to a specific version of .NET Standard, it must support all the APIs defined in that version.

Think of .NET Standard as a common denominator. If you build a class library that targets a specific version of .NET Standard (e.g., .NET Standard 2.0), you can be confident that this library can be used by applications built with different .NET implementations that also target or are compatible with that version of .NET Standard.

For example, if you're building a library that contains your core business logic and you want it to be usable in both an ASP.NET Core web application (running on Linux) and a .NET MAUI mobile application (running on iOS and Android), you would target a .NET Standard version that is supported by all these platforms. This allows you to share a significant portion of your code across your different applications, maximizing code reuse and reducing development effort.

While .NET Standard provides a great way to share code, it's important to note that it doesn't include all the APIs available in specific .NET implementations. For example, UI-specific APIs like WPF (Windows Presentation Foundation) or UIKit (for iOS) are not part of .NET Standard because they are inherently platform-specific.

With the evolution towards .NET 5 and later (including .NET 9), Microsoft's strategy has shifted somewhat. Instead of targeting .NET Standard as the primary way to achieve cross-platform compatibility within the unified .NET platform, you can now often target the specific .NET TFM (Target Framework Moniker) directly (e.g., net9.0). This .NET TFM implicitly includes support for Windows, macOS, and Linux. However, .NET Standard still plays a crucial role for libraries that need to maintain compatibility with older .NET Framework versions or with other .NET implementations that might not be part of the unified .NET platform.

8.2 Exploring Target Framework Monikers (TFMs)

Alright, let's talk about a seemingly small but incredibly important concept when it comes to cross-platform .NET development: Target Framework Monikers (TFMs). Think of a TFM as a special label that you put on your project, telling the .NET SDK exactly which version (or flavor) of .NET your code is designed to run on.

It's like specifying the precise dialect of the .NET language your project is speaking. This ensures that your project is built against the correct set of libraries and runtime components.

You specify the TFM in your project file, which is the .csproj file for C# projects.[1] It's usually found within the <PropertyGroup> tags. For a simple, single-target project, you'll see an element like <TargetFramework>net9.0</TargetFramework>. This tells the .NET SDK that this project is targeting .NET 9.

Now, why are TFMs so important for cross-platform development? Because they are the key to telling the .NET SDK which set of platform-specific implementations of the base class libraries and which version of the .NET runtime your application or library is expecting. When you target a specific TFM, the .NET SDK will ensure that your build process uses the correct reference assemblies (which contain the metadata for the .NET APIs) and that your application is packaged in a way that's compatible with the target runtime.

Let's explore some of the common TFMs you'll encounter in cross-platform .NET development:

First, there's .NET Standard (e.g., netstandard2.0, netstandard2.1). As we discussed earlier, .NET Standard is a specification of .NET APIs that are guaranteed to be available across all compliant .NET implementations.[2] When you target a specific version of .NET Standard (like netstandard2.0, which has broad support across .NET Framework, .NET Core, and .NET 9), you're essentially saying, "My library uses only these common APIs, so it should be usable by any application that also targets or is compatible with this version of .NET Standard." Libraries that contain your core business logic and need to be shared across different types of .NET applications (e.g., a class library used by both a web API and a mobile app) will often target a .NET Standard TFM.

Then, there's .NET (e.g., net9.0). This TFM targets the unified .NET platform, which currently is .NET 9. When you target net9.0, you're saying, "My application is designed to run on the modern, cross-platform .NET runtime." The .NET 9 SDK includes platform-specific implementations of the base class libraries for Windows, macOS, and Linux. So, an application targeting net9.0 can run on any of these operating systems without needing to be recompiled for each one. This is the primary TFM you'll likely use for your cross-platform console applications, background services, and even the backend of your web applications built with ASP.NET Core.

Finally, there are platform-specific TFMs (e.g., net9.0-windows, net9.0-macos, net9.0-android, net9.0-ios).[3] These TFMs allow you to target a specific operating system or platform and gain access to APIs that are unique to that platform. For example, if you target net9.0-windows, your application can use Windows-specific APIs that are not available on macOS or Linux.[4] Similarly, if you're building a user interface application with .NET MAUI, you'll use net9.0-android and net9.0-ios to target those mobile platforms and access their specific UI toolkits and device features through the .NET MAUI abstraction layer.[5]

The choice of TFM for your project is crucial. If you're building a reusable library, targeting .NET Standard provides the widest compatibility. If you're building an application that needs to run cross-platform without accessing platform-specific APIs, targeting .NET 9 is usually the way to go. If you need to leverage platform-specific features (like Windows-only APIs or Android-specific functionalities), you'll use the corresponding platform-specific TFM.

Understanding TFMs is the first step in controlling the cross-platform reach of your .NET applications and libraries. It dictates the set of APIs you can use and the runtime environment your code is built for. In the next section, we'll explore how you can even target multiple TFMs within a single project to offer different levels of compatibility or to include platform-specific code.

8.3 Multi-Targeting in .NET Projects

Alright, let's talk about a really powerful technique that takes cross-platform development in .NET a step further: multi-targeting. Think of multi-targeting as the ability for a single project to be built against multiple .NET frameworks simultaneously. It's like having your project speak multiple dialects of the .NET language at the same time, allowing it to be consumed by a wider range of applications and libraries built on different .NET implementations or versions. This can be particularly useful when you're creating libraries that you want to share across different parts of your ecosystem or with the broader .NET community.

Why would you want to multi-target? Consider a scenario where you're building a class library that contains some core utility functions. You might want this library to be usable by your existing applications that are still running on older versions of the .NET Framework for compatibility reasons. At the same time, you also want it to leverage the latest performance improvements and features available in .NET 9 for your newer applications. Multi-targeting allows you to achieve both of these goals with a single project.

To enable multi-targeting in your .NET project, you'll modify your project file (.csproj). Instead of using the <TargetFramework> element (singular) to specify a single target framework moniker (TFM), you'll use the <TargetFrameworks> element (plural). Within this element, you list the different TFMs you want to target, separated by semicolons.

Here's a simple example of a project file that is configured to multi-target both .NET 9 and .NET Standard 2.0:

XML

```xml
<Project Sdk="Microsoft.NET.Sdk">

  <PropertyGroup>


<TargetFrameworks>net9.0;netstandard2.0</TargetFrameworks>

  </PropertyGroup>

</Project>
```

When the .NET SDK builds this project, it will essentially perform the build process twice: once for net9.0 and once for netstandard2.0. The output will typically be two separate sets of compiled assemblies, one for each target framework. When a consuming project references this multi-targeted library, the .NET runtime will automatically pick the assembly that is the best match for the consuming project's target framework. For example, a project targeting net9.0 will use the net9.0 version of your library, while a project targeting .NET Framework 4.8 (which is compatible with .NET Standard 2.0) will use the .NET Standard 2.0 version.

Multi-targeting becomes particularly interesting when you need to write code that behaves differently or utilizes APIs that are specific to a particular target framework. For instance, you might want to use some of the newer performance-oriented APIs available in .NET 9 when your library is consumed by a .NET 9 application, but fall back to more widely compatible APIs when it's used by an application targeting .NET Standard 2.0.

You can achieve this conditional behavior using conditional compilation with preprocessor directives. The .NET SDK automatically defines certain preprocessor symbols based on the target framework your code is being compiled against. You can use the #if, #elif, #else, and #endif directives along with these symbols to include or exclude specific blocks of code during compilation for each target framework.

Here's an example of a library that multi-targets .NET 9 and .NET Standard 2.0 and uses conditional compilation to provide a platform-specific string:

C#

```csharp
using System;


public class PlatformInfo

{

    public static string GetPlatformName()

    {
#if NET9_0

        return
System.Runtime.InteropServices.RuntimeInformation
.OSDescription;

#elif NETSTANDARD2_0

        return ".NET Standard 2.0";

#else

        return "Unknown Platform";
```

```
#endif

    }

}
```

When this code is compiled targeting net9.0, the code within the #if NET9_0 block will be included, and it will use the System.Runtime.InteropServices.RuntimeInformation.OSDescript ion property (which provides information about the operating system the application is running on). When the same code is compiled targeting netstandard2.0, the #elif NETSTANDARD2_0 block will be included, and it will simply return the string ".NET Standard 2.0". The #else block acts as a fallback for any other target frameworks.

The .NET SDK defines various preprocessor symbols based on the TFM. For example, for .NET Standard 2.0, the symbol NETSTANDARD2_0 is defined. For .NET 9, the symbol NET9_0 is defined. You can find a comprehensive list of these predefined symbols in the .NET documentation. You can also define your own custom preprocessor symbols in your project file if needed.

Multi-targeting allows you to create versatile libraries that can cater to a broad range of .NET applications, taking advantage of the specific capabilities of each targeted framework while still providing a baseline level of functionality across all of them. It's a powerful tool for library authors and for teams that need to maintain compatibility with different .NET versions within their own codebase.

8.5 Sharing Code Effectively Across Platforms

Alright, let's talk about a core goal in cross-platform development: sharing code effectively between your applications that target different operating systems or platforms. Think of it as having a common codebase for the parts of your application that are platform-agnostic, allowing you to write that code once and reuse it across your Windows, macOS, Linux, iOS, and Android projects. This not only saves you a significant amount of development time and effort but also helps ensure consistency in the logic and behavior of your application across all the platforms it runs on.

There are primarily two main strategies for sharing code effectively across platforms in .NET 9: utilizing .NET Standard libraries and creating platform-specific implementations via interfaces. Let's explore each of these in detail.

Utilizing .NET Standard Libraries

As we've discussed before, .NET Standard is a formal specification of .NET APIs that are guaranteed to be available across all compliant .NET implementations. This makes it an excellent choice for creating class libraries that contain your core business logic, data models, utility functions, and other platform-independent code. If you build a library that targets a specific version of .NET Standard (like netstandard2.0 or netstandard2.1), you can be confident that this library can be referenced and used by applications built with different .NET implementations (like .NET Framework, .NET Core, .NET 9, Xamarin, and .NET MAUI) that are compatible with that version of .NET Standard.

Consider a real-world example: you're building a multi-platform application for managing a user's tasks. You might have a core library that handles the business logic for creating, updating, and categorizing tasks, as well as the data models that represent a task. This core library doesn't need to know anything about the user interface or the specific operating system the application is running on. By targeting a .NET Standard TFM for this core library, you can then reference it from your Windows desktop application (using WPF or WinForms), your macOS application (using .NET MAUI), your Android and iOS mobile applications (also using .NET MAUI), and even a backend web API (using ASP.NET Core running on Linux). This allows you to share all that essential task management logic and data structures across all these different platforms without having to rewrite it for each one.

Here's a simplified example of a .NET Standard library containing a Task data model and a basic TaskManager class:

C#

```
// MyTaskLibrary.csproj (Target Framework:
netstandard2.1)

<Project Sdk="Microsoft.NET.Sdk">

  <PropertyGroup>


<TargetFramework>netstandard2.1</TargetFramework>

  </PropertyGroup>

</Project>
```

C#

```
// Task.cs

using System;


namespace MyTaskLibrary.Models

{
```

```csharp
    public class Task

    {

        public Guid Id { get; set; }

        public string Title { get; set; }

        public string Description { get; set; }

        public DateTime DueDate { get; set; }

        public bool IsCompleted { get; set; }

    }

}


// TaskManager.cs

using System;

using System.Collections.Generic;

using MyTaskLibrary.Models;


namespace MyTaskLibrary.Services

{

    public class TaskManager

    {

        private readonly List<Task> _tasks = new
List<Task>();
```

```csharp
public void AddTask(Task task)

{

    task.Id = Guid.NewGuid();

    _tasks.Add(task);

}


public Task GetTaskById(Guid id)

{

    return _tasks.Find(t => t.Id == id);

}



public IEnumerable<Task>
GetIncompleteTasks()

    {

        return _tasks.FindAll(t =>
!t.IsCompleted);

    }

    }

}
```

This MyTaskLibrary, targeting .NET Standard 2.1, can now be referenced and used by various applications targeting compatible

.NET implementations, allowing them to share the task management logic and data models.

Creating Platform-Specific Implementations via Interfaces

While .NET Standard allows you to share a lot of code, there will inevitably be situations where you need to interact with platform-specific features or APIs. For example, accessing the device's camera on a mobile phone, interacting with the Windows registry on a desktop application, or using specific Linux system calls. In these cases, you can't rely solely on .NET Standard.

A powerful pattern for handling such scenarios while still maintaining a good degree of code sharing is to define interfaces in your .NET Standard library that describe the platform-specific functionality you need. Then, you can create concrete implementations of these interfaces in your platform-specific application projects. Your core, platform-agnostic code in the .NET Standard library can then depend on these interfaces. At runtime, you'll need a mechanism (often dependency injection) to provide the appropriate platform-specific implementation based on the operating system the application is running on.

Consider a scenario where you need to access the device's local storage. The way you do this is very different on iOS, Android, Windows, and macOS.

You can define an ILocalStorageService interface in your .NET Standard library:

C#

```
// MyCoreLibrary.csproj (Target Framework:
netstandard2.1)

public interface ILocalStorageService
```

```
{

    Task<string> ReadFileAsync(string filename);

    Task WriteFileAsync(string filename, string
content);

}
```

Then, in your platform-specific application projects, you can create concrete implementations of this interface:

C#

```
// MyAndroidApp.csproj (Target Framework:
net9.0-android)

public class AndroidLocalStorageService :
ILocalStorageService

{

    public async Task<string>
ReadFileAsync(string filename)

    {

        // Android-specific implementation using
Android APIs

        return await
Android.OS.Environment.ExternalStorageDirectory.P
ath.ReadFileAsync(filename);

    }
```

```csharp
    public async Task WriteFileAsync(string
filename, string content)

    {

        // Android-specific implementation using
Android APIs

        await
Android.OS.Environment.ExternalStorageDirectory.P
ath.WriteFileAsync(filename, content);

    }

}
```

C#

// MyiOSApp.csproj (Target Framework: net9.0-ios)

```csharp
public class iOSLocalStorageService :
ILocalStorageService

{

    public async Task<string>
ReadFileAsync(string filename)

    {

        // iOS-specific implementation using iOS
APIs

        return await
Foundation.NSFileManager.DefaultManager.GetUrlFor
UbiquityContainer(null,
true).Path.ReadFileAsync(filename);
```

```csharp
    }

    public async Task WriteFileAsync(string
filename, string content)

    {

        // iOS-specific implementation using iOS
APIs

        await
Foundation.NSFileManager.DefaultManager.GetUrlFor
UbiquityContainer(null,
true).Path.WriteFileAsync(filename, content);

    }

}


// Similar implementations for Windows and macOS
```

In your core, platform-agnostic code (in the .NET Standard library or a shared project), you would depend on the ILocalStorageService interface. At runtime, you would use a dependency injection container to register the appropriate platform-specific implementation based on the operating system your application is running on. This way, your core logic remains platform-agnostic, while the platform-specific details are handled by the concrete implementations.

This approach allows you to share a significant amount of code (the interfaces and the core logic that depends on them) while still being able to leverage platform-specific capabilities when necessary. It promotes a clean separation of concerns and makes your codebase more maintainable and testable across different platforms.

Chapter 9: Building Desktop Applications with .NET 9 (Windows, macOS, Linux)

Alright, let's shift our focus to the exciting world of building desktop applications that can run natively on Windows, macOS, and Linux using .NET 9. Think of desktop applications as the software you install and run directly on your computer, offering rich user interfaces and powerful capabilities. While the web and mobile have become dominant, there's still a strong need for well-crafted desktop applications, and .NET 9 provides several compelling options for creating them in a cross-platform manner.

9.1 Introduction to Modern .NET UI Frameworks for Desktop

Alright, let's get acquainted with the exciting landscape of building user interfaces for desktop applications that can run on Windows, macOS, and Linux using .NET 9. Think of desktop applications as the software you install and run directly on your computer – the kind that offers rich, interactive experiences tailored to the power and capabilities of a personal computer. While the web browser has become a ubiquitous platform, and mobile apps dominate our pockets, there's still a significant need for well-crafted desktop applications for various tasks, from productivity tools to creative software. The good news is that .NET 9 provides us with some really compelling options for creating these applications in a way that isn't tied to just one operating system.

In the past, if you wanted to build a .NET desktop application, you might have primarily thought of Windows-specific technologies like WPF (Windows Presentation Foundation) or WinForms. These are powerful frameworks, but they inherently limit your application to running only on Windows. The modern .NET ecosystem, however, offers UI frameworks that are specifically designed with cross-platform capabilities in mind. These frameworks allow you to write a significant portion of your UI code once and have it run on Windows, macOS, and Linux, saving you considerable time and effort compared to building separate applications for each platform.

Let's explore two of the most prominent and actively developed players in this space: .NET MAUI and Avalonia UI. These frameworks take different architectural approaches to achieve cross-platform UI development, and understanding their philosophies and capabilities will help you choose the right tool for your specific needs.

First, let's talk about .NET MAUI (Multi-platform App UI). This is Microsoft's evolution of Xamarin.Forms, and it represents a significant step towards unifying .NET development across mobile and desktop platforms. While its initial focus was heavily on enabling developers to build native iOS and Android mobile applications from a shared C# codebase, .NET MAUI has expanded its reach to include support for desktop operating systems, specifically macOS and Windows (using WinUI 3, which is the latest native UI framework for Windows). Linux support is also under active development by the community and is becoming increasingly mature.

The core idea behind .NET MAUI's approach to cross-platform UI is to provide an abstraction layer over the native user interface controls of each target platform. When you build your UI in .NET MAUI, you use a set of platform-agnostic controls provided by the framework – things like Label for displaying text, Button for user interaction, Entry for text input, and CollectionView for displaying lists of data. At runtime, when your .NET MAUI application runs on a specific platform, these abstract controls are translated into the actual native UI elements of that platform. For example, a .NET MAUI Button will become a native UIButton on iOS, an android.widget.Button on Android, a WinUI Button on Windows, and a Cocoa NSButton on macOS. The goal is to provide a truly native look and feel on each platform, ensuring that your application adheres to the platform's UI conventions and offers optimal performance by leveraging the underlying native UI infrastructure.

This abstraction extends beyond just the visual appearance. .NET MAUI also provides abstractions for accessing various platform-specific features, such as the device's camera, GPS, and sensors, through a set of cross-platform APIs. While the underlying implementation of these APIs will be platform-specific, your core application logic can interact with them in a consistent way.

Here's a very basic example of how you might define a simple user interface page in .NET MAUI using XAML (Extensible Application Markup Language):

XML

```
<ContentPage
xmlns="http://schemas.microsoft.com/dotnet/2021/m
aui"


xmlns:x="http://schemas.microsoft.com/winfx/2009/
xaml"

          x:Class="MauiDesktopApp.MainPage">


     <VerticalStackLayout Padding="20">

        <Label Text="Welcome to .NET MAUI
Desktop!"
```

```
                    FontSize="24"

HorizontalOptions="CenterAndExpand" />


        <Button Text="Click Me"

            Clicked="OnCounterClicked"

            HorizontalOptions="Center" />


        <Label x:Name="CounterLabel"

            Text="Clicked 0 times"

            FontSize="18"

            HorizontalOptions="Center" />

    </VerticalStackLayout>


</ContentPage>
```

This XAML markup describes a simple layout with a label displaying a welcome message, a button that can be clicked, and another label to display a counter. When this page is rendered on Windows, .NET MAUI will use WinUI 3 to create native Windows controls that correspond to these elements. On macOS, it will use native Cocoa controls, and on Linux (when support is fully mature), it will likely use GTK+ or another native Linux UI toolkit. The C# code-behind file (MainPage.xaml.cs) would contain the application logic, such as the OnCounterClicked event handler that updates the CounterLabel. This C# code can be largely shared across all the target platforms.

Now, let's look at Avalonia UI. This is another powerful and actively developed open-source cross-platform UI framework for .NET. Unlike .NET MAUI, which primarily acts as an abstraction over native UI, Avalonia UI is a fully independent, rendered UI framework. It has its own comprehensive set of controls, layout system, styling mechanisms, and its own rendering engine. This engine is designed to provide a consistent look and feel for your application across all the platforms it supports, which currently include Windows, macOS, Linux, WebAssembly, Android, and iOS.

The key advantage of Avalonia UI's approach is its consistent appearance across platforms. If you have a strong need for your application to look and behave the same way on Windows as it does on Linux or macOS, without necessarily adhering strictly to each platform's native UI conventions, Avalonia UI can be a very compelling choice. It offers a rich set of features, including a flexible layout system, powerful data binding capabilities, extensive styling and theming options (including support for CSS-like styles), and support for modern UI concepts like vector graphics and animations.

Here's a basic example of an Avalonia UI window with similar elements to the .NET MAUI example, defined using Avalonia's XAML-based markup:

XML

```
<Window xmlns="https://github.com/avaloniaui"

xmlns:x="http://schemas.microsoft.com/winfx/2006/
xaml"
```

```xml
        x:Class="AvaloniaDesktopApp.MainWindow">


    <StackPanel Margin="20">

        <TextBlock Text="Welcome to Avalonia UI
Desktop!"

                FontSize="24"

                HorizontalAlignment="Center"
/>


        <Button Content="Click Me"

                Click="OnCounterClicked"

                HorizontalAlignment="Center" />


        <TextBlock x:Name="CounterTextBlock"

                Text="Clicked 0 times"

                FontSize="18"

                HorizontalAlignment="Center"
/>
    </StackPanel>

</Window>
```

This XAML defines a window containing a text block and a button within a stack panel. The rendering and styling of these elements are handled by Avalonia UI's own rendering engine, ensuring a consistent visual appearance regardless of the underlying operating system. The C# code-behind (MainWindow.xaml.cs) would contain the application logic for the OnCounterClicked event.

Both .NET MAUI and Avalonia UI provide excellent options for building cross-platform desktop applications with .NET 9. The choice between them often hinges on whether you prioritize a native look and feel (leaning towards .NET MAUI) or a consistent look and feel across all platforms (leaning towards Avalonia UI). Both frameworks are actively developed and have vibrant communities, offering a solid foundation for building modern desktop experiences. You might also encounter other cross-platform .NET UI frameworks, such as the Uno Platform, which allows you to build applications based on the Windows UI Library (WinUI) that can run on various platforms, including WebAssembly, Linux, macOS, iOS, and Android. The key takeaway is that you have powerful choices beyond the traditional Windows-only UI frameworks when building .NET desktop applications today.

9.2 Architecting Cross-Platform Desktop Applications

Alright, now that we've explored some of the modern UI frameworks available for building cross-platform desktop applications with .NET 9, let's talk about how to structure your application's code in a way that promotes maintainability, testability, and, most importantly, maximizes code sharing across those different platforms (Windows, macOS, and Linux). Think of architecting your application as creating a solid blueprint before you start building the actual structure. A well-thought-out architecture will make your cross-platform development much smoother in the long run.

One of the most widely adopted and highly recommended architectural patterns for building modern UI applications, including cross-platform desktop apps with frameworks like .NET MAUI and Avalonia UI, is the Model-View-ViewModel (MVVM) pattern. Let's break down what MVVM is and why it's so beneficial for our purposes.

Model-View-ViewModel (MVVM) Pattern

The MVVM pattern is a design pattern that separates the different concerns within your application's user interface code into three distinct parts:

- Model: This part represents your application's data and business logic. It's responsible for holding and manipulating the data. Ideally, the Model should be completely independent of the View and the ViewModel. It shouldn't have any specific knowledge of how the data is presented or how the user interacts with it. Think of your data entities (like Customer, Order, Product) and the services that operate on that data as belonging to the Model.
- View: This is your application's user interface – what the user sees and interacts with. In the context of .NET MAUI and Avalonia UI, the View is typically defined using XAML. The View is responsible for the visual presentation of the data and for relaying user input (like button clicks or text changes). Importantly, the View should have minimal to no business logic directly within it. Its primary responsibility is to present the data provided by the ViewModel and to notify the ViewModel of user actions.
- ViewModel: This acts as an intermediary between the Model and the View. The ViewModel exposes data from the Model in a way that is easily consumable by the View. It also contains the presentation logic – the logic that determines

how the data is presented and how the View reacts to user input. The ViewModel doesn't have direct knowledge of the View itself, but it provides properties and commands that the View can bind to. When the View interacts with the ViewModel (e.g., a button is clicked), the ViewModel can then interact with the Model to perform business operations and update the data. The ViewModel then notifies the View of any changes in the data, typically through mechanisms like data binding and change notifications.

So, how does MVVM help with cross-platform development?

- Separation of Concerns: By clearly separating the data and business logic (Model), the presentation logic (ViewModel), and the UI (View), you make your codebase more organized and easier to maintain. Changes to the UI on one platform are less likely to affect your core business logic.
- Testability: The ViewModel is a plain C# class that doesn't have any direct dependencies on UI elements. This makes it very easy to unit test your presentation logic in isolation, without having to instantiate or interact with UI controls. This significantly improves the testability of your application.
- Code Reusability: Because the ViewModel is platform-agnostic and the Model contains your core logic, a significant portion of your code (ViewModel and Model) can often be shared directly across your Windows, macOS, and Linux desktop applications (and even mobile applications if you're using .NET MAUI). You would primarily need to create platform-specific Views using the native UI elements of each operating system (via .NET MAUI's abstraction or separate XAML for Avalonia UI).
- Maintainability: When you need to make changes to the UI, you can focus on the View layer. If you need to update the business logic or presentation logic, you can work within the

Model and ViewModel respectively, with less risk of accidentally breaking other parts of the application.

Separation of Concerns

The MVVM pattern is a prime example of the broader architectural principle of Separation of Concerns (SoC). SoC advocates for dividing your application into distinct sections, each addressing a specific responsibility. This makes your application more modular, easier to understand, and less prone to ripple effects when you make changes.

In the context of cross-platform desktop development, SoC helps you isolate the platform-specific UI code from your core application logic. Your business rules, data access, and other platform-independent functionalities can reside in shared libraries (often targeting .NET Standard or just .NET 9), while the UI layer in each platform-specific application (or within .NET MAUI's platform-specific implementations) handles the presentation and user interaction using the native widgets of that operating system.

For example, if you need to implement a feature that downloads data from the internet, the core logic for making the network request, handling the response, and processing the data can reside in a shared service. Your ViewModel can then orchestrate this service and expose the results to the View. The View, whether it's a WinUI 3 window on Windows or a Cocoa window on macOS (via .NET MAUI), simply binds to the properties exposed by the ViewModel to display the downloaded data. The underlying mechanism of how the data is fetched remains platform-agnostic.

Adhering to SoC principles, often through patterns like MVVM, is crucial for building robust and maintainable cross-platform desktop applications. It allows you to maximize code reuse, improve testability, and simplify the complexities of targeting multiple operating systems with a single .NET codebase.

9.3 Handling Platform-Specific UI Elements and APIs

Alright, while the beauty of cross-platform development lies in sharing as much code as possible, the reality is that sometimes you'll need to interact with UI elements or access APIs that are specific to a particular operating system (Windows, macOS, or Linux). Think of these as the unique features and controls that make each platform distinct. Handling these platform-specific needs gracefully while still maintaining a significant amount of shared code is a key challenge in cross-platform desktop development with .NET 9. Let's explore some common approaches to tackle this.

One common scenario arises when you want to use a UI control that is available natively on one platform but doesn't have a direct equivalent in your chosen cross-platform UI framework (.NET MAUI or Avalonia UI). For example, Windows might have a specific type of date picker control with unique features that isn't available in the cross-platform abstraction. In such cases, you might need to find a way to use the native control on Windows while providing a suitable alternative or a more generic control on macOS and Linux.

Another situation is when you need to access platform-specific APIs for functionalities beyond the core UI. This could include interacting with the operating system's file system in a more advanced way, accessing system sensors, handling notifications in a platform-native style, or leveraging other OS-level features. These APIs are inherently different across operating systems.

One approach to handle these platform-specific needs is through conditional compilation using preprocessor directives, as we touched on earlier. You can use #if directives along with target framework monikers (TFMs) to include or exclude specific blocks of code based on the platform your application is being built for.

For example, if you wanted to use a Windows-specific API, you could wrap that code in an #if NET9_0_WINDOWS block. When your project is built for Windows, this code will be included. When it's built for macOS or Linux (targeting net9.0 or their specific TFMs), this code will be excluded. You would then provide alternative implementations (if necessary) for those other platforms within their own #if blocks.

Here's a conceptual example:

```csharp
C#

public class PlatformSpecificFeatures
{
    public string GetSpecialPlatformFeature()
    {
#if NET9_0_WINDOWS
        // Windows-specific API call
(hypothetical)
        return
Windows.System.OperatingSystem.GetSpecialWindowsInfo();
#elif NET9_0_MACOS
        // macOS-specific API call (hypothetical)
        return
AppKit.NSProcessInfo.ProcessInfo.GetSpecialMacInfo();
#elif NET9_0_LINUX
        // Linux-specific API call (hypothetical)
        return
Linux.Sysinfo.GetSpecialLinuxInfo();
#else
        return "No special platform feature
available on this OS.";
#endif
    }
```

```
}
```

While conditional compilation can be straightforward for simple cases, it can quickly become unwieldy if you have a lot of platform-specific code scattered throughout your codebase. It can also make your code harder to read and maintain.

A more structured and often preferred approach is to use interfaces defined in your shared, platform-agnostic code (e.g., a .NET Standard library or a shared project) to represent the platform-specific functionality you need. Then, you create concrete implementations of these interfaces in your platform-specific application projects. Your core, shared code can then depend on these interfaces. At runtime, you use a mechanism like dependency injection to provide the appropriate platform-specific implementation based on the operating system your application is running on.

We saw a similar pattern earlier with the ILocalStorageService. Let's consider another example: accessing a specific hardware sensor that might have different APIs on different operating systems.

First, you define an interface in your shared code:

C#

```csharp
public interface ISensorService
{
    double GetSensorReading();
}
```

Then, in your platform-specific projects, you create implementations:

C#

```csharp
// Windows-specific implementation
```

```csharp
public class WindowsSensorService :
ISensorService
{
    public double GetSensorReading()
    {
        // Use Windows-specific sensor APIs
        return
Windows.Devices.Sensors.MySpecificSensor.GetCurre
ntValue();
    }
}


// macOS-specific implementation
public class MacSensorService : ISensorService
{
    public double GetSensorReading()
    {
        // Use macOS-specific sensor APIs
        return
AppKit.MyMacSensor.ReadSensorData();
    }
}


// Linux-specific implementation
public class LinuxSensorService : ISensorService
{
    public double GetSensorReading()
    {
        // Use Linux-specific sensor APIs (e.g.,
reading from a file)
        return
System.IO.File.ReadAllText("/sys/devices/mysensor
/value");
    }
}
```

In your shared code, you would depend on the ISensorService interface:

C#

```csharp
public class DataProcessor
{
    private readonly ISensorService
_sensorService;

    public DataProcessor(ISensorService
sensorService)
    {
        _sensorService = sensorService;
    }

    public void ProcessSensorData()
    {
        double reading =
_sensorService.GetSensorReading();
        // Process the sensor reading
    }
}
```

Finally, in your platform-specific application startup (e.g., in your .NET MAUI MauiProgram.cs or your Avalonia UI App.xaml.cs code-behind), you would register the appropriate implementation of ISensorService with your dependency injection container based on the operating system the application is running on. For example, on Windows, you would register WindowsSensorService, on macOS, MacSensorService, and so on. The DataProcessor class would then automatically receive the correct platform-specific implementation through its constructor.

In the context of .NET MAUI, it provides a mechanism called Platform Services that simplifies accessing platform-specific functionality. You can define an interface in your shared code, and then in your platform-specific projects, you can register implementations of this interface. .NET MAUI then provides a way to resolve these platform-specific services at runtime. This is essentially a built-in dependency injection mechanism tailored for platform-specific implementations.

For example, if you wanted to access the device's battery level, you could define an IBatteryService interface in your shared code and then provide AndroidBatteryService, iOSBatteryService, WindowsBatteryService, and MacBatteryService implementations in your respective platform projects. .NET MAUI would then allow you to easily retrieve the correct implementation at runtime.

In conclusion, handling platform-specific UI elements and APIs in cross-platform .NET 9 desktop applications requires a thoughtful approach. While conditional compilation can be used for simple cases, the interface-based approach with dependency injection (or .NET MAUI's Platform Services) offers a more structured, maintainable, and testable way to isolate platform-specific code while maximizing code sharing in your core application logic.

9.4 Deployment Considerations for Different Desktop Operating Systems

Alright, you've built your fantastic cross-platform desktop application with .NET 9, and now comes the crucial step of getting it into the hands of your users, no matter if they're on Windows, macOS, or Linux. Think of deployment as packaging up your application and all its necessary components in a way that's easily installable and runnable on the target operating system. Each of these platforms has its own conventions and expectations for how applications are packaged and distributed, so understanding these nuances is key to providing a smooth and user-friendly installation experience. Let's explore some of the common deployment considerations for each of these desktop environments.

Creating Installers for Windows (MSI, ClickOnce)

On Windows, the two most common ways to distribute desktop applications are through MSI (Microsoft Installer) packages and ClickOnce deployment.

MSI packages provide a standard way to install, uninstall, and manage Windows applications. They can include all the necessary files, registry entries, shortcuts, and other configuration settings for your application. Creating MSI installers often involves using specialized tools like the WiX Toolset (a free and powerful command-line tool) or Visual Studio Installer Projects (an extension for Visual Studio). MSI installers offer a robust and reliable way to deploy applications, and they are often preferred for more complex applications or enterprise deployments. They allow for administrative installation, silent installation, and integration with the Windows Installer service.

Consider a large enterprise application built with .NET MAUI for Windows. You might create an MSI installer that bundles the application executable, .NET runtime components (if you're doing a self-contained deployment), any required libraries, and sets up Start Menu shortcuts and file associations. Users can then run this MSI file, and the Windows Installer will guide them through the installation process.

ClickOnce deployment is a deployment technology specifically designed for .NET applications. It allows for easy installation and automatic updates of Windows desktop applications with minimal user interaction. ClickOnce applications are typically deployed from a web server or a network file share. When a user clicks a link or runs a setup file, the application is installed (often without requiring administrative privileges) and can be launched directly. ClickOnce also handles automatic updates in the background, ensuring users always have the latest version. This makes it particularly convenient for distributing and maintaining applications for a wider audience.

Imagine a smaller utility application built with Avalonia UI that you want to distribute to a group of users. You could publish it using ClickOnce. Users could then install it with a few clicks from a webpage or a shared folder, and any subsequent updates you release could be applied automatically without requiring them to manually download and reinstall.

When deploying .NET 9 applications to Windows, you also have the choice between a framework-dependent deployment and a self-contained deployment.

- Framework-dependent deployment: This requires the .NET 9 runtime to be already installed on the user's machine. Your installer (MSI or ClickOnce) will typically only include your application's compiled code and any third-party libraries it uses. This results in a smaller installer size, but it relies on the user having the correct .NET runtime version installed.
- Self-contained deployment: This bundles the necessary parts of the .NET 9 runtime along with your application in the installer. This results in a larger installer size but ensures that the application will run even if the user doesn't have .NET 9 installed. This is often preferred for end-user applications where you can't assume the .NET runtime is present.

Packaging for macOS (DMG, PKG)

On macOS, applications are typically distributed as DMG (Disk Image) files or PKG (Package) installers.

DMG files are virtual disk images that, when opened, mount as a volume in the Finder. They often contain the application bundle (a directory structure that holds the application executable and its resources) and sometimes a shortcut to the Applications folder, making installation as simple as dragging and dropping the application bundle to the Applications folder. Creating DMG files can be done using the built-in Disk Utility application on macOS or through command-line tools.

Consider a creative application built with Avalonia UI for macOS. You might package it as a DMG file. When a user downloads and opens the DMG, a Finder window appears with the application icon and a link to the Applications folder. The user simply drags the application icon to the Applications folder to install it.

PKG installers are similar to MSI installers on Windows. They are used for more complex installations that might involve installing frameworks, libraries, or setting up system services. The macOS Installer application guides the user through the installation process. You can create PKG installers using Apple's Xcode tools (like the Package product) or third-party tools.

For a larger, more complex .NET MAUI application for macOS that relies on specific native libraries or frameworks, you might choose to distribute it as a PKG installer to ensure all dependencies are correctly installed.

Similar to Windows, you also have the choice between framework-dependent and self-contained deployments for .NET 9 applications on macOS. Self-contained deployments will bundle the .NET runtime within the application bundle.

Packaging for Linux (DEB, RPM, Snap, AppImage)

The Linux ecosystem has a more diverse range of packaging formats due to the different distributions. Some of the most common formats you'll encounter are DEB (Debian packages), RPM (Red Hat Package Manager packages), Snap packages, and AppImage files.

DEB packages are used by Debian-based distributions like Ubuntu and Mint. They are typically managed by the apt package manager. You can create DEB packages using tools like the Debian Package Control Files (.control) and packaging utilities.

RPM packages are used by Red Hat-based distributions like Fedora and CentOS and are managed by the yum or dnf package managers. You can create RPM packages using tools like rpmbuild.

Snap packages are a universal package format that aims to work across many different Linux distributions. They bundle all the necessary dependencies within the package and are managed by the snapd service. You can create Snap packages using the snapcraft tool.

AppImage files are another universal format that aims for simplicity. An AppImage is a self-contained executable that includes all the libraries and dependencies needed to run the application. Users typically just need to make the AppImage executable and run it, without needing to install it through a package manager.

For a .NET MAUI or Avalonia UI application targeting Linux, you might choose to package it as a DEB for Ubuntu users, an RPM for Fedora users, or explore universal formats like Snap or AppImage to reach a wider audience with a single package.

Again, you'll need to consider framework-dependent versus self-contained deployments. For Linux, self-contained deployments can be quite large due to the size of the .NET runtime and platform-specific native libraries. You might lean towards framework-dependent deployments and rely on the user having the appropriate .NET 9 runtime installed on their Linux distribution, providing clear instructions on how to install it.

Deploying cross-platform .NET 9 desktop applications requires understanding the packaging conventions and tools for each target operating system. Windows uses MSI and ClickOnce, macOS uses DMG and PKG, and Linux has a variety of formats like DEB, RPM, Snap, and AppImage. Additionally, you'll need to decide between framework-dependent and self-contained deployments based on your target audience and the ease of installation you want to provide. Planning your deployment strategy early in your development process will help ensure a smooth release for your users on their chosen desktop platform.

Chapter 10: Building Mobile Applications with .NET 9 (iOS & Android)

Alright, let's shift gears again and venture into the exciting space of building mobile applications that can run on both iOS and Android using .NET 9. Think of mobile development as reaching users where they spend a significant amount of their time – on their smartphones and tablets. .NET MAUI (Multi-platform App UI) is the key technology here, providing a unified framework to create native mobile apps from a single C# codebase. Understanding how .NET MAUI works and the specific considerations for mobile development is crucial for reaching this vast audience effectively.

10.1 Deep Dive into .NET MAUI for Mobile Development

Alright, let's really immerse ourselves in the world of building mobile applications that can run on both iOS and Android using .NET 9, and the key technology that makes this happen: .NET MAUI (Multi-platform App UI). Think of .NET MAUI as your unified toolkit for crafting native mobile experiences with the power of C# and the .NET ecosystem. It's not just about writing code once and having it magically appear on different phones; it's about intelligently leveraging the underlying capabilities of each platform while sharing a significant portion of your development effort.

.NET MAUI is the evolution of Xamarin.Forms, building upon its years of experience in cross-platform mobile development. However, it's more than just a rebranding. .NET MAUI aims to simplify and enhance the process of creating native user interfaces for iOS and Android (with desktop support for Windows and macOS also a core part of its vision). It provides an abstraction layer over the native UI toolkits of these mobile platforms – UIKit on iOS and the Android UI framework.

At its core, .NET MAUI gives you a set of platform-agnostic UI controls. These are the building blocks you use to construct your application's user interface. Think of familiar elements like Label for displaying text, Button for user interaction, Entry for single-line text input, Image for displaying graphics, and more complex controls like CollectionView for presenting lists of data. When you use these .NET MAUI controls in your code (typically in XAML, the Extensible Application Markup Language), the framework takes care of translating them into the native UI elements of the specific mobile platform your application is running on *at runtime*.

For example, when your .NET MAUI application runs on an iPhone, a <Button> control you defined in your shared XAML will be rendered as a native UIButton – the standard button control on iOS. Similarly, when the same code runs on an Android device, that <Button> will become an android.widget.Button – the native button component in the Android UI system. This translation happens seamlessly behind the scenes, allowing your application to not only look and feel like a native app on each platform but also to benefit from the underlying performance and accessibility features that those native UI toolkits provide.

The architecture that enables this involves a shared UI layer, which you write in XAML or C#. This shared UI is then rendered using platform-specific handlers. Handlers are a crucial concept in .NET MAUI and represent a more modern and efficient approach compared to the "renderers" used in Xamarin.Forms. For every .NET MAUI control, there's a corresponding handler for iOS and another for Android (and eventually for other platforms). These handlers are the bridge between the cross-platform abstraction and the native implementation.

When a .NET MAUI control needs to be displayed on a specific platform, the appropriate handler is responsible for creating the actual native UI control instance. It then takes the properties you've set on the .NET MAUI control (like the Text of a Button or the Source of an Image) and maps them to the corresponding properties or methods of the native control. For example, setting the Text property of a .NET MAUI Button will result in the handler setting the setTitle:forState: method on a UIButton in iOS or the setText() method on an android.widget.Button in Android.

Handlers also play a vital role in handling events. When a user interacts with a native UI control (like tapping a button), the native control generates an event. The handler is responsible for capturing this native event and routing it back to the corresponding .NET MAUI event in your shared code (like the Clicked event of a Button).

The handler architecture in .NET MAUI is designed to be more performant and flexible than the older renderer system. Handlers follow a more streamlined lifecycle and introduce the concept of a mapper. A mapper is essentially a dictionary that defines how the properties of the .NET MAUI control should be mapped to actions on the underlying native control. This allows for more targeted updates. When a property of a .NET MAUI control changes, only the specific action defined in the mapper for that property needs to be executed on the native control, rather than potentially recreating or reconfiguring larger parts of the native view. This leads to more efficient UI updates and better overall performance.

Understanding handlers becomes particularly important when you need to customize the native appearance or behavior of a .NET MAUI control beyond what the cross-platform API readily provides. You can create custom handlers to intercept the creation of the native control, modify its properties directly, or add platform-specific logic for certain events. This gives you a powerful way to fine-tune the user interface for each mobile platform when necessary, ensuring that your application feels truly integrated with the operating system while still allowing you to share the majority of your UI and all of your core application logic in C#.

In essence, .NET MAUI for mobile development provides a sophisticated yet approachable way to build native iOS and Android applications from a shared C# codebase. By abstracting away the complexities of the underlying native UI toolkits through platform-agnostic controls and efficiently mapping these to native elements via handlers, .NET MAUI allows you to reach a broad mobile audience with a significant amount of code reuse and a truly native user experience on each platform.

10.2 Working with UI Controls, Layouts, and Navigation in .NET MAUI

Alright, let's get into the practical aspects of building the user interface for your .NET MAUI mobile applications. Think of UI controls as the individual elements your users interact with – the buttons they tap, the text they read, the images they see. Layouts are how you arrange these controls on the screen, ensuring they adapt well to different screen sizes and orientations. And navigation is how users move between different screens or sections of your application. Mastering these three areas is fundamental to creating engaging and usable mobile experiences with .NET MAUI.

Common UI Elements and Their Cross-Platform Abstraction

.NET MAUI provides a rich set of UI controls that abstract away the platform-specific differences between iOS and Android, allowing you to define your UI once in XAML or C# and have it render as native controls on both platforms.

Let's explore some of the most commonly used elements:

For displaying information to the user, you have controls like Label, which is used to show text. You can customize its font, size, color, and alignment. Image is used to display static images from various sources (local files, embedded resources, or the web). WebView allows you to embed web content within your native mobile application, which can be useful for displaying HTML pages or integrating with web-based services.

For gathering user input, you have Button for triggering actions when tapped. You can customize its text, appearance, and the event that fires when it's clicked. Entry provides a single-line text input field for things like usernames or short answers. Editor offers a multi-line text input area, suitable for longer text like notes or descriptions. CheckBox allows users to toggle a boolean value, while RadioButton provides a set of mutually exclusive options. Slider lets users select a value from a continuous range. For selecting specific dates and times, DatePicker and TimePicker provide platform-native picker interfaces.

When it comes to displaying lists or collections of data, ListView and, the more modern and performant, CollectionView are your go-to controls. CollectionView offers more flexibility in terms of layout (supporting grids and custom layouts) and provides better performance for large datasets through features like virtualization (only rendering items that are currently visible).

To arrange these controls on the screen, .NET MAUI provides a variety of layout controls. These layouts act as containers for your UI elements and define how their children are positioned and sized.

Some of the most common layouts include:

- StackLayout: Arranges its child elements in a single line, either horizontally or vertically. You can control the spacing between elements and how they expand to fill the available space. Think of it like stacking items either on top of each other or side by side.

- Grid: Arranges its child elements in a two-dimensional grid of rows and columns. This is very powerful for creating more complex and structured layouts, similar to tables in HTML. You define the rows and columns, and then you can specify in which cell each control should reside.
- FlexLayout: A more flexible layout container inspired by CSS Flexbox. It allows you to arrange children in a line (horizontally or vertically) and provides sophisticated ways to distribute space among them, align them, and handle different screen sizes.
- AbsoluteLayout: Allows you to position and size child elements using absolute coordinates and dimensions. This is less common for creating responsive layouts as it doesn't adapt well to different screen sizes.
- RelativeLayout: Positions and sizes child elements relative to each other or to the parent layout. This can be useful for creating layouts where the position of one element depends on the size or position of another.

When building your UI, you'll typically nest these layout controls and place your UI controls within them to achieve the desired visual structure. .NET MAUI handles the translation of these layouts into efficient native layout mechanisms on iOS and Android.

Navigation Patterns (Stack Navigation, Tabbed Navigation)

Moving between different screens or sections of your mobile application is a fundamental aspect of user experience. .NET MAUI provides several built-in navigation patterns to handle this:

Stack Navigation is a hierarchical model where you navigate through a series of pages. When you navigate to a new page, it's pushed onto a navigation stack. To go back, the current page is popped off the stack, revealing the previous page. This is commonly used for flows where you drill down into details, like navigating from a list of items to the specifics of a selected item. In .NET MAUI, the NavigationPage control provides this stack-based navigation. You typically wrap your root page within a NavigationPage to enable push and pop navigation using the Navigation property available on each Page.

For example, to navigate from MainPage to a DetailPage, you might use code like this in your MainPage's code-behind:

C#

```
await Navigation.PushAsync(new
DetailPage(selectedItem));
```

And to go back to the MainPage from the DetailPage:

C#

```
await Navigation.PopAsync();
```

Tabbed Navigation presents multiple top-level content areas as tabs, typically displayed at the bottom of the screen on iOS and often at the top on Android. This pattern allows users to easily switch between different primary sections of the application, such as different feeds, settings, or features. In .NET MAUI, the TabbedPage control enables this. You add different ContentPage instances as children of the TabbedPage, and .NET MAUI will render them as tabs.

Here's a simple example of a TabbedPage in XAML:

XML

```
<TabbedPage
xmlns="http://schemas.microsoft.com/dotnet/2021/m
aui"

xmlns:x="http://schemas.microsoft.com/winfx/2009/
xaml"

xmlns:local="clr-namespace:MauiTabbedApp"

        x:Class="MauiTabbedApp.MainPage">


    <local:HomePage Title="Home"
IconImageSource="home.png" />

    <local:SettingsPage Title="Settings"
IconImageSource="settings.png" />

    <local:ProfilePage Title="Profile"
IconImageSource="profile.png" />


</TabbedPage>
```

In this example, HomePage, SettingsPage, and ProfilePage are different ContentPage instances that will be displayed as separate tabs within the TabbedPage. You can also specify icons for each tab.

Beyond these primary navigation patterns, .NET MAUI also supports other models like Flyout Navigation (often used for application-level menus, sometimes referred to as hamburger menus) using the FlyoutPage. The framework provides a consistent way to define and manage navigation across both iOS and Android, while the underlying implementation leverages the native navigation mechanisms of each platform (like UINavigationController on iOS and FragmentTransaction on Android). This abstraction allows you to focus on the user flow of your application without getting bogged down in platform-specific navigation code for the majority of cases.

10.3 Accessing Platform-Specific Features in a Cross-Platform Way

Alright, while the goal of .NET MAUI is to abstract away platform differences and allow you to share as much code as possible between iOS and Android, the reality of mobile development is that you'll often encounter situations where you need to tap into features that are specific to one platform or the other. Think of these as the unique capabilities and APIs that make iOS feel like iOS and Android feel like Android. Handling these platform-specific needs in a cross-platform application requires a thoughtful approach to maintain code sharing while still leveraging the full potential of each operating system.

.NET MAUI provides a couple of key mechanisms to help you access these platform-specific features in a more or less cross-platform way: .NET MAUI Essentials and Platform Invocation (P/Invoke) for directly calling native APIs. Let's explore each of these.

Using .NET MAUI Essentials

.NET MAUI Essentials is a fantastic set of cross-platform APIs that provides a unified way to access many common device features from your shared .NET MAUI code.

It acts as a bridge, abstracting away the underlying platform-specific implementations for things like:

- Battery Information: Getting the current battery level, charge state, and monitoring for changes.

- Connectivity: Checking network status (Wi-Fi, cellular), detecting changes, and even accessing Wi-Fi information.
- Geolocation: Obtaining the device's current location and monitoring location updates.
- Sensors: Accessing device sensors like the accelerometer, compass, gyroscope, and magnetometer.
- File System Access: Interacting with the device's file system in a platform-agnostic way for common tasks.
- Preferences: Storing and retrieving simple key-value data in platform-specific settings.
- Haptic Feedback: Providing tactile feedback to the user.
- Share: Allowing users to share text, files, and URIs with other applications.
- Browser: Opening web pages in the device's default browser.
- Email: Composing and sending emails.
- Phone Dialer: Initiating phone calls.
- SMS: Sending SMS messages.
- Clipboard: Getting and setting text on the device's clipboard.

For example, if you want to get the current battery level in your .NET MAUI application, you can use the Battery.ChargeLevel property in your shared C# code, and .NET MAUI Essentials will handle the platform-specific calls to retrieve this information from iOS and Android. You don't need to write separate code for each platform for this common task.

Here's a simple code snippet demonstrating how to get the battery level:

```csharp
C#

using Microsoft.Maui.Controls;

using Microsoft.Maui.Essentials;
```

```csharp
using System;

public class BatteryInfoPage : ContentPage
{
    private Label batteryLabel;

    public BatteryInfoPage()
    {
        batteryLabel = new Label
        {
            Text = $"Battery Level:
{Battery.ChargeLevel * 100}%"
        };

        Content = new StackLayout
        {
            Padding = new Thickness(20),
            Children = { batteryLabel }
        };
```

```
        Battery.BatteryInfoChanged +=
Battery_BatteryInfoChanged;

    }



    private void
Battery_BatteryInfoChanged(object sender,
BatteryInfoChangedEventArgs e)

    {

        batteryLabel.Text = $"Battery Level:
{e.ChargeLevel * 100}%";

    }

}
```

In this example, the Battery.ChargeLevel property and the BatteryInfoChanged event from .NET MAUI Essentials provide a cross-platform way to access battery information without writing any iOS or Android-specific code.

.NET MAUI Essentials covers a wide range of common device functionalities, significantly simplifying cross-platform mobile development. It's always worth checking if a particular feature you need is available through Essentials before resorting to platform-specific code.

Platform Invocation (P/Invoke) for Native APIs

For more advanced or highly platform-specific features that are not exposed by .NET MAUI Essentials, you can use Platform Invocation (P/Invoke). P/Invoke is a technology in .NET that allows you to call native code (written in Objective-C or Swift for iOS and Java or Kotlin for Android) directly from your C# code.

This gives you access to the full power of the underlying operating system APIs.

However, using P/Invoke comes with a few caveats. It requires a deeper understanding of the native APIs you're trying to call, including their function signatures, data types, and memory management conventions. You also need to handle the process of marshalling data between the .NET managed environment and the native unmanaged environment, which can be complex and error-prone if not done correctly. Furthermore, P/Invoke inherently introduces platform-specific code into your application, which can make it harder to maintain and less portable.

To use P/Invoke, you typically declare the signature of the native function you want to call in your C# code using the DllImport attribute (even for iOS and Android, the concept of a "DLL" is used metaphorically to represent the native library). You specify the name of the native library and the function name, and then you can call this declared C# method as if it were a regular .NET method. The .NET runtime handles the necessary interactions with the native library behind the scenes.

Here's a very simplified, conceptual example of calling a hypothetical native iOS function to get the device's model name:

C#

```
using System.Runtime.InteropServices;


public static class NativeiOS

{

    [DllImport("__Internal")] // Special
identifier for iOS native library
```

```
    public static extern string GetDeviceModel();

}


public class DeviceInfo

{

    public static string GetiOSModel()

    {

        return NativeiOS.GetDeviceModel();

    }

}
```

Similarly, you can use P/Invoke to call Android native functions, specifying the appropriate Android library name.

While P/Invoke provides immense power and access to platform-specific features, it should be used judiciously. It's generally recommended to first explore if .NET MAUI Essentials provides the functionality you need. If not, consider if there's a cross-platform .NET library or plugin available that wraps the native functionality in a more manageable way. Only when those options are exhausted should you resort to direct P/Invoke calls. When using P/Invoke, thorough testing on each target platform is crucial to ensure correctness and stability.

.NET MAUI offers a great balance between cross-platform code sharing and the ability to leverage platform-specific features on iOS and Android. .NET MAUI Essentials covers many common device functionalities in a platform-agnostic way, while P/Invoke provides a powerful escape hatch to access the full spectrum of native APIs when necessary. By understanding and utilizing these mechanisms effectively, you can build rich, performant mobile applications that feel truly native on each platform while maximizing your code reuse.

10.4 Performance Optimization Techniques for Mobile

Alright, let's talk about a critical aspect of mobile development with .NET MAUI: performance optimization. Think of performance on mobile devices as even more crucial than on desktop. Users expect apps to be fast, fluid, and responsive, and they are particularly sensitive to battery drain and excessive data usage. A poorly performing mobile app can lead to frustration, negative reviews, and uninstalls. Therefore, understanding and applying performance optimization techniques is paramount when building for iOS and Android with .NET MAUI.

UI Performance Considerations

The user interface is what your users directly interact with, so ensuring its performance is smooth and responsive is key to a good user experience. Here are some important UI performance considerations in .NET MAUI mobile development:

One common area to focus on is minimizing UI complexity. Deeply nested layouts with a large number of elements can increase the time it takes for the UI to render and update. Each layout and control adds overhead. Try to keep your visual hierarchy as flat as possible by using layouts efficiently. For example, instead of nesting multiple StackLayout controls, consider using a Grid or FlexLayout which might achieve the same visual result with fewer elements. Tools within your development environment (like Visual Studio's Live Visual Tree) can help you inspect the visual hierarchy of your application.

Optimize image usage is another significant factor. Images are often a large part of mobile app UIs, and using them inefficiently can lead to slow loading times and increased memory consumption. Ensure you are using images at the appropriate resolution for their display size on the target devices. Providing unnecessarily high-resolution images wastes bandwidth and memory. Use appropriate image formats (like JPEG for photographs and PNG for graphics with transparency). Consider compressing images to reduce their file size without significant loss of visual quality. For frequently displayed images, implement image caching so they don't need to be reloaded from disk or the network every time they are needed. .NET MAUI provides mechanisms for image caching, especially for images loaded via the Image control.

When displaying lists or collections of data using ListView or, preferably, CollectionView, it's crucial to employ techniques for efficient rendering, especially for large datasets. Virtualization is a key optimization here. Instead of creating and rendering UI elements for all the items in your collection at once (which can be very memory-intensive and slow), virtualization only creates and renders the items that are currently visible on the screen. As the user scrolls, new items are rendered, and items that are no longer visible are recycled. CollectionView in .NET MAUI has built-in support for virtualization, so using it over ListView for large lists is generally recommended.

Finally, it's paramount to avoid blocking the main UI thread. The main UI thread is responsible for handling user interactions and updating the UI. If you perform long-running operations (like network requests, file I/O, or intensive computations) synchronously on the main thread, your application will become unresponsive, leading to a frozen or "not responding" state. Always perform such operations asynchronously using the async and await keywords. This allows the main thread to remain free to handle UI updates and user input, providing a smooth and responsive experience.

Battery Optimization

Mobile devices have limited battery capacity, and users are very aware of applications that drain their battery quickly. Optimizing your application for battery usage is crucial for user satisfaction and the longevity of your app on their devices. Here are some key considerations:

Minimize background activity. Avoid performing unnecessary tasks or keeping active network connections when your application is in the background or not actively being used by the user. Schedule background tasks only when absolutely necessary and try to perform them in a batch or in a way that minimizes the impact on battery life. Be mindful of background location updates, sensor monitoring, and network polling, as these can be significant battery drainers.

Optimize network usage. Reduce the frequency and size of network requests. Only fetch data when you truly need it and try to batch multiple requests into a single one whenever feasible. Compress data being sent and received to reduce bandwidth and energy consumption. Be smart about when you perform network operations – for example, deferring large downloads to when the device is connected to Wi-Fi and is charging.

Use location services judiciously. Continuously tracking the user's location can be one of the biggest battery drains. Only request location updates when your application actively needs them, and use the lowest acceptable accuracy and frequency for your use case. Stop location updates when they are no longer required. Consider using significant location change monitoring, which uses less power than continuous tracking but notifies you when the user has moved a significant distance.

Be mindful of sensor usage. Similar to location services, continuously polling sensors like the accelerometer or gyroscope can consume battery. Only enable sensors when you need their data and disable them when you don't. Use the lowest acceptable sampling rate for your needs.

Optimize background processing. If your application needs to perform background tasks, use the platform's recommended mechanisms for background processing (like WorkManager on Android or Background Tasks on iOS). These mechanisms are designed to be more power-efficient by allowing the system to schedule tasks intelligently and perform them in a way that minimizes battery impact.

By paying close attention to both UI and battery performance, you can build .NET MAUI mobile applications that are not only feature-rich and engaging but also provide a smooth, responsive, and power-efficient experience for your users on both iOS and Android devices. Profiling your application's performance on actual devices is crucial to identify and address any bottlenecks in these areas.

Chapter 11: Building Web Applications and APIs with ASP.NET Core 9

Alright, let's shift our focus to the powerful capabilities of .NET 9 for building web applications and APIs that can run seamlessly across Windows, macOS, and Linux. Think of web applications as the interactive experiences you access through your browser, and APIs as the backend services that power these applications and often mobile apps too. ASP.NET Core 9 is Microsoft's modern, cross-platform framework for building these types of networked applications with .NET. Understanding how to leverage its features for cross-platform development is key to reaching a wide audience and building scalable, robust web solutions.

11.1 Leveraging ASP.NET Core for Cross-Platform Web Development

Alright, let's really get into the core of building web applications and APIs that aren't tied to just one operating system, and the key player in the .NET ecosystem for this: ASP.NET Core 9. Think of ASP.NET Core as the modern, re-architected successor to the original ASP.NET Framework. One of its fundamental design goals was to be truly cross-platform, meaning that the applications you build with it can run seamlessly on Windows, macOS, and Linux. This is a game-changer for web development with .NET, opening up a vast landscape of deployment options and allowing you to choose the operating system that best suits your technical requirements, budget, and team expertise.

The original ASP.NET Framework, while powerful, was deeply integrated with the Windows operating system. This meant that if you wanted to host your ASP.NET applications, you generally had to do so on a Windows Server. ASP.NET Core broke free from this limitation by being built on top of .NET Core (now simply .NET), which, as we've discussed, is the cross-platform implementation of the .NET runtime. This foundational shift allows ASP.NET Core 9 applications to run wherever the .NET runtime is supported, giving you unprecedented flexibility in your deployment choices.

Consider a real-world scenario: you're building a backend API to power a mobile application that will be used by people on iPhones and Android devices. You might prefer to host your API on a Linux server because of its cost-effectiveness or your team's familiarity with the Linux environment. With ASP.NET Core 9, you can develop your API using C# on your Windows or macOS machine and then deploy it to a Linux server without having to rewrite a significant portion of your code or deal with major compatibility issues. This flexibility allows you to choose the best tools and infrastructure for each part of your application stack, rather than being locked into a single operating system.

This cross-platform capability isn't just about deployment. It also impacts your development workflow. You and your team can use your preferred development operating systems (Windows, macOS, or Linux) to build and test ASP.NET Core applications. The consistent .NET development experience across these platforms streamlines collaboration and reduces the friction that can sometimes arise when teams are forced to use a specific OS.

Furthermore, ASP.NET Core's architecture is designed with modern web development needs in mind. It's modular, meaning you only include the components your application actually uses, leading to smaller application sizes and faster startup times. It also embraces open-source principles, with the framework itself being open and actively contributed to by the community. This fosters innovation and provides a rich ecosystem of libraries and tools that are also often cross-platform.

In essence, leveraging ASP.NET Core 9 for cross-platform web development means you're choosing a framework that gives you:

- Deployment Flexibility: Run your web applications and APIs on Windows, macOS, or Linux servers.
- Development Choice: Use your preferred development operating system.
- Modern Architecture: Benefit from a modular, performant, and open framework.
- Vibrant Ecosystem: Access a wide range of cross-platform libraries and tools.

This foundational cross-platform nature makes ASP.NET Core 9 a cornerstone for building modern web solutions that can reach a broad audience and be deployed in a variety of environments. In the subsequent sections, we'll explore some of the key architectural elements of ASP.NET Core that contribute to this flexibility and power.

ASP.NET Core Architecture and Middleware Pipeline

To understand how ASP.NET Core achieves its flexibility and cross-platform capabilities, it's helpful to grasp its core architecture, particularly the middleware pipeline. When a request comes into your ASP.NET Core application, it doesn't directly hit your application code. Instead, it flows through a series of components called middleware. Each middleware component in the pipeline has the opportunity to process the request, perform some action (like authentication, logging, serving static files), and then either pass the request on to the next middleware in the pipeline or short-circuit the pipeline and return a response directly.

This middleware pipeline is highly configurable, allowing you to add and arrange components to handle various aspects of your web application. Because these middleware components are built with cross-platform compatibility in mind, your core request processing logic can run consistently across different operating systems. ASP.NET Core provides built-in middleware for many common tasks, and you can also create your own custom middleware to handle application-specific requirements.

Razor Pages vs. MVC

When building web applications with ASP.NET Core, you have two primary programming models to choose from: Razor Pages and Model-View-Controller (MVC). Both are built on top of the same ASP.NET Core foundation and are cross-platform. The choice between them often comes down to the complexity of your UI and your preferred way of organizing code.

Razor Pages provide a more page-centric approach, making it easier to build simple, form-based web pages. The logic for a specific page is typically contained within a single .cshtml.cs file (the PageModel) that handles requests to that page. Razor Pages can be a great choice for applications with a straightforward page structure.

MVC (Model-View-Controller) is a more traditional architectural pattern that separates the application into three interconnected parts: the Model (data), the View (UI), and the Controller (handling user input and updating the Model). MVC is well-suited for building more complex web applications with clear separation of concerns and better testability for the UI logic.

Both Razor Pages and MVC Views are built using Razor syntax, which allows you to embed C# code directly within your HTML markup to dynamically generate web content. Because ASP.NET Core itself is cross-platform, both Razor Pages and MVC applications you build with it will also be cross-platform.

Building RESTful APIs with Web API Controllers

Beyond traditional web applications, ASP.NET Core is also excellent for building RESTful APIs (Representational State Transfer Application Programming Interfaces). APIs are the backbone of modern web applications and are often used to power single-page applications (SPAs) built with frameworks like Angular, React, or Vue.js, as well as mobile applications.

ASP.NET Core Web API controllers provide a way to handle HTTP requests and return data in formats like JSON. You can define routes, handle different HTTP methods (GET, POST, PUT, DELETE), and serialize/deserialize data using built-in features. Because ASP.NET Core runs cross-platform, the Web APIs you build with it will also be cross-platform, capable of running on Windows, macOS, or Linux servers and serving clients on any operating system.

11.2 Architecting Cross-Platform Web Applications

Alright, now that we've established the fundamental cross-platform nature of ASP.NET Core 9, let's talk about how to structure your web applications and APIs in a way that truly embraces this capability. Think of architecting your application as creating a solid foundation and a clear blueprint that allows your codebase to run smoothly and consistently across different operating systems (Windows, macOS, and Linux) without being tightly coupled to any one of them. A well-designed architecture will not only make your application more portable but also easier to maintain, test, and scale.

One of the primary principles to keep in mind when architecting cross-platform web applications with ASP.NET Core 9 is to strive for a platform-agnostic backend. Your core application logic – the business rules, data access, services, and domain models – should ideally be independent of the underlying operating system. This means relying on the standard .NET 9 base class libraries and avoiding direct dependencies on Windows-specific APIs or libraries if you intend to run your application on macOS or Linux.

Consider a real-world example: you're building an e-commerce platform with ASP.NET Core 9. The core logic for handling orders, managing inventory, processing payments, and calculating shipping costs should be the same regardless of whether your application is hosted on a Windows Server or a Linux instance in the cloud. This core logic should reside in class libraries that target .NET 9 (which inherently supports cross-platform execution) or .NET Standard for even broader compatibility. These libraries should use platform-agnostic APIs for tasks like file manipulation (if needed for temporary processing or logging), basic networking (if communicating with other internal services), and data handling.

Now, inevitably, you might encounter situations where you need to interact with features that are inherently operating system-specific. A common example in web applications is handling file system operations beyond basic reading and writing, or perhaps interacting with system-level services. When you face such requirements, the key is to abstract these OS-specific interactions behind interfaces. Your core, platform-agnostic code can then depend on these interfaces, and you can provide concrete implementations of these interfaces that are specific to each operating system you need to support.

Let's take file system operations as an example. Suppose your application needs to generate thumbnails of uploaded images. The underlying image processing libraries you use might be cross-platform, but the exact way you access temporary storage or handle file permissions might differ slightly between Windows and Linux.

You could define an IThumbnailService interface in your core project:

C#

```csharp
public interface IThumbnailService

{

    Task<string> GenerateThumbnailAsync(string
sourceImagePath, string destinationPath, int
size);

    Task DeleteTemporaryFileAsync(string
filePath);

}
```

Then, in your Windows-specific deployment or within a platform-specific implementation if you're using a multi-targeting project, you would create a WindowsThumbnailService that implements this interface using Windows-specific file system APIs if needed. Similarly, you would create a LinuxThumbnailService that implements the same interface but uses Linux-specific file system interactions. Your core application logic that needs to generate thumbnails would then depend on the IThumbnailService interface, and at runtime, the appropriate implementation would be injected based on the operating system the application is running on (often handled by your dependency injection container).

This approach of abstracting platform-specific concerns behind interfaces allows you to keep your core application logic clean and portable while still being able to leverage the unique capabilities of each operating system when necessary. It also makes your code more testable, as you can easily provide mock implementations of these platform-specific interfaces for unit testing.

Another important consideration for cross-platform web applications is being mindful of file paths and case sensitivity. Windows uses backslashes (\) as directory separators, while macOS and Linux use forward slashes (/). When constructing file paths, it's best to use System.IO.Path.Combine() and System.IO.Path.DirectorySeparatorChar to ensure your code works correctly on all platforms. Additionally, remember that file systems on Windows are generally case-insensitive, while macOS and Linux file systems are case-sensitive. This can lead to subtle bugs if you're not careful with file names and paths in your code. Always treat file paths consistently with regards to casing, or better yet, avoid hardcoding case-sensitive file names in your platform-agnostic code.

Architecting cross-platform web applications with ASP.NET Core 9 involves designing a core backend that is as platform-agnostic as possible, abstracting away OS-specific interactions behind interfaces with platform-specific implementations, and being mindful of file path conventions and case sensitivity. By following these principles, you can build robust and maintainable web applications that run consistently and efficiently across Windows, macOS, and Linux.

Designing Platform-Agnostic Backends

Your core application logic, including business rules, data access, and services, should ideally be designed to be as platform-agnostic as possible. Rely on the .NET Standard libraries or the core .NET 9 libraries for these parts of your application. Avoid using Windows-specific APIs directly in your core logic if you intend to run on other operating systems. Abstract platform-specific needs behind interfaces, as we discussed in the context of desktop applications, and provide platform-specific implementations if necessary.

Handling File System and OS-Specific Interactions

While ASP.NET Core provides cross-platform APIs for many common tasks, you might encounter situations where you need to interact with the file system in a more advanced way or access other OS-specific features. When doing so, be mindful of the differences between operating systems. For example, file paths use different separators (\ on Windows, / on macOS and Linux). You can use System.IO.Path.DirectorySeparatorChar to handle this in a platform-agnostic way. Be aware of case sensitivity in file systems (Windows is generally case-insensitive, while macOS and Linux are case-sensitive). When dealing with more advanced OS-specific features, you might need to use conditional compilation or platform-specific implementations via interfaces.

11.3 Authentication and Authorization in a Cross-Platform Context

Alright, let's tackle a crucial aspect of building modern web applications and APIs with ASP.NET Core 9 that needs careful consideration in a cross-platform environment: authentication (verifying who the user is) and authorization (determining what a verified user is allowed to do). Think of authentication as checking the user's ID and authorization as checking their permissions to access certain resources or perform specific actions. Implementing these securely and consistently across different operating systems is paramount for protecting your application and its data.

The good news is that ASP.NET Core 9 provides robust, built-in support for various authentication schemes that work seamlessly across Windows, macOS, and Linux.[1] The underlying mechanisms for handling user credentials, issuing cookies, and validating tokens are all implemented within the framework itself and are not tied to any specific operating system. This means you can implement your authentication and authorization logic once in your ASP.NET Core application and have it function consistently regardless of where your application is deployed.

For traditional web applications where users interact through a browser, cookie-based authentication is a common approach.[2] When a user logs in successfully, the server issues a session cookie that is stored in the user's browser. For subsequent requests from the same browser, the browser automatically sends this cookie back to the server.[3] ASP.NET Core can then use this cookie to identify the authenticated user and maintain their session.[4] The framework provides middleware for handling cookie creation, encryption, and validation, and this middleware works identically across all supported operating systems.[5]

Consider a simple e-commerce website built with ASP.NET Core Razor Pages. When a user logs in with their username and password, the server can create an authentication cookie and send it back to the browser.[6] For every subsequent page request the user makes, the browser will include this cookie, and ASP.NET Core will use it to recognize the user and maintain their logged-in state.[7] This process is the same whether the ASP.NET Core application is running on a Windows Server, a Linux instance in the cloud, or even being tested on your local macOS development machine.

For APIs, especially those powering single-page applications (SPAs) or mobile applications, token-based authentication is often preferred.[8] A common standard here is JSON Web Tokens (JWTs). When a user authenticates against your API (usually by sending their credentials in a POST request), the server issues a JWT.[9] This JWT is a compact, self-contained way of securely transmitting information between parties as a JSON object.[10] The client (e.g., the SPA or mobile app) then typically includes this JWT in the headers of subsequent requests to the API.[11] The API can then validate the JWT to authenticate the user and determine their permissions. ASP.NET Core has excellent built-in support for generating, signing, and validating JWTs through its authentication and authorization middleware.[12] This mechanism is also completely cross-platform.

Imagine a mobile application built with .NET MAUI that needs to access data from an ASP.NET Core Web API. When the user logs in on the mobile app, the API can return a JWT. The mobile app then stores this JWT and includes it in the Authorization header (usually with the Bearer scheme) of all subsequent API requests.[13] The ASP.NET Core API, running on any supported operating system, can then validate this JWT to ensure the user is authenticated and authorized to access the requested resources.[14]

For more complex authentication and authorization scenarios, especially in microservices architectures or when you need to integrate with external identity providers (like Google, Facebook, or Azure Active Directory), frameworks like IdentityServer are often used. IdentityServer is an open-source framework that runs on ASP.NET Core and implements the OpenID Connect and OAuth 2.0 protocols.[15] These are industry-standard protocols for federated authentication and authorization. Because IdentityServer is built on ASP.NET Core, it is also inherently cross-platform, allowing you to centralize your authentication and authorization logic across your entire ecosystem, regardless of the operating systems your various services and applications are running on.

Consider a scenario with multiple microservices built with ASP.NET Core, some running on Windows and others on Linux, all needing to authenticate users and protect their APIs. You could use IdentityServer, running on a separate server (which could be Windows or Linux), to handle user authentication and issue security tokens (like JWTs).[16] All your microservices can then validate these tokens to authenticate users and authorize access to their specific resources.

Implementing authentication and authorization in your cross-platform ASP.NET Core 9 web applications and APIs is greatly simplified by the framework's built-in, OS-agnostic support for various authentication schemes like cookie-based and JWT authentication.[17] For more complex scenarios, cross-platform frameworks like IdentityServer provide robust solutions based on industry standards. This allows you to focus on securely protecting your application and its data without having to worry about the underlying operating system differences affecting your authentication and authorization logic.

IdentityServer and OpenID Connect

For more complex authentication and authorization scenarios, especially in microservices architectures or when you need to integrate with external identity providers, IdentityServer is a popular open-source framework that runs on ASP.NET Core and is cross-platform. It implements the OpenID Connect and OAuth 2.0 protocols, providing a secure and standardized way to handle user authentication and API authorization.

JWT Authentication

JSON Web Tokens (JWTs) are a common standard for securing APIs. ASP.NET Core has excellent support for generating and validating JWTs, allowing you to implement stateless authentication for your APIs that can be consumed by clients on any platform.

11.4 Deployment Options for ASP.NET Core Applications

Alright, you've built your fantastic web application or API with ASP.NET Core 9, and now comes the crucial step of making it accessible to the world – deployment. Think of deployment as taking your carefully crafted application and setting it up to run in a live environment, whether that's on a traditional server or in the cloud. One of the significant advantages of ASP.NET Core is its flexibility when it comes to deployment, allowing you to choose the option that best fits your needs, infrastructure, and target audience, regardless of the underlying operating system of your server. Let's explore some of the common deployment options available for your cross-platform ASP.NET Core 9 applications.

One of the most traditional ways to host web applications on Windows Server is using IIS (Internet Information Services), Microsoft's powerful web server. You can configure IIS to host your ASP.NET Core application by setting up an application pool that's configured to run .NET Core. Often, you'll also configure IIS as a reverse proxy. In this setup, IIS listens for incoming HTTP requests on standard ports (like 80 for HTTP and 443 for HTTPS) and then forwards those requests to your ASP.NET Core application, which typically runs as a separate process on a specific port. IIS then handles the response from your application and sends it back to the client. This setup allows IIS to handle tasks like process management, request logging, and potentially SSL termination, while your ASP.NET Core application focuses on handling the application logic.

Consider a large enterprise running a mix of legacy ASP.NET applications and newer ASP.NET Core microservices on their existing Windows Server infrastructure. They can leverage IIS to host both types of applications, using its robust management tools and security features.

For those who prefer the open-source world or are deploying to Linux servers, Nginx and Apache are two of the most popular and widely used web servers. You can configure these web servers as reverse proxies in a similar way to IIS. They listen for incoming web requests and forward them to your ASP.NET Core application, which again runs as a standalone process, often managed by a service like Systemd (on modern Linux distributions). Nginx and Apache are known for their performance, stability, and extensive feature sets, making them excellent choices for hosting ASP.NET Core applications on Linux.

Imagine a startup deploying their ASP.NET Core-based SaaS platform to a cloud provider that primarily uses Linux servers.

They might choose to use Nginx as their reverse proxy due to its performance characteristics and ease of configuration in a Linux environment.

Increasingly popular for modern web applications is containerization using Docker. Docker allows you to package your entire application, including all its dependencies (like the .NET runtime, libraries, and even the operating system environment it needs), into a self-contained unit called a Docker image. This image can then be run as an isolated process called a container on any operating system that supports Docker (Windows, macOS, Linux). This provides a consistent and reproducible deployment environment, eliminating many of the "it works on my machine" problems. For ASP.NET Core applications, you can create a Dockerfile that specifies how to build a Docker image containing your application and the necessary .NET runtime. This containerized application can then be easily deployed to various environments, including your local machine for testing, traditional servers running Docker, or container orchestration platforms like Kubernetes.

Consider a development team that wants to ensure their ASP.NET Core microservices have a consistent deployment environment across their development, staging, and production servers, which might be a mix of Windows and Linux. They can use Docker to containerize each microservice, ensuring that the exact same runtime and dependencies are used in all environments, simplifying deployment and reducing the risk of environment-specific bugs.

Finally, cloud providers like Azure, AWS, and GCP offer excellent and often highly scalable options for hosting ASP.NET Core applications.

- Azure provides services like Azure App Service, a platform-as-a-service (PaaS) offering specifically designed for hosting web applications and APIs. It simplifies deployment, scaling, and management of your ASP.NET Core applications, often handling the underlying infrastructure for you. You can deploy directly from Visual Studio or using various deployment pipelines.

- AWS (Amazon Web Services) offers services like AWS Elastic Beanstalk and AWS Fargate (for containerized applications) that provide similar PaaS capabilities for deploying and managing ASP.NET Core applications on the AWS infrastructure.

- GCP (Google Cloud Platform) offers services like Google Cloud Run (for containerized applications) and Google App Engine that provide scalable and managed environments for hosting your ASP.NET Core web workloads.

These cloud platforms often provide built-in features for auto-scaling, load balancing, and monitoring, making it easier to run your cross-platform ASP.NET Core applications at scale.

Deploying your ASP.NET Core 9 applications across different operating systems offers a wealth of options. You can leverage traditional web servers like IIS (on Windows) and Nginx/Apache (on Linux), embrace the consistency of containerization with Docker, or take advantage of the managed services offered by major cloud providers. The choice depends on your specific requirements, infrastructure, team expertise, and scalability needs. The key takeaway is that ASP.NET Core's cross-platform nature gives you the freedom to choose the deployment environment that best suits your application.

Deploying to Windows Servers (IIS)

You can deploy ASP.NET Core applications to Windows servers using IIS (Internet Information Services), Microsoft's web server. This often involves setting up an application pool and configuring IIS to host your ASP.NET Core application, often using a reverse proxy configuration.

Deploying to Linux Servers (Nginx, Apache)

For Linux servers, popular choices for hosting ASP.NET Core applications include Nginx and Apache. You typically configure these web servers as reverse proxies to forward requests to your ASP.NET Core application, which usually runs as a standalone process managed by a service like Systemd.

Containerization with Docker for Web Applications

Containerization using Docker has become a very popular way to deploy web applications, including ASP.NET Core applications, across different environments. You can create a Docker image of your application that includes all its dependencies, including the .NET runtime, and then run this container on any operating system that supports Docker (Windows, macOS, Linux). This provides a consistent and isolated deployment environment.

Cloud Deployment (Azure, AWS, GCP)

All major cloud providers (Azure, AWS, GCP) offer excellent support for hosting ASP.NET Core applications on Linux-based or Windows-based virtual machines, as well as through platform-as-a-service (PaaS) offerings like Azure App Service, AWS Elastic Beanstalk, and Google Cloud Run, which often simplify deployment and scaling.

ASP.NET Core 9 provides a powerful and versatile framework for building cross-platform web applications and APIs. By understanding its architecture, choosing appropriate programming models, handling platform-specific needs carefully, and leveraging its flexible deployment options, you can build web solutions that reach a wide audience on their preferred operating systems.

Chapter 12: Testing and Quality Assurance in Cross-Platform .NET Development

Alright, let's talk about a crucial aspect of building robust and reliable applications, especially when you're targeting multiple platforms with .NET 9: testing and quality assurance. Think of testing as your safety net, ensuring that the code you've written actually works as expected across Windows, macOS, Linux, iOS, and Android. A comprehensive testing strategy is essential for catching bugs early, preventing regressions, and delivering a high-quality user experience on every platform.

12.1 Strategies for Writing Unit Tests

Alright, let's talk about the bedrock of software quality: unit tests. Think of unit tests as small, focused checks that verify the behavior of individual pieces of your code – typically a single method or a small class. They are the first line of defense against bugs and play a crucial role in ensuring that your cross-platform .NET 9 applications function correctly on Windows, macOS, Linux, iOS, and Android. Writing effective unit tests for your core, shared logic is paramount for building robust and reliable software.

The fundamental goal of a unit test is to isolate a specific part of your code and verify that it behaves as expected under a variety of conditions. This isolation is key. You want to test the unit without being influenced by the complexities or potential failures of its dependencies (other classes or services it interacts with). If a test fails, you want to be able to pinpoint the issue directly to the unit under test, rather than having to unravel a chain of interactions between multiple components.

A well-written unit test typically follows a pattern known as Arrange-Act-Assert (AAA):

- Arrange: In this phase, you set up the necessary preconditions for your test. This might involve creating instances of the class you're testing, initializing input parameters, and configuring any dependencies that the unit under test relies on (often using mocking, which we'll discuss shortly). The goal is to get everything into a known state before you execute the code you want to test.
- Act: This is where you perform the actual action you want to test. This usually involves calling a method on the class you're testing with the arranged inputs. You capture the result of this action (e.g., the return value, any exceptions thrown, or changes to the object's state).
- Assert: In this final phase, you verify that the outcome of the action matches your expectations. You use assertion methods provided by your chosen testing framework to check if the actual result is equal to the expected result, if a specific exception was thrown, or if the state of an object has changed in the way you anticipated.

Let's consider a real-world example. Suppose you have a simple StringReverser class with a method that reverses a given string:

C#

```
public class StringReverser

{

    public string Reverse(string input)

    {

        if (input == null)
```

```
        {

            return null;

        }

        char[] charArray = input.ToCharArray();

        Array.Reverse(charArray);

        return new string(charArray);

    }

}
```

Here's how you might write a unit test for the Reverse method using xUnit.net:

C#

```csharp
using Xunit;


public class StringReverserTests

{

    [Fact]

    public void Reverse_NullInput_ReturnsNull()

    {

        // Arrange

        var reverser = new StringReverser();

        string input = null;
```

```csharp
    // Act

    string result = reverser.Reverse(input);


    // Assert

    Assert.Null(result);

}


[Fact]
public void
Reverse_EmptyString_ReturnsEmptyString()

{

    // Arrange

    var reverser = new StringReverser();

    string input = "";


    // Act

    string result = reverser.Reverse(input);


    // Assert

    Assert.Equal("", result);
```

```csharp
        }


    [Fact]

    public void
Reverse_RegularString_ReturnsReversedString()

        {

            // Arrange

            var reverser = new StringReverser();

            string input = "hello";

            string expectedResult = "olleh";


            // Act

            string result = reverser.Reverse(input);


            // Assert

            Assert.Equal(expectedResult, result);

        }


    [Fact]

    public void
Reverse_StringWithSpaces_ReturnsReversedStringWit
hSpaces()
```

```
    {
        // Arrange

        var reverser = new StringReverser();

        string input = "hello world";

        string expectedResult = "dlrow olleh";


        // Act

        string result = reverser.Reverse(input);


        // Assert

        Assert.Equal(expectedResult, result);

    }

}
```

In this example, we have multiple test methods, each focusing on a specific scenario (null input, empty string, regular string, string with spaces). Each test follows the Arrange-Act-Assert pattern to clearly define the input, the action, and the expected outcome.

Now, let's talk about mocking dependencies. Often, the class you're testing will rely on other classes or services to perform its work. To keep your unit tests isolated and focused on the behavior of the unit under test, you use mock objects (or stubs) to simulate the behavior of these dependencies.

Consider a UserService that, as we saw before, depends on an IUserRepository to interact with user data. When you're unit testing the logic within UserService (e.g., its CreateUser method), you don't want your test to actually interact with a real database through UserRepository. That would make your test slow, brittle (dependent on the database being available and in a specific state), and not truly a *unit* test. Instead, you would use a mocking library (like Moq, NSubstitute, or FakeItEasy) to create a mock implementation of IUserRepository. You can then set up expectations on this mock – for example, specifying that when the AddUser method is called with a certain User object, it should behave in a specific way (e.g., not throw an exception). You can also verify that the UserService correctly interacts with its dependency (e.g., that it calls the AddUser method on the repository).

Here's a reminder of the UserService and a unit test for its CreateUser method using Moq:

C#

```csharp
using Moq;

using Xunit;


public interface IUserRepository

{

    User GetUserById(int id);

    void AddUser(User user);

}


public class UserService
```

```csharp
{
    private readonly IUserRepository
_userRepository;

    public UserService(IUserRepository
userRepository)
    {
        _userRepository = userRepository;
    }


    public void CreateUser(int id, string name)
    {
        var user = new User { Id = id, Name =
name };

        _userRepository.AddUser(user);

        // ... other logic
    }
}


public class User
{
    public int Id { get; set; }
```

```csharp
    public string Name { get; set; }

}


public class UserServiceTests

{

    [Fact]

    public void
CreateUser_ValidInput_CallsUserRepositoryAddUser(
)

    {

        // Arrange

        var mockRepo = new
Mock<IUserRepository>();

        var userService = new
UserService(mockRepo.Object);

        int userId = 123;

        string userName = "New User";


        // Act

        userService.CreateUser(userId, userName);


        // Assert
```

```
        mockRepo.Verify(repo =>
repo.AddUser(It.Is<User>(u => u.Id == userId &&
u.Name == userName)), Times.Once);

    }


    // ... other tests for UserService

}
```

In this test, we mock IUserRepository and verify that when CreateUser is called on the UserService, the AddUser method of the mock repository is called exactly once with a User object that has the correct Id and Name. This ensures that the UserService is correctly interacting with its dependency.

Writing comprehensive and well-isolated unit tests like these for your core, platform-agnostic code is a cornerstone of building high-quality cross-platform .NET applications. They provide confidence that your fundamental logic works correctly, regardless of the specific operating system or UI framework your application is running on.

Using xUnit.net and NUnit

.NET provides several popular testing frameworks to help you write and run unit tests. Two of the most widely used are xUnit.net and NUnit. Both frameworks provide a structured way to define test cases using attributes, assert expected outcomes, and organize your tests. They also integrate well with popular .NET IDEs like Visual Studio and Rider, as well as with command-line tools for running tests in your CI/CD pipelines.

Here's a simple example of a unit test using xUnit.net:

C#

```csharp
using Xunit;

public class CalculatorTests
{
    [Fact]
    public void
Add_TwoPositiveNumbers_ReturnsCorrectSum()
    {
        // Arrange
        var calculator = new Calculator();
        int a = 5;
        int b = 10;
        int expectedSum = 15;

        // Act
        int actualSum = calculator.Add(a, b);

        // Assert
        Assert.Equal(expectedSum, actualSum);
    }

    public class Calculator
    {
        public int Add(int x, int y)
        {
            return x + y;
        }
    }
}
```

In this example, the [Fact] attribute marks the Add_TwoPositiveNumbers_ReturnsCorrectSum method as a test case. The test follows the Arrange-Act-Assert pattern: setting up the necessary conditions (Arrange), performing the action being tested (Act), and verifying the outcome (Assert). xUnit.net provides various Assert methods to check for expected results.

NUnit provides similar functionality using attributes like [Test] and its own set of assertion methods (Assert.AreEqual, etc.). The choice between xUnit.net and NUnit often comes down to team preference or specific features of the framework. Both are excellent for writing unit tests for your cross-platform .NET code.

Mocking Dependencies

When unit testing a class, it often has dependencies on other classes or services. To test the unit in isolation, you typically use mocking. Mocking involves creating substitute objects (mocks or stubs) that mimic the behavior of the real dependencies, allowing you to control their responses and verify how the unit under test interacts with them. This is crucial for ensuring that your unit tests are focused and not affected by the behavior or state of their dependencies.

Popular .NET mocking libraries include Moq, NSubstitute, and FakeItEasy. These libraries provide fluent APIs for creating mocks, setting up expectations on their method calls, and verifying interactions.

Consider a UserService that depends on an IUserRepository to access user data:

C#

```
public interface IUserRepository
{
    User GetUserById(int id);
    void AddUser(User user);
}

public class UserService
{
    private readonly IUserRepository
_userRepository;
```

```csharp
    public UserService(IUserRepository
userRepository)
    {
        _userRepository = userRepository;
    }

    public User GetUser(int id)
    {
        return _userRepository.GetUserById(id);
    }

    public void CreateUser(int id, string name)
    {
        var user = new User { Id = id, Name =
name };
        _userRepository.AddUser(user);
        // ... other logic
    }
}

public class User
{
    public int Id { get; set; }
    public string Name { get; set; }
}
```

To unit test the UserService, you would typically mock the IUserRepository:

C#

```csharp
using Moq;
using Xunit;

public class UserServiceTests
{
```

```csharp
    [Fact]
    public void
GetUser_ExistingId_ReturnsUserFromRepository()
    {
        // Arrange
        var mockRepo = new
Mock<IUserRepository>();
        var expectedUser = new User { Id = 123,
Name = "Test User" };
        mockRepo.Setup(repo =>
repo.GetUserById(123)).Returns(expectedUser);
        var userService = new
UserService(mockRepo.Object);

        // Act
        var actualUser =
userService.GetUser(123);

        // Assert
        Assert.Equal(expectedUser, actualUser);
        mockRepo.Verify(repo =>
repo.GetUserById(123), Times.Once);
    }

    // ... other tests for UserService
}
```

Here, we use Moq to create a mock implementation of IUserRepository. We set up an expectation that when GetUserById(123) is called, the mock should return a specific User object. Then, we verify that GetUserById was indeed called once. This allows us to test the UserService in isolation, without relying on a real database implementation.

12.2 Integration Testing Cross-Platform Components

Alright, now that we've covered the importance of unit testing individual pieces of code, let's talk about the next level of testing: integration testing. Think of integration tests as verifying that different parts of your application work correctly *together*. While unit tests focus on isolated units, integration tests examine the interactions between two or more components to ensure they collaborate as expected. This is particularly important in cross-platform .NET 9 development, where you might have shared business logic interacting with platform-specific services or APIs.

The scope of an integration test is typically broader than a unit test. Instead of just testing a single method in isolation, you might be testing the flow of data and control through several interacting classes or even across different layers of your application. For example, you might want to test how your platform-agnostic data processing logic interacts with a platform-specific file storage implementation, or how your shared business rules are enforced when data is retrieved from a platform-specific data access layer.

Consider a real-world scenario: you're building a photo editing application with .NET MAUI that runs on both iOS and Android. You have a core image processing library (likely targeting .NET Standard or just .NET 9) that handles tasks like applying filters and resizing images. This core library might need to interact with the underlying file system to load and save images. However, the way you access the file system is different on iOS and Android.

To ensure that your core image processing logic correctly interacts with the platform-specific file system implementations, you would write integration tests. These tests would involve using the actual file system APIs of iOS and Android (or abstractions that mimic them) in conjunction with your core image processing code. You would then assert that images are loaded and saved correctly on both platforms.

Here's a conceptual example. Let's say you have an IFileSystemService interface in your shared code with platform-specific implementations (AndroidFileSystemService and iOSFileSystemService). You also have an ImageProcessor class in your shared code that uses IFileSystemService to load and save images.

An integration test for this scenario might look like this (using xUnit.net):

C#

```csharp
using Xunit;

using Moq; // Assuming you might still use mocks
for parts of the integration


// Shared interface

public interface IFileSystemService

{

    byte[] ReadFile(string path);

    void WriteFile(string path, byte[] content);

}


// Shared image processor

public class ImageProcessor
```

```csharp
{
    private readonly IFileSystemService
_fileSystemService;


    public ImageProcessor(IFileSystemService
fileSystemService)
    {
        _fileSystemService = fileSystemService;

    }


    public byte[] LoadImage(string path)
    {
        return _fileSystemService.ReadFile(path);

    }


    public void SaveImage(string path, byte[]
content)
    {
        _fileSystemService.WriteFile(path,
content);

    }

}
```

```csharp
public class
CrossPlatformImageProcessingIntegrationTests

{

    [Fact]
    public void
ImageProcessor_LoadsAndSavesImage_SuccessfullyOnA
ndroid()

    {
        // Arrange (setting up an Android-like
file system service)
        var mockAndroidFileSystem = new
Mock<IFileSystemService>();
        byte[] dummyImageBytes = { 0x01, 0x02,
0x03 };
        mockAndroidFileSystem.Setup(fs =>
fs.ReadFile("test_android.png")).Returns(dummyIma
geBytes);
        var imageProcessor = new
ImageProcessor(mockAndroidFileSystem.Object);


        // Act
        byte[] loadedImage =
imageProcessor.LoadImage("test_android.png");
```

```
        imageProcessor.SaveImage("saved_android.png",
loadedImage);


        // Assert (verifying interactions with
the Android-like file system service)

        Assert.Equal(dummyImageBytes,
loadedImage);

        mockAndroidFileSystem.Verify(fs =>
fs.ReadFile("test_android.png"), Times.Once);

        mockAndroidFileSystem.Verify(fs =>
fs.WriteFile("saved_android.png",
dummyImageBytes), Times.Once);

    }



    [Fact]

    public void
ImageProcessor_LoadsAndSavesImage_SuccessfullyOni
OS()

    {

        // Arrange (setting up an iOS-like file
system service)

        var mockiOSFileSystem = new
Mock<IFileSystemService>();

        byte[] dummyImageBytes = { 0x04, 0x05,
0x06 };
```

```
        mockiOSFileSystem.Setup(fs =>
fs.ReadFile("test_ios.png")).Returns(dummyImageBy
tes);

        var imageProcessor = new
ImageProcessor(mockiOSFileSystem.Object);


        // Act

        byte[] loadedImage =
imageProcessor.LoadImage("test_ios.png");

        imageProcessor.SaveImage("saved_ios.png",
loadedImage);


        // Assert (verifying interactions with
the iOS-like file system service)

        Assert.Equal(dummyImageBytes,
loadedImage);

        mockiOSFileSystem.Verify(fs =>
fs.ReadFile("test_ios.png"), Times.Once);

        mockiOSFileSystem.Verify(fs =>
fs.WriteFile("saved_ios.png", dummyImageBytes),
Times.Once);

    }


    // More integration tests covering different
scenarios and interactions
```

}

In this conceptual example, we're using mocks to simulate the platform-specific file system services. While this isn't testing the actual native file system, it allows us to verify that our shared ImageProcessor correctly interacts with the *abstractions* of these platform-specific components. For truly end-to-end integration testing with the actual native file systems, you would likely need to run your tests on actual Android and iOS environments (or emulators/simulators), which can be more involved to set up.

Key aspects of integration testing for cross-platform components include:

- Focus on Interactions: Verify that different parts of your application communicate and work together correctly.
- Realistic Environments: Try to set up testing environments that closely resemble your target platforms, especially when testing platform-specific integrations. This might involve using test doubles (like mocks or stubs) that mimic the behavior of platform-specific APIs.
- Broader Scope: Integration tests typically cover more code paths and involve more components than unit tests.
- Slower Execution: Integration tests often take longer to run than unit tests due to the setup of the testing environment and the broader scope of the tests.

By writing effective integration tests, you can gain confidence that your cross-platform .NET 9 application will function correctly as a whole, ensuring that your shared logic and platform-specific implementations work harmoniously on each target operating system. This is a crucial step in delivering a high-quality and reliable cross-platform experience for your users.

12.3 UI Testing for Desktop and Mobile Applications

Alright, let's talk about the visual and interactive heart of your cross-platform .NET 9 applications: the user interface. Ensuring that your UI looks right, behaves as expected, and provides a smooth experience on Windows, macOS, Linux, iOS, and Android is paramount. This is where UI testing comes in. Think of UI tests as simulating real user interactions with your application's interface to verify that everything renders correctly and responds appropriately to clicks, taps, typing, and gestures.

Testing the UI across different platforms presents unique challenges. Each operating system has its own native UI toolkit (WinUI on Windows, Cocoa on macOS, GTK+ on Linux, UIKit on iOS, Android UI), and while frameworks like .NET MAUI and Avalonia UI aim to abstract away many of these differences, subtle variations in rendering, behavior, and user expectations can still exist. Therefore, having a strategy for UI testing on each target platform is crucial for delivering a consistent and high-quality user experience.

Introduction to Playwright for .NET

Playwright for .NET is a powerful, open-source testing framework developed by Microsoft. While its primary focus is on end-to-end testing of web applications across all major browsers (Chromium, Firefox, and WebKit), it's also emerging as a valuable tool for testing desktop applications, particularly those built with technologies like Electron or those embedding web-based components.

Think of Playwright as a browser automation tool on steroids. It allows you to write tests in C# that can launch and interact with web browsers in a headless (without a visible UI) or headed (with a visible UI) mode. You can automate user actions like clicking buttons, filling out forms, navigating between pages, and asserting on the content and state of the rendered web pages.

While Playwright doesn't directly interact with the native UI controls of .NET MAUI or Avalonia UI desktop applications in the same way it interacts with HTML elements in a browser, if parts of your desktop application's UI are rendered using web technologies (for instance, if you're embedding a Blazor component or using a WebView), Playwright can be an excellent choice for automating and testing those parts of the interface.

For example, if you have a settings screen in your .NET MAUI desktop application that uses a WebView to display some web-based configuration options, you could use Playwright to write tests that navigate to this settings screen, interact with the web elements within the WebView, and verify the resulting behavior.

Playwright provides a rich API for interacting with the browser DOM (Document Object Model), allowing you to locate elements using CSS selectors or XPath expressions. It also supports advanced features like auto-waits (automatically waiting for elements to become visible or enabled before interacting with them), handling dialogs, and taking screenshots.

Here's a very basic conceptual example of a Playwright test in C# that navigates to a webpage and asserts on its title:

C#

```csharp
using Microsoft.Playwright;

using System.Threading.Tasks;

using Xunit;
```

```csharp
public class WebUITests

{

    [Fact]

    public async Task HomePage_HasCorrectTitle()

    {

        using var playwright = await
Playwright.CreateAsync();

        await using var browser = await
playwright.Chromium.LaunchAsync();

        await using var context = await
browser.NewContextAsync();

        await using var page = await
context.NewPageAsync();


        await
page.GotoAsync("https://example.com");


        Assert.Equal("Example Domain", await
page.TitleAsync());

    }

}
```

While this example targets a web page, the same principles of using Playwright to automate browser interactions and assert on the UI state can be applied to any web-based components embedded within your desktop applications.

Testing Native Mobile UI with Appium (Overview)

For testing the native user interfaces of your .NET MAUI iOS and Android mobile applications, Appium is a widely adopted open-source framework. Appium allows you to write tests that interact with your mobile app's UI elements in a way that mimics real user behavior, without requiring you to modify your app's code specifically for testing purposes. It supports testing native, hybrid (apps that contain web views), and mobile web applications running on real devices (both physical and virtual) and simulators/emulators.

Appium works by using platform-specific drivers. For iOS, it uses the XCUITest framework provided by Apple. For Android, it can use either UIAutomator or Espresso, depending on the version of Android and your specific needs. These drivers communicate with your mobile application running on the device or simulator/emulator, allowing you to find UI elements and perform actions on them.

You can write your Appium tests in various programming languages, including C#, using client libraries like DotNetSeleniumExtras.Appium. Your tests can then locate UI elements based on their properties, such as their text content, accessibility identifiers, class names, or XPath expressions. Once an element is located, your tests can perform actions on it, such as tapping buttons, entering text into input fields, swiping, and scrolling.

Furthermore, Appium allows you to assert on the state of UI elements to verify that they are displayed correctly. You can check if an element is visible, enabled, if its text content is as expected, or if its position and size are correct.

Setting up Appium for mobile UI testing can involve a more involved configuration process compared to unit tests. You'll typically need to install the Appium server, configure the necessary drivers for your target platforms (iOS and Android), and set up emulators or connect to real devices. Writing effective Appium tests requires understanding how to identify UI elements on iOS and Android (often using tools provided with the platform SDKs) and how to simulate realistic user interactions.

Here's a very basic conceptual example of an Appium test in C# that finds a button by its accessibility identifier and performs a click:

```csharp
C#

using OpenQA.Selenium.Appium;

using OpenQA.Selenium.Appium.iOS;

using OpenQA.Selenium.Appium.Android;

using System;

using System.Threading.Tasks;

using Xunit;



public class MobileUITests

{

    private AppiumDriver driver; // Could be
IOSDriver or AndroidDriver
```

```csharp
    // Setup method to initialize the driver
before each test


    [Fact]

    public async Task
ButtonClick_CounterIncrements()

    {

        // Find the button element by its
accessibility identifier

        var button =
driver.FindElement(AppiumBy.AccessibilityId("MyCo
unterButton"));


        // Perform a click action

        button.Click();


        // Find the label displaying the counter
value

        var counterLabel =
driver.FindElement(AppiumBy.AccessibilityId("Coun
terValueLabel"));


        // Assert that the counter value has
increased
```

```
      Assert.Equal("Clicked 1 times",
counterLabel.Text);

    }



    // Teardown method to quit the driver after
each test

}
```

This example illustrates the basic idea of using Appium to interact with UI elements in a mobile application. You would need to configure the driver (either IOSDriver or AndroidDriver) to connect to your running application on a simulator, emulator, or real device.

UI testing for cross-platform desktop applications might involve tools like Playwright if web technologies are part of the UI. For testing the native UIs of .NET MAUI iOS and Android applications, Appium provides a powerful framework for simulating user interactions and verifying the UI's state. Investing in UI testing is crucial for ensuring a consistent and high-quality user experience across all the platforms you target.

Introduction to Playwright for .NET

Playwright for .NET is a powerful, open-source testing framework by Microsoft that enables reliable end-to-end testing for web applications across all major browsers (Chromium, Firefox, WebKit). While primarily focused on web testing, Playwright can also be used for testing desktop applications (built with technologies like Electron or potentially web-based components embedded in desktop apps). It provides a high-level API to interact with the UI, automate user actions (like clicks, typing, and navigation), and assert on the state of the UI.

While not directly testing native .NET MAUI or Avalonia UI desktop controls, if parts of your desktop application involve embedded web views or if you are using a framework like Electron, Playwright can be a valuable tool for UI automation.

12.4 Continuous Integration and Continuous Deployment (CI/CD)

Alright, let's talk about a set of practices that are absolutely essential for maintaining the quality and velocity of your cross-platform .NET 9 development efforts: Continuous Integration (CI) and Continuous Deployment (CD). Think of CI/CD as an automated pipeline that takes your code changes and systematically builds, tests, and deploys your application across all your target platforms (Windows, macOS, Linux, iOS, and Android) with minimal manual intervention.[1] Implementing a robust CI/CD pipeline is a game-changer for ensuring that your application is always in a releasable state and that new features and bug fixes can be delivered to your users quickly and reliably.[2]

Continuous Integration (CI) is a development practice where developers frequently integrate their code changes into a shared repository,[3] ideally multiple times a day.[4] Each integration is then automatically verified by an automated build process that includes compiling the code, running unit tests, and often performing static code analysis to catch potential issues early. The key goal of CI is to detect and address integration errors as soon as they occur, preventing them from becoming more complex and harder to fix later in the development cycle.[5]

Consider a team of developers working on a .NET MAUI application. Each developer might be working on a different feature branch. With CI, every time a developer pushes their changes to the main branch (or merges a feature branch), an automated build process is triggered.[6] This process would compile the .NET MAUI project for iOS and Android, run all the unit tests written for the shared business logic, and potentially perform UI tests on emulators or simulators. If any of these steps fail, the team is immediately notified, allowing them to fix the issues before they become deeply integrated into the codebase.[7]

Continuous Deployment (CD) builds upon CI by automatically deploying the application to various environments after the automated build and testing phases are successful.[8] This can include testing environments, staging environments, and ultimately production environments. The goal of CD is to have a deployment pipeline that can release new versions of your application to users with minimal manual effort, making the release process faster, more reliable, and less prone to human error.[9]

Following our .NET MAUI example, if the CI pipeline successfully builds the iOS and Android apps and all tests pass, the CD pipeline could then automatically package the application for distribution to test devices, upload it to a staging environment for further testing, or even release it to the iOS App Store and Google Play Store (though the final step often involves some manual approval).[10]

Implementing a CI/CD pipeline for cross-platform .NET 9 applications typically involves using a CI/CD platform. These platforms provide the infrastructure and tools to automate your build, test, and deployment processes.[11] Here are a few popular options that work well with .NET projects and support building and testing on different operating systems:

Azure DevOps Pipelines

Azure DevOps provides a comprehensive CI/CD platform that is tightly integrated with Azure Repos (Git repositories) but can also work with other Git providers like GitHub.[12] You define your CI/CD workflows as pipelines, which are a series of steps or tasks.[13] Azure DevOps offers hosted build agents that can run on Windows, macOS, and Linux, allowing you to build your .NET 9 applications for all your target platforms. For mobile development with .NET MAUI, you can configure pipelines to build and sign iOS and Android applications using hosted macOS agents (for iOS builds) and hosted Linux or Windows agents (for Android builds). You can also integrate various testing frameworks (like xUnit.net and NUnit) and UI testing tools (like Appium for mobile) into your pipelines. For deployment, Azure DevOps offers tasks for publishing to app stores, deploying to Azure services, and more.[14]

GitHub Actions

GitHub Actions is a CI/CD platform directly integrated into GitHub repositories.[15] You define your workflows in YAML files within your repository. GitHub provides hosted runners (virtual machines) that can run on Linux, macOS, and Windows, making it suitable for building and testing cross-platform .NET 9 applications. For .NET MAUI mobile development, you can use macOS runners to build and sign iOS apps and Linux or Windows runners for Android builds. GitHub Actions has a large marketplace of pre-built actions that you can use in your workflows for common tasks like building, testing, packaging, and deploying .NET applications to various platforms and app stores.[16]

GitLab CI/CD

GitLab CI/CD is a powerful CI/CD platform integrated directly into GitLab.[17] You define your CI/CD pipelines in a .gitlab-ci.yml file within your repository.[18] GitLab provides its own runners (agents that execute your pipeline jobs), which can be configured to run on various operating systems, including Linux, macOS, and Windows.[19] You can set up your pipelines to build and test your .NET 9 applications for all your target platforms.[20] For mobile development, you can use macOS runners for iOS builds and Linux or Windows runners for Android builds. GitLab CI/CD offers a wide range of features, including parallel execution of jobs, caching, and deployment integrations.

Implementing a CI/CD pipeline for your cross-platform .NET 9 applications provides numerous benefits:

- Automation: Automates the build, test, and deployment processes, reducing manual effort and the risk of human error.[21]
- Faster Feedback: Quickly identifies integration issues and build failures, allowing developers to address them promptly.[22]
- Improved Quality: Ensures that every code change is automatically tested, leading to a more stable and reliable application across all platforms.[23]
- Faster Releases: Enables you to deliver new features and bug fixes to your users more frequently and with greater confidence.[24]
- Consistency: Provides a consistent and repeatable process for building and deploying your application across different environments.[25]

Establishing a robust CI/CD pipeline is a cornerstone of modern software development, and it's particularly crucial for cross-platform .NET 9 applications. By automating the build, test, and deployment processes for Windows, macOS, Linux, iOS, and Android, you can significantly improve the quality, stability, and delivery speed of your applications on all the platforms your users rely on.[26]

Chapter 13: Deployment and Distribution of Cross-Platform .NET Applications

Alright, you've successfully built your amazing cross-platform .NET 9 applications, and now the final piece of the puzzle is getting them into the hands of your users. This chapter focuses on deployment and distribution, which involves packaging your application and all its necessary components in a way that's suitable for installation and running on each of your target platforms (Windows, macOS, Linux for desktop; iOS and Android for mobile). Think of this as preparing your carefully crafted product for its grand entrance into the market, ensuring it's packaged and presented in a way that resonates with users on each platform.

13.1 Deployment Models for Desktop Applications

Alright, you've poured your heart and soul into crafting a fantastic .NET 9 desktop application that's ready to run on Windows, macOS, and Linux. Now comes the crucial step of getting it onto the computers of your users. Think of deployment models as the different ways you can package and deliver your application and its dependencies to these various desktop operating systems. Choosing the right deployment model is key to providing a smooth and hassle-free installation and execution experience for your users on their preferred platform.

When deploying .NET 9 desktop applications, one of the first and most fundamental decisions you'll need to make is around how you handle the .NET runtime itself. Does your application bring the runtime with it, or does it rely on the user having it installed already? This leads us to the two primary deployment models: self-contained deployment and framework-dependent deployment.

Let's first explore Self-Contained Deployment (SCD). In this model, you essentially create a complete package of your application that includes not only your compiled code and any third-party libraries you're using but also a copy of the specific .NET 9 runtime and the .NET libraries that your application depends on. Think of it like bundling all the necessary ingredients and the cooking instructions together in one box. When a user installs your self-contained application, they don't need to worry about whether they have .NET 9 installed on their system or not. Everything your application needs to run is included within its installation directory.

The primary advantage of SCD is its simplicity for the end-user. They download your application's installer, run it, and the application just works. There are no additional prerequisites for them to install. This can be particularly appealing for applications targeting a wide audience, where you can't assume a certain level of technical expertise or a pre-existing .NET installation.

However, this convenience comes at a cost: larger application sizes. Because you're including the entire .NET runtime (or at least the parts your application uses), the size of your application's installer and its footprint on the user's disk will be significantly larger compared to a framework-dependent deployment. Additionally, because the .NET runtime is platform-specific, you'll typically need to create separate self-contained deployment packages for each target operating system you want to support. For example, you'll build one package for Windows x64, another for macOS x64 (or ARM64), and yet another for Linux x64 (or other Linux architectures).

Now, let's consider Framework-Dependent Deployment (FDD). In this model, you only package your application's compiled code (the .dll files) and any third-party libraries it relies on. You do *not* include the .NET 9 runtime itself. Instead, you rely on the user having the .NET 9 runtime already installed on their machine.

Think of this like providing the recipe and expecting the user to have the basic ingredients in their pantry.

The main advantage of FDD is the smaller application size. Your deployment package will be much smaller because it doesn't include the potentially large .NET runtime. This can lead to faster download times and a smaller disk footprint. However, the significant drawback is the prerequisite for the user to have the correct version of the .NET 9 runtime installed on their operating system. If they don't, your application won't be able to run. This model is often preferred for internal applications within an organization where the IT department can manage the deployment of the .NET runtime across all machines, or for more technical users who are comfortable with installing software prerequisites.

Once you've decided on your deployment model (self-contained or framework-dependent), the next step is to package your application in a way that's standard and user-friendly for each target desktop operating system. This usually involves creating an installer.

For Windows, as we discussed earlier, the two primary ways to distribute desktop applications are through MSI (Microsoft Installer) packages and ClickOnce deployment. MSI installers provide a robust and standard way to install, uninstall, and manage applications, often preferred for complex applications. ClickOnce offers a simpler installation and automatic updates specifically for .NET applications. Tools like the WiX Toolset or Visual Studio Installer Projects can help you create MSI installers. Visual Studio provides built-in support for ClickOnce publishing.

For macOS, the common formats are DMG (Disk Image) files and PKG (Package) installers. DMGs are often used for simpler applications, where the user just drags and drops the application bundle to their Applications folder. PKG installers are used for more complex installations. Apple's Xcode tools can be used to create PKG installers, and the Disk Utility can create DMGs.

For Linux, the landscape is more diverse. Common formats include DEB packages (for Debian-based systems like Ubuntu), RPM packages (for Red Hat-based systems like Fedora), Snap packages, and AppImage files. Snap and AppImage aim to be more universal, bundling dependencies within the package. Tools like dpkg, rpmbuild, snapcraft, and utilities for creating AppImages are used for packaging.

When creating these platform-specific installers, you'll typically bundle your application's executable, any necessary configuration files, resources (like images and localization files), and the .NET runtime if you're doing a self-contained deployment. You'll also define how the application should be installed, including creating shortcuts, registering file associations, and handling uninstallation. The specific tools and processes for creating these installers are platform-dependent and often involve using utilities provided by the operating system or third-party packaging tools.

13.2 Deployment Models for Mobile Applications

Alright, let's now turn our attention to the world of getting your .NET MAUI applications onto the mobile devices of your users, specifically those running iOS and Android. Think of this as preparing your mobile app for its debut in the Apple App Store and the Google Play Store. The process here is quite different from deploying desktop applications, largely due to the centralized nature of app distribution on these platforms, which involves specific building, signing, and submission procedures.

When you're ready to share your .NET MAUI mobile application with the world, the first crucial step is to build and sign your application for the specific target platform. This process creates the installable package that users will download from the app stores, and the signing verifies your identity as the developer and ensures the integrity of your application.

For iOS, the entire process of building and signing your application revolves around Apple's ecosystem and tools. You'll need to have an Apple Developer account and utilize Xcode, which runs exclusively on macOS. Xcode provides the necessary tools to build your .NET MAUI iOS project into an application bundle (.app directory) and then package it into an IPA (iOS App Archive) file, which is the format used for distributing iOS applications.

A critical part of this process is code signing. Apple requires all iOS applications to be digitally signed with a certificate issued by Apple. This certificate is linked to your Apple Developer account and ensures that the application comes from a trusted source. You'll also need to create a provisioning profile, which is a file that contains information about your app's bundle identifier, the devices it's allowed to run on (for development builds), and the signing certificate. The build process in Xcode (or the .NET MAUI build process when configured on a Mac) uses your signing certificate and provisioning profile to sign the IPA file. Without proper signing, your iOS application cannot be installed on a real device or submitted to the App Store.

Consider a .NET MAUI application you've built. When you're ready to release it for iPhones and iPads, you'll use Xcode on a Mac to create an IPA file. This file will be signed using the certificate associated with your Apple Developer account and will be provisioned for either development/testing on specific devices or for distribution through the App Store.

For Android, the process is a bit more platform-agnostic in terms of the development machine. You can build your .NET MAUI Android project on Windows, macOS, or Linux using the .NET SDK. The build process will generate an APK (Android Package Kit) file, which is the standard format for distributing Android applications, or the more modern AAB (Android App Bundle) format, which is now the recommended format for publishing to the Google Play Store.

Similar to iOS, Android applications also need to be digitally signed. You'll use a keystore file (a .keystore or .jks file) to store your signing certificate and private key. You'll create this keystore file using the Java Keytool, which is part of the Java Development Kit (JDK). You then configure your .NET MAUI Android project's build settings to use your keystore file and password to sign the APK or AAB file. Signing ensures the integrity of your application and verifies your identity as the developer. The Android App Bundle (.aab) format allows the Google Play Store to generate optimized APKs for different device configurations, resulting in smaller download sizes for users.

Imagine the same .NET MAUI application. When you're ready to release it for Android devices, you'll use the .NET SDK to build an AAB file. This file will be signed using the keystore file you created, and you'll then upload this AAB file to the Google Play Store.

Once you have your signed application package (IPA for iOS, AAB for Android), the next step is submitting it to the respective app stores: the Apple App Store for iOS users and the Google Play Store for Android users. Each store has its own set of guidelines, requirements, and submission processes that you must meticulously follow. This includes providing detailed information about your app, such as its title, description, keywords, screenshots, privacy policy, support contact information, and setting pricing and availability.

For the Apple App Store, the submission process involves using Xcode and the Transporter application (or the upload functionality within Xcode itself) to upload your IPA file to App Store Connect, which is Apple's web-based platform for managing your iOS apps. Your app will then go through a review process by Apple to ensure it complies with their guidelines. This review process can take anywhere from a few days to a couple of weeks or longer, so it's crucial to submit your app well in advance of any planned release date.

For the Google Play Store, you upload your APK or AAB file through the Google Play Console, which is Google's web-based platform for managing your Android apps. The review process on the Play Store is generally faster than on the App Store, often taking a few hours to a day. However, you still need to ensure your app adheres to Google's policies regarding content, privacy, and security.

Both app stores also require you to provide metadata about your app in various languages, manage your app's versions, handle updates, and monitor user reviews and ratings. The submission process is a critical final step in getting your .NET MAUI mobile application into the hands of your users worldwide.

13.3 Deployment Models for Web Applications and APIs

Alright, let's shift our focus to the world of making your ASP.NET Core 9 web applications and APIs accessible over the internet. Think of this as setting up your digital storefront or your backend service so that users and other applications can interact with it. The way you deploy your web applications and APIs can significantly impact their performance, scalability, reliability, and maintainability. Fortunately, ASP.NET Core offers a range of flexible deployment models that cater to various needs and infrastructure setups, and these models work seamlessly across Windows, macOS, and Linux server environments.

One of the most straightforward ways to host ASP.NET Core applications, especially if you're already familiar with the Windows ecosystem, is by deploying to Windows Servers using IIS (Internet Information Services). IIS has been a staple web server on Windows for a long time, and it has excellent integration with the .NET platform. To host an ASP.NET Core application on IIS, you typically need to install the ASP.NET Core Hosting Bundle on your server. This bundle includes the .NET runtime, the ASP.NET Core

Module (a native IIS module that allows IIS to forward requests to your ASP.NET Core application), and other necessary components.

The typical setup involves configuring an application pool in IIS that's set to "No Managed Code" because ASP.NET Core runs as an out-of-process application (using its own self-contained web server like Kestrel by default). You then create a website in IIS and configure it to point to the directory where you've published your ASP.NET Core application. Often, you'll also configure IIS as a reverse proxy. In this role, IIS listens for incoming HTTP(S) requests on standard ports (80 and 443) and then forwards those requests to your ASP.NET Core application, which is running as a separate process on a specific port (often a higher-numbered port). IIS then takes the response from your ASP.NET Core application and sends it back to the client. This setup allows IIS to handle tasks like process management (ensuring your application restarts if it crashes), request logging, handling static files, and managing SSL certificates, while your ASP.NET Core application focuses on processing the application logic and generating dynamic content or API responses.

Consider a large organization with existing Windows Server infrastructure. They might choose to host their new ASP.NET Core 9 web applications on IIS to leverage their existing investment and expertise in Windows Server administration. They can use IIS's management tools to configure the applications, manage security, and monitor performance.

For those who prefer the open-source world or are deploying to Linux servers, Nginx and Apache are two of the most popular and widely used web servers. Just like with IIS, you can configure these web servers as reverse proxies to host your ASP.NET Core applications. You would install Nginx or Apache on your Linux server and then configure it to listen for incoming web requests and forward them to your ASP.NET Core application, which runs as a standalone process, often managed by a system service like

Systemd. Your ASP.NET Core application will typically be configured to listen on a specific port (e.g., port 5000 for Kestrel). Nginx or Apache will then act as the entry point for all web traffic to your application, handling things like static file serving, SSL termination, and load balancing if needed, before passing the relevant requests to your ASP.NET Core process.

Imagine a startup deploying their ASP.NET Core 9-based API to a cloud provider that primarily uses Linux instances. They might opt for Nginx as their reverse proxy due to its lightweight nature and high performance in serving web traffic on Linux. They would configure Nginx to forward API requests to their ASP.NET Core application running as a Systemd service.

A highly flexible and increasingly popular way to deploy ASP.NET Core applications across different environments is through containerization using Docker. Docker allows you to package your entire application, including all its dependencies – the .NET 9 runtime, any required libraries, your application's code, and even a minimal operating system environment – into a self-contained unit called a Docker image. This image can then be run as an isolated process called a container on any operating system that supports Docker (Windows, macOS, Linux). This provides a consistent and reproducible deployment environment, eliminating many of the environment-specific configuration issues that can arise with traditional deployments. For ASP.NET Core applications, you typically create a Dockerfile that specifies how to build the Docker image, including which base image to use (e.g., an official .NET 9 runtime image from Microsoft), how to copy your application code into the image, and how to run your application. This containerized ASP.NET Core application can then be easily deployed to various environments, from your local development machine for testing to production servers running Docker or container orchestration platforms like Kubernetes.

Consider a development team that wants to ensure their ASP.NET Core 9 microservices have a consistent deployment environment across their local development setups, staging servers running Linux, and production clusters managed by Kubernetes on a cloud provider. They can use Docker to create container images for each microservice, ensuring that the exact same runtime and dependencies are used in all environments, simplifying deployment and reducing the risk of environment-specific bugs.

Finally, all major cloud providers (Azure, AWS, GCP) offer excellent and often highly scalable options for hosting ASP.NET Core applications.

- Azure provides Azure App Service, a fully managed platform-as-a-service (PaaS) offering specifically designed for hosting web applications and APIs, including those built with ASP.NET Core. It simplifies deployment, scaling, and management, often handling the underlying infrastructure for you. You can deploy directly from Visual Studio, using CI/CD pipelines, or through other deployment tools.
- AWS (Amazon Web Services) offers services like AWS Elastic Beanstalk and AWS Fargate (for containerized applications) that provide similar PaaS capabilities for deploying and managing ASP.NET Core applications on the AWS infrastructure.
- GCP (Google Cloud Platform) offers services like Google Cloud Run (for containerized applications) and Google App Engine that provide scalable and managed environments for hosting your ASP.NET Core web workloads.

These cloud platforms often provide built-in features for auto-scaling, load balancing, monitoring, and security, making it easier to run your cross-platform ASP.NET Core 9 applications at scale and with high availability.

Deploying your ASP.NET Core 9 web applications and APIs offers a wide range of choices, from traditional web servers like IIS and Nginx/Apache to the modern approach of containerization with Docker and the fully managed services of cloud providers. The best option for you will depend on your specific requirements, existing infrastructure, team expertise, scalability needs, and budget. The key takeaway is that ASP.NET Core's cross-platform nature gives you the freedom to choose the deployment environment that best suits your application and your organization.

13.4 Considerations for Application Updates and Maintenance

Alright, you've successfully deployed your cross-platform .NET 9 applications, and users are starting to interact with them. However, the journey doesn't end there. Software is rarely static; you'll likely need to release updates with new features, bug fixes, and security patches. Think of application updates and maintenance as the ongoing care and evolution of your application after its initial release, ensuring it remains relevant, reliable, and secure across all the platforms it supports (Windows, macOS, Linux, iOS, and Android). Having a well-defined strategy for updates and maintenance is crucial for the long-term success and user satisfaction of your cross-platform applications.

When it comes to desktop applications (built with .NET MAUI or Avalonia UI), the update mechanisms can vary depending on the platform and how you initially distributed your application.

On Windows, if you used ClickOnce deployment, it offers built-in support for automatic updates. When you publish a new version of your application to the ClickOnce deployment location (e.g., a web server or network share), the next time a user launches the application, ClickOnce can automatically check for updates and prompt the user to install them. This provides a seamless way to keep your users on the latest version. For applications deployed via

MSI installers, updates are typically handled by creating a new MSI package for the updated version. Users might need to manually download and run this new MSI, or you could potentially use technologies like Microsoft Update or third-party update frameworks to automate the process.

For macOS, a common approach for handling updates is using Sparkle, an open-source update framework specifically designed for macOS applications. You integrate Sparkle into your application, and it handles checking for updates from a designated feed (often an XML file on your server), downloading the new version (usually packaged as a DMG or ZIP file), and prompting the user to install it. For applications distributed through the Mac App Store, updates are handled automatically by the store itself.

On Linux, the update process often depends on how you packaged your application. If you used distribution-specific package formats like DEB or RPM, users will typically receive updates through their system's package manager (apt or yum/dnf) if you provide a software repository. For universal formats like Snap and AppImage, they often have their own built-in update mechanisms. Snap packages can be automatically updated in the background, while AppImages might require users to download a new version.

When dealing with mobile applications (built with .NET MAUI for iOS and Android), the primary mechanism for distributing updates is through the respective app stores: the Apple App Store and the Google Play Store. To release an update to your app, you typically build a new, signed version of your application package (IPA for iOS, AAB for Android) and submit it through the app store's developer console. You'll need to provide information about the update, and it will usually go through a review process (especially on the App Store). Once approved, the update will be made available to your users, who can then download and install it through the app store. Both stores often provide mechanisms for automatic updates if users have enabled that setting.

For web applications and APIs (built with ASP.NET Core 9), the update and maintenance process typically involves deploying a new version of your application to your web servers or containers. This might involve stopping the old version, deploying the new files, and then restarting the application. If you're using containerization with Docker and orchestration platforms like Kubernetes, updates can often be rolled out more seamlessly using techniques like rolling updates or blue/green deployments, which minimize downtime. Cloud platforms like Azure App Service and AWS Elastic Beanstalk also offer features to simplify the deployment and updating of web applications.

Regardless of the platform, there are some general considerations for application updates and maintenance:

- Planning for Updates: Design your application with updates in mind. Consider how new features will be introduced without breaking existing functionality. Use modular design and feature flags to control the rollout of new features.
- Testing Updates: Thoroughly test your updates on all target platforms before releasing them to your users. This includes unit tests, integration tests, and ideally some form of user acceptance testing (UAT) or beta testing.
- Version Control: Use a robust version control system (like Git) to manage your codebase and track changes between releases. Use branching strategies to isolate development of new features and bug fixes.
- Rollback Strategy: Have a plan in place to roll back to a previous stable version of your application if a critical issue is discovered after an update.
- Monitoring and Logging: Implement comprehensive logging and monitoring in your application to track its health, identify errors, and understand user behavior after an update. This will help you quickly detect and address any issues that might arise.

- User Communication: Keep your users informed about upcoming updates, new features, and bug fixes. Provide clear instructions on how to update their applications if it's not an automatic process.
- Security Updates: Stay vigilant about security vulnerabilities in your application and its dependencies. Apply security patches promptly across all your deployed versions.

Maintaining cross-platform applications requires a consistent and well-planned approach to updates and ongoing support. By leveraging the update mechanisms provided by each platform and following best practices for version control, testing, monitoring, and user communication, you can ensure the long-term success and satisfaction of your users on Windows, macOS, Linux, iOS, and Android.

Chapter 14: Advanced Performance Tuning and Optimization

Alright, you've got a solid foundation in writing performant cross-platform .NET 9 applications and know how to identify common bottlenecks. Now, let's delve into some more advanced techniques for squeezing every last drop of performance out of your code. Think of this chapter as moving from general best practices to more specialized strategies for those truly performance-critical sections of your application.

14.1 In-Depth Exploration of Span<T> and Memory<T>

Alright, let's really get into the weeds of two powerful tools in the .NET memory management API arsenal: Span<T> and Memory<T>. Think of these as providing a way to interact with contiguous regions of memory with a level of control and efficiency that goes beyond traditional arrays and collections. They are particularly valuable when you're striving for high performance, especially in scenarios involving data processing, I/O operations, and interop with native code. Understanding their nuances and capabilities can unlock significant performance gains in your .NET 9 applications.

As we touched on earlier, the primary goal of Span<T> and Memory<T> is to provide a zero-overhead abstraction over contiguous blocks of memory, whether that memory is managed by the .NET runtime (like arrays) or resides in unmanaged memory. This "zero-overhead" aspect is crucial – these types themselves are lightweight value types (struct), meaning that creating and manipulating them generally doesn't involve allocations on the managed heap, thus reducing pressure on the garbage collector.

Let's start with Span<T>. Imagine you have an array, which is a contiguous block of memory holding elements of a specific type. Span<T> gives you a view into a portion of this array (or the entire array) without copying the underlying data.[1] It's like having a window into the array. You can read and write elements through the Span<T>, and these changes directly affect the original array.[2]

Consider a real-world example: you're processing a large image represented as a byte array. You might want to work with a specific row or a rectangular region of this image. With traditional array manipulation, you might end up creating new arrays to represent these sub-regions, leading to memory allocations and copying. Span<byte> allows you to create a view (a slice) of the original byte array that represents just the row or the rectangle you're interested in, without allocating any new memory for the view itself. You can then operate directly on this slice.

Here's a code example illustrating this:

C#

```
using System;


public class SpanImageProcessing

{

    public static void ProcessRow(Span<byte>
imageData, int rowNumber, int rowWidth, byte
color)

    {

        int startIndex = rowNumber * rowWidth;
```

```csharp
        var rowSpan = imageData.Slice(startIndex,
rowWidth);

        for (int i = 0; i < rowSpan.Length; i++)

        {

            rowSpan[i] = color; // Modify the
original image data directly

        }

    }


    public static void Main(string[] args)

    {

        int imageWidth = 100;

        int imageHeight = 50;

        byte[] imageData = new byte[imageWidth *
imageHeight];


        // Initialize image data (e.g., with some
initial pixel values)

        for (int i = 0; i < imageData.Length;
i++)

        {

            imageData[i] = (byte)(i % 256);

        }
```

```
        int rowToProcess = 25;

        byte newColor = 200;



        var imageDataSpan = new
Span<byte>(imageData);

        ProcessRow(imageDataSpan, rowToProcess,
imageWidth, newColor);



        // Now, the 'imageData' array will have
the specified row modified directly

        Console.WriteLine($"Row {rowToProcess} of
the image data has been processed.");

    }

}
```

In this example, imageData.AsSpan() creates a Span<byte> over the imageData array. The ProcessRow method then uses Slice() to get a Span<byte> representing a specific row. Importantly, when we modify the elements within rowSpan, we are directly modifying the elements in the original imageData array. No new array or memory allocation occurred for rowSpan.

Now, let's consider Memory<T>. Memory<T> is similar to Span<T> in that it represents a contiguous region of memory. However, Memory<T> has a key difference: it can own the memory it points to. While Span<T> is always a view over existing memory, Memory<T> can be created from managed memory (like arrays) or it can be allocated directly using MemoryPool<T>. This makes Memory<T> more versatile, especially when dealing with asynchronous operations and managing the lifetime of the underlying memory.

You can easily get a Span<T> from a Memory<T> using its .Span property. This allows you to use the efficient Span<T> APIs for synchronous operations on the memory represented by a Memory<T>.

Consider a scenario involving asynchronous I/O. When you perform an asynchronous read operation (e.g., from a NetworkStream using ReadAsync), the data is often read into a buffer that needs to persist across the asynchronous operation. Memory<byte> is often used to represent this buffer.

Here's a conceptual example:

C#

```
using System;

using System.Buffers;

using System.IO.Pipelines;

using System.Net.Sockets;

using System.Threading.Tasks;



public class MemoryAsyncIO

{

    public static async Task
ProcessNetworkStreamAsync(NetworkStream stream,
MemoryPool<byte> pool)
```

```csharp
    {
        using IMemoryOwner<byte> memoryOwner =
pool.Rent(1024);

        Memory<byte> buffer = memoryOwner.Memory;


        while (true)
        {
            int bytesRead = await
stream.ReadAsync(buffer);

            if (bytesRead == 0)
                break;


            ReadOnlySpan<byte> receivedData =
buffer.Span.Slice(0, bytesRead);

            // Process the receivedData
Span<byte> efficiently

            Console.WriteLine($"Received
{bytesRead} bytes:
{System.Text.Encoding.UTF8.GetString(receivedData
)}");

        }

    }
```

```
    // ... (NetworkStream setup would be needed
for a runnable example)

}
```

In this example, MemoryPool<byte>.Shared.Rent(1024) rents a block of memory represented by an IMemoryOwner<byte>, from which we can get a Memory<byte>.[3] The asynchronous stream.ReadAsync operation writes data directly into this Memory<byte>. We then obtain a Span<byte> (receivedData) to efficiently process the received data. The MemoryPool<T> helps manage the allocation and pooling of memory, further optimizing memory usage in I/O-bound scenarios.[4]

Span<T> and Memory<T> are powerful tools for achieving high-performance, zero-copy operations in .NET 9. Span<T> provides a lightweight, safe view over existing contiguous memory, while Memory<T> offers a more versatile abstraction that can own memory and is particularly useful in asynchronous scenarios. By understanding and leveraging these types, you can significantly improve the efficiency of your applications when dealing with memory-intensive tasks.

14.2 Understanding and Mitigating Interop Performance Costs

Alright, let's delve into a topic that becomes relevant when your cross-platform .NET 9 applications need to interact with code written in other languages, often referred to as interoperability or interop. This is particularly common when you need to access platform-specific APIs that aren't directly available through the .NET base class libraries or when you're integrating with existing native libraries for performance reasons or access to specialized functionalities. The primary mechanism for achieving this in .NET is Platform Invocation Services (P/Invoke). However, crossing the boundary between the managed .NET environment and the unmanaged world of native code comes with inherent performance costs, and understanding these costs, along with strategies to mitigate them, is crucial for building efficient applications that rely on interop.

The performance overhead of P/Invoke stems largely from the process of data marshalling. When you call a native function from your .NET code, the .NET runtime needs to convert the data between the managed types used in .NET (which are under the control of the garbage collector) and the unmanaged types used by the native code (where memory management is manual).

This marshalling process can involve several steps:

1. Type Conversion: .NET types might not have a direct equivalent in the unmanaged world. The runtime needs to figure out how to represent the data in a way that the native function understands. For simple types like integers or booleans, this conversion is usually straightforward. However, for more complex types like strings, arrays, and structs, the conversion can be more involved.

2. Memory Allocation: Unmanaged code operates on raw memory addresses. The .NET runtime might need to allocate unmanaged memory to hold the data being passed to the native function. For example, when passing a .NET string to a native function that expects a null-terminated character array, the runtime will allocate unmanaged memory, copy the string content, and add the null terminator.

3. Data Copying: Once the unmanaged memory is allocated, the data from the managed object needs to be copied into this unmanaged buffer. This copying takes time, especially for large data structures.

4. Garbage Collection Considerations: The garbage collector can move managed objects in memory. If a native function holds a pointer to managed memory, this can lead to crashes. To prevent this, you might need to "pin" the

managed memory, which tells the GC not to move it. Pinning can, however, impact the GC's efficiency.

5. Transition Overhead: There's also a small overhead associated with the actual transition of execution from managed to unmanaged code and back.

The impact of these costs can vary greatly depending on the frequency of your P/Invoke calls and the complexity of the data being marshalled. If you're making many P/Invoke calls with complex data structures in performance-critical sections of your code, the overhead can become significant.

So, how can you mitigate these performance costs? Here are some best practices to consider:

- Minimize the Number of P/Invoke Calls: The overhead of crossing the managed/unmanaged boundary exists for each call. Therefore, it's often more efficient to design your interop layer to make fewer, larger calls rather than many small ones. If you need to perform a series of related operations in native code, consider creating a single native function that performs the entire sequence, if feasible. For instance, if you need to process multiple elements of an array in native code, try to pass the entire array in one P/Invoke call instead of calling the native function for each element.

- Optimize Data Marshalling: Carefully choose the data types you use in your .NET signatures for the native functions and pay close attention to the default marshalling behavior. Use the [MarshalAs] attribute to explicitly specify how data should be marshalled if the default is not the most efficient for your scenario. For example, if a native function only reads a string, you might be able to use an IntPtr and manually marshal the string as a read-only pointer to avoid unnecessary copying. For arrays that are only read by the native code, you might be able to pass an IntPtr to the first element and the array length, letting the native code directly access the managed memory (with appropriate pinning).

- Avoid Unnecessary String Conversions: String marshalling can be particularly expensive due to encoding conversions and memory allocations. If the native code works with a specific encoding (like UTF-8), ensure your .NET strings are in that encoding to avoid redundant conversions. If the native code only needs a pointer to a null-terminated string, use [MarshalAs(UnmanagedType.LPStr)] or similar attributes. However, be very careful with the lifetime of the managed string in this case – it must live at least as long as the native function is using the pointer.

- Pin Memory Judiciously: When you need to pass managed objects like arrays or structs to unmanaged code that will access them directly, you might need to pin the memory to prevent the garbage collector from moving it during the native call. You can do this using the fixed keyword (for stack-allocated memory or array elements within a fixed block) or GCHandle.Alloc(object, GCHandleType.Pinned) (for heap-allocated objects). However, pinning can fragment the managed heap and hinder the GC's efficiency, so use it sparingly and for the shortest possible duration. For example, if you're passing a byte array to a native function for processing, pin it just before the call and unpin it immediately afterwards.

- Cache Native Function Pointers: Looking up the address of a native function each time you call it via P/Invoke has a small overhead. If you're calling the same native function many times, especially in a loop, consider obtaining the function pointer once (e.g., using Marshal.GetFunctionPointerForDelegate) and storing it in a static field. You can then create a .NET delegate from this function pointer and call the delegate directly, avoiding the repeated lookup.

- Profile Your Interop Code: The most important step is to profile your application and identify if P/Invoke calls are indeed a significant performance bottleneck. Use profiling tools that can track the time spent in P/Invoke calls and the amount of data being marshalled. If interop is a hotspot, then focus your optimization efforts on the most frequently called interop methods and the data types being passed. Sometimes, the best solution might involve restructuring your code or the native library interaction to reduce the frequency or complexity of P/Invoke calls.

By understanding the performance costs associated with P/Invoke and applying these mitigation strategies, you can build cross-platform .NET 9 applications that effectively leverage native code when necessary without sacrificing overall performance. The key is to be mindful of the managed/unmanaged boundary and to optimize the data flow and the frequency of transitions across this boundary.

14.3 Advanced Profiling and Tracing Techniques

Alright, we've touched on the basics of profiling your .NET 9 applications to identify performance bottlenecks. Now, let's explore some more advanced techniques that can give you even deeper insights into your application's runtime behavior. Think of these as going beyond the surface-level metrics and really understanding the intricate dance of your code execution, memory usage, and resource consumption.

Deep Dive into PerfView Analysis

As we discussed earlier, PerfView is a phenomenal free tool for performance analysis on Windows. Mastering its advanced features can be a game-changer when you're tackling complex performance mysteries. Beyond just looking at CPU usage and memory allocation, PerfView allows you to analyze various aspects of your application with incredible granularity.

For instance, you can perform a deep dive into garbage collection (GC) behavior. PerfView provides detailed information about every GC event, including the generation being collected, the reason for the collection, the duration of the pause, the size of the heap before and after the collection, and even the fragmentation of the heap. By analyzing this data over time, you can understand if your application is putting undue pressure on the GC, if you're experiencing long GC pauses that are impacting responsiveness, or if memory fragmentation might be an issue. You can also see object survival rates across generations, which can give you clues about the lifetime of your objects and potential areas for optimization.

Another powerful area is analyzing JIT (Just-In-Time) compilation. PerfView can show you which methods are being JIT-compiled, how frequently they are being compiled, and how long the compilation takes. This can be particularly useful for understanding application startup performance. If certain methods are being compiled very late in the application's lifecycle or are taking a long time to compile, you might consider strategies like forcing early JIT compilation or restructuring your code to improve startup times.

PerfView also provides rich insights into threading. You can analyze thread activity, including when threads are created and destroyed, how long they spend running, how often they are blocked (waiting on locks or other synchronization primitives), and the number of context switches. This information can be invaluable for diagnosing concurrency issues, identifying potential deadlocks, or understanding if your parallel or asynchronous code is behaving as expected.

Furthermore, PerfView can track exceptions that are thrown and caught within your application. While not always a direct performance bottleneck, a high rate of exceptions, even if handled, can consume significant CPU resources. Analyzing the types and frequency of exceptions can sometimes reveal underlying performance problems or areas in your code that could be made more robust.

Finally, if you've instrumented your application with custom Event Tracing for Windows (ETW) events, PerfView is the tool you'll use to analyze this application-specific tracing information. This allows you to track the flow of execution through your own components and measure the duration of critical operations with high precision.

To really leverage PerfView's advanced capabilities, it takes time and practice to become familiar with its various views, the different types of events it collects, and its powerful filtering and grouping features. However, the level of insight it provides can be indispensable for tackling complex performance challenges on Windows.

Using Event Tracing for Windows (ETW)

As mentioned, Event Tracing for Windows (ETW) is the underlying, powerful tracing mechanism on Windows that PerfView utilizes. You can also interact with ETW programmatically within your .NET applications to emit custom events that are specific to your application's logic and performance metrics. This gives you a very detailed and low-level way to trace the execution flow and measure the timing of critical operations.

You typically use the System.Diagnostics.Tracing.EventSource class to define and emit your custom ETW events. You create a class that inherits from EventSource and define methods that correspond to the events you want to log. These methods use the WriteEvent method to emit the event data, which can include various payloads (strings, numbers, etc.).

Here's a simplified example of a custom EventSource:

C#

```csharp
using System.Diagnostics.Tracing;


[EventSource(Name = "MyApp-Performance")]

public class MyAppPerformanceSource : EventSource

{

    public static MyAppPerformanceSource Log =
new MyAppPerformanceSource();


    [Event(1, Level = EventLevel.Informational,
Message = "Operation started: {0}")]

    public void OperationStarted(string
operationName)

    {

        WriteEvent(1, operationName);

    }


    [Event(2, Level = EventLevel.Informational,
Message = "Operation completed in {1}ms: {0}")]

    public void OperationCompleted(string
operationName, long durationMilliseconds)

    {

        WriteEvent(2, operationName,
durationMilliseconds);
```

```
        }

    }
```

In your application code, you would then use the **MyAppPerformanceSource.Log** instance to emit these events:

```csharp
using System.Diagnostics;


public class MyComponent
{
    public void PerformTimedOperation(string
operationName)

    {

        var stopwatch = Stopwatch.StartNew();


MyAppPerformanceSource.Log.OperationStarted(opera
tionName);

        // Perform the operation here

        stopwatch.Stop();


MyAppPerformanceSource.Log.OperationCompleted(ope
rationName, stopwatch.ElapsedMilliseconds);

    }
```

}

You can then collect and analyze these "MyApp-Performance" events in PerfView, allowing you to see when your operations started and how long they took. This level of custom tracing can be invaluable for understanding the performance of specific parts of your application logic.

For a more cross-platform approach to tracing that can be consumed by various monitoring backends (not just ETW), consider using System.Diagnostics.Activity to represent operations and System.Diagnostics.DiagnosticSource to publish events related to these activities. Many modern .NET libraries and frameworks are adopting these APIs for providing rich tracing information.

Mastering advanced profiling with PerfView and leveraging custom tracing with ETW (or Activity/DiagnosticSource for cross-platform scenarios) can provide you with the deep insights needed to tackle the most challenging performance bottlenecks in your .NET 9 applications. These techniques allow you to go beyond simple metrics and truly understand the runtime behavior of your code.

14.4 Optimizing Garbage Collection Behavior (Advanced Configuration)

Alright, let's venture into a more nuanced area of performance tuning: directly influencing the behavior of the .NET garbage collector (GC) through advanced configuration. Think of the GC as a highly sophisticated automatic system, and in most cases, it does an excellent job of managing memory without requiring any intervention. However, for very specific and demanding scenarios, particularly in high-performance or latency-sensitive applications, you might consider tweaking some of its advanced settings. It's crucial to understand that these are advanced techniques and should be approached with extreme caution, backed by thorough profiling and a deep understanding of your application's memory usage patterns. Incorrectly configured GC settings can actually worsen performance.

These advanced GC configurations are typically specified in your application's runtime configuration file, which is usually named runtimeconfig.json and resides alongside your application's main executable. This file allows you to control various aspects of the .NET runtime, including the garbage collector.

One of the fundamental choices you can make is between Server GC and Workstation GC, which we discussed earlier. For server applications that prioritize throughput and can tolerate slightly longer but less frequent GC pauses, enabling Server GC by adding the following to your runtimeconfig.json might be beneficial:

JSON

```json
{

  "runtimeOptions": {

    "configProperties": {

      "System.GC.Server": true

    }

  }

}
```

Conversely, for interactive client applications (like desktop or mobile apps) where responsiveness is paramount and shorter, more frequent GC pauses are preferred, ensuring Workstation GC is enabled (which is often the default) or explicitly setting it to false in the configuration might be appropriate.

For server GC on multi-core machines, you can also influence the number of GC heaps created. By default, server GC tries to create one GC heap per logical processor. In some high-workload scenarios with significant concurrent memory allocation, you might experiment with increasing the number of heaps using the System.GC.HeapCount setting:

JSON

```json
{

  "runtimeOptions": {

    "configProperties": {

      "System.GC.Server": true,

      "System.GC.HeapCount": 12 // Example:
setting to 12 heaps

    }

  }

}
```

However, increasing the heap count also increases the resources used by the GC, so it's essential to profile your application under realistic load to determine if this setting provides a net benefit.

Another advanced setting to be aware of is Retained Mode. This is a more specialized option primarily aimed at reducing GC pauses in certain latency-sensitive applications that experience high allocation rates of short-lived objects. When retained mode is enabled, the GC might try to avoid moving objects during collection, potentially leading to shorter pauses but possibly at the cost of increased memory fragmentation over time.

You can enable retained mode with the System.GC.RetainVM setting:

JSON

```json
{

  "runtimeOptions": {

    "configProperties": {

      "System.GC.RetainVM": true

    }

  }

}
```

Using retained mode should be approached with caution and is typically only considered for very specific performance-critical scenarios where latency is a primary concern. Thorough profiling and understanding of the application's memory behavior are crucial.

Finally, you can influence the behavior of the Large Object Heap (LOH). Objects larger than a certain threshold (around 85,000 bytes) are allocated on the LOH, which is collected less frequently and is not compacted by default in all scenarios. Fragmentation on the LOH can sometimes lead to OutOfMemoryException errors even if there's enough total free memory, as the free blocks might not be contiguous enough to satisfy a large allocation request.

You can configure whether and when the LOH is compacted using the System.GC.LOHCompactionMode setting:

JSON

```
{

    "runtimeOptions": {

        "configProperties": {

            "System.GC.LOHCompactionMode": 2 // 2 means
always compact LOH on full GC

        }

    }

}
```

Setting System.GC.LOHCompactionMode to 2 forces a compaction of the LOH during every full (Generation 2) garbage collection. While this can help reduce fragmentation and prevent OutOfMemoryException errors in some cases, LOH compaction is an expensive operation and can significantly increase GC pause times. Therefore, it should only be enabled if you've identified LOH fragmentation as a clear problem through profiling and understand the potential trade-offs with GC pause duration.

It's paramount to reiterate that these advanced GC configuration options should not be tweaked without a solid understanding of your application's specific memory usage patterns and a clear performance problem that you are trying to address. You should always profile your application extensively with and without these settings to measure their actual impact and ensure that you are indeed achieving a net performance improvement without introducing other issues like increased GC pauses or excessive resource consumption. The default GC behavior in .NET is generally well-tuned for a wide range of applications, so proceed with caution when considering these advanced configurations.

14.5 Native AOT Compilation (Ahead-of-Time) for Performance

Alright, let's explore a cutting-edge technique in the .NET performance landscape that can offer significant advantages, especially for applications with strict startup time requirements or those being deployed to platforms with limited support for Just-In-Time (JIT) compilation: Native Ahead-of-Time (AOT) compilation. Think of AOT as compiling your .NET code directly to native machine code *before* your application is run, rather than relying on the JIT compiler to do this during runtime. This fundamental difference in compilation timing can have profound implications for performance, particularly in the areas of startup speed and memory usage.

To understand the benefits, let's quickly recap how the traditional .NET execution model works. When you run a .NET application, your C# or F# code is first compiled to an intermediate language (IL). Then, when your application starts and as different parts of your code are executed for the first time, the JIT compiler translates this IL into native machine code that your processor can understand. This JIT compilation happens during runtime, which introduces a startup delay – the time it takes for the JIT compiler to do its work before your application code can actually run at full speed. Additionally, the JIT compiler needs to reside in memory while your application is running, contributing to the application's memory footprint.

Native AOT compilation bypasses this runtime JIT compilation. Instead, the entire application (or a significant portion of it) is compiled directly to native machine code as part of the build process. The result is a standalone executable that contains the native code for your application and the necessary parts of the .NET runtime. When you run an AOT-compiled application, there's no JIT compilation phase at startup. The native code is ready to execute immediately, leading to significantly faster startup times. This can be a huge win for applications where quick startup is critical, such as command-line tools, serverless functions, and mobile applications (especially on platforms like iOS where JIT is heavily restricted).

Beyond faster startup, Native AOT compilation can also lead to reduced memory usage. Because the JIT compiler doesn't need to be present in memory at runtime, and in some cases, the AOT compiler can perform more aggressive optimizations than the JIT compiler, the overall memory footprint of an AOT-compiled application can be smaller.

However, Native AOT compilation also comes with certain trade-offs and considerations:

- Larger Executable Size: The AOT-compiled executable will typically be larger than a JIT-compiled application because it includes the native code for the .NET runtime and your application.
- Longer Build Times: AOT compilation is a more involved process than IL compilation, so the build times for AOT-compiled applications can be significantly longer.
- Limitations on Reflection and Dynamic Code: Native AOT compilation has limitations on the use of reflection and other dynamic code generation techniques. Because the code is compiled ahead of time, the compiler needs to know all the types and members that will be used. Highly dynamic code patterns that rely on runtime type discovery can be problematic. You might need to use techniques like trimming and reflection metadata inclusion to make such code work with AOT.
- Platform Specificity: The native code generated by the AOT compiler is specific to the target operating system and architecture. If you want to run your application on different platforms, you'll need to compile it ahead of time for each target.

As of .NET 9, Native AOT compilation is a feature that continues to evolve. While it offers compelling performance benefits for certain scenarios, it's not a one-size-fits-all solution. The .NET team is actively working on improving its capabilities and reducing its limitations.

Consider a real-world example: you're building a command-line tool with .NET 9 that needs to execute very quickly. The startup time of a traditional JIT-compiled .NET application might introduce an undesirable delay. By AOT-compiling your command-line tool, you can achieve near-instantaneous startup, making it feel much more responsive to the user.

Another example is deploying serverless functions to platforms with "cold start" penalties. AOT-compiling your .NET serverless function can significantly reduce the cold start time, leading to better performance and potentially lower costs.

While providing a complete working example of Native AOT compilation within this context is complex due to the setup and platform-specific nature, the general process involves publishing your .NET 9 application with the PublishAot flag set to true in your project file:

XML

```
<PropertyGroup>

  <PublishAot>true</PublishAot>

  <OutputType>Exe</OutputType>

  <TargetFramework>net9.0</TargetFramework>


<RuntimeIdentifier>linux-x64</RuntimeIdentifier>
<SelfContained>true</SelfContained>
</PropertyGroup>
```

You would then use the dotnet publish command with the specified RuntimeIdentifier to perform the AOT compilation for that target platform.

Native AOT compilation is a powerful advanced technique in .NET 9 that can offer significant performance improvements in terms of startup time and memory usage by compiling your code directly to native machine code ahead of time. While it comes with trade-offs like larger executable sizes and limitations on dynamic code, it's a valuable tool to consider for performance-critical scenarios, especially when targeting platforms with JIT restrictions or when fast startup is paramount. As .NET continues to evolve, Native AOT is likely to become an even more important part of the performance optimization landscape.

Chapter 15: The Future of Modern .NET Development

Alright, as we reach the end of our exploration into mastering modern .NET, let's take a moment to gaze into the crystal ball and discuss the future of modern .NET development. Think of this as looking at the horizon, trying to anticipate the emerging trends, new technologies, and evolving paradigms that will shape how we build applications with .NET in the years to come. Staying aware of these developments will help you prepare for what's next and ensure your skills and applications remain relevant and cutting-edge.

15.1 Exploring Emerging Trends in the .NET Ecosystem

Alright, let's peer into what the future might hold for the .NET ecosystem. Think of this as a friendly chat about the directions technology is heading and how .NET is positioning itself to be a key player in those advancements. The world of software development is in constant motion, and staying aware of these emerging trends will help you make informed decisions about the technologies you learn and the architectures you adopt for your future projects.

One of the most significant shifts we're seeing, and one that will undoubtedly continue to shape .NET development, is the move towards cloud-native development and microservices architectures. Cloud-native isn't just about hosting applications in the cloud; it's a whole paradigm around building and running applications that are specifically designed to leverage the benefits of cloud environments. This includes things like containerization (using Docker), orchestration (with Kubernetes), serverless functions, and a focus on scalability, resilience, and agility.

Consider a large e-commerce platform. Instead of a single, massive application (a monolith), they might break it down into smaller, independent services – one for managing user profiles, another for handling orders, another for processing payments, and so on. Each of these services is a microservice. Cloud-native principles dictate that these microservices would likely be packaged as Docker containers, orchestrated by Kubernetes for deployment and scaling, and might even include serverless functions for event-driven tasks. .NET 9 and its future iterations are increasingly focusing on providing excellent tools and libraries for building these kinds of distributed systems. Expect to see further enhancements in areas like building lightweight microservices with ASP.NET Core, improved integration with container registries and orchestration platforms, and better support for observability – the ability to monitor and understand the health and performance of your distributed application through logging, tracing, and metrics.

Another very exciting trend is the rise of Blazor and its use of WebAssembly (Wasm). For a long time, building interactive frontend web applications meant primarily using JavaScript. Blazor offers a compelling alternative for .NET developers: the ability to write your client-side web UI using C# instead of JavaScript. WebAssembly is a binary instruction format that allows code written in languages like C# (via Blazor) to run directly in the user's web browser at near-native speed.

Think about a complex data visualization dashboard that traditionally might have required a significant amount of JavaScript code. With Blazor, you can build the entire frontend using C#, leveraging your existing .NET skills and potentially sharing code with your backend. As WebAssembly continues to evolve and gain even broader support across web browsers, and as its performance improves, Blazor is poised to become an increasingly significant player in web development. Expect to see further advancements in Blazor's tooling, performance (especially around Wasm), and its ability to integrate with existing JavaScript ecosystems.

Finally, the integration of Artificial Intelligence (AI) and Machine Learning (ML) into applications is no longer a futuristic concept; it's becoming a standard expectation. .NET has its own cross-platform machine learning library, ML.NET, which allows .NET developers to build, train, and deploy machine learning models within their .NET applications. As AI and ML become more pervasive, the .NET ecosystem is likely to see even tighter integration in this space. This could involve more streamlined APIs for common ML tasks, better tooling within .NET development environments for working with ML models, and closer integration with cloud-based AI and ML services offered by platforms like Azure AI, AWS AI, and Google Cloud AI.

Consider a scenario where you're building an e-commerce application. You might want to implement a recommendation engine that suggests products to users based on their browsing history. With ML.NET, you can build the machine learning model using C# and then integrate it directly into your ASP.NET Core backend to provide these personalized recommendations. The future of .NET development will likely see even smoother ways to incorporate such intelligent features into a wide range of applications.

These trends – cloud-native development and microservices, Blazor and WebAssembly, and AI/ML integration – represent significant shifts in the software development landscape, and the .NET ecosystem is actively evolving to embrace and empower developers in these areas. Staying aware of these directions will be crucial for building modern, scalable, and intelligent applications with .NET in the years to come.

15.2 Considerations for Adopting New .NET Features and Technologies

Alright, as the .NET platform and its associated technologies continue their rapid evolution, you'll inevitably face decisions about when and how to incorporate these new features and tools into your projects. Think of this as deciding which new gadgets to add to your developer toolkit. While shiny new features can be tempting, a thoughtful approach to adoption is key to ensuring stability, maintainability, and long-term success for your applications. Let's explore some important considerations to keep in mind.

First and foremost, it's essential to stay informed about the latest developments in the .NET ecosystem. Microsoft regularly announces new features, updates, and even entirely new technologies through official channels like the .NET Blog, release notes, and the annual .NET Conf event. Beyond the official sources, the vibrant .NET community also plays a crucial role in disseminating information through blogs, podcasts, and open-source projects. Regularly engaging with these resources will give you a good overview of what's new and what's on the horizon.

However, just because something is new doesn't automatically mean you should rush to use it in your current or future projects. The next crucial step is to evaluate the relevance of these new features and technologies to your specific needs and the types of applications you build. For example, if you primarily work on backend APIs, a new UI framework might not be immediately relevant. Similarly, a feature aimed at optimizing garbage collection for high-throughput servers might not be a priority for a small desktop application. Take the time to understand what problem a new feature solves and whether that problem is one you are currently facing or anticipate facing.

Once you've identified a new feature or technology that seems promising, consider adopting it gradually. Avoid rewriting large portions of an existing, stable application to use the latest and greatest just for the sake of it. Instead, try incorporating new features in smaller, less critical parts of your codebase or in new projects. This allows you to gain practical experience with the technology, understand its nuances, and assess its real-world benefits and potential drawbacks in a controlled environment. Think of it as trying out a new tool on a small task before committing to using it for a major project.

Team training and knowledge sharing are also vital when adopting new technologies. If a new feature or paradigm is deemed important for your team's future development, ensure that everyone has the opportunity to learn about it and become comfortable using it. This might involve dedicated training sessions, internal workshops, or simply encouraging team members to explore the new technology and share their findings. A team that's collectively proficient in new tools will be much more effective at leveraging them.

Another important consideration is long-term support and stability. While the .NET platform generally has excellent backward compatibility, new features and even entire technologies can have varying levels of maturity. Consider the support lifecycle for a new framework or library. Is it backed by Microsoft or a strong community? Is it likely to be actively maintained and updated in the future? Adopting a technology that might become obsolete or unsupported can lead to significant maintenance headaches down the line. Look for signals of stability and a clear roadmap for future development.

Finally, performance implications should always be evaluated. While new features are often introduced with performance improvements in mind, this isn't always the case, or the performance benefits might only be realized in specific scenarios.

Thoroughly test the performance of any new features or libraries you adopt in the context of your own application's workload to ensure they are indeed providing the benefits you expect and not introducing unexpected performance regressions.

Adopting new .NET features and technologies should be a deliberate and informed process. Stay up-to-date, evaluate relevance, adopt gradually, invest in team training, consider long-term support, and always measure the performance impact. By following these considerations, you can strategically enhance your development capabilities and build modern, efficient applications without unnecessary risk or disruption.

15.3 The Evolution of C# and the .NET Platform

Alright, let's take a step back and appreciate the incredible journey that the C# language and the .NET platform have been on, and how their continuous evolution shapes the way we develop software today and will continue to do so in the future. Think of C# and .NET as a dynamic duo, each constantly pushing the boundaries of what's possible and providing us with increasingly powerful and developer-friendly tools.

From its initial release in the early 2000s as a key part of the .NET Framework, C# was envisioned as a modern, object-oriented language that aimed to balance power with ease of use. It drew inspiration from languages like C++, Java, and Smalltalk, incorporating features like garbage collection, a rich type system, and strong support for component-based development. The .NET Framework itself provided a vast set of libraries that allowed developers to build a wide range of applications, primarily for Windows.

Over the years, both C# and the .NET platform have undergone significant transformations. With the rise of cross-platform needs and the desire for a more modular and performant runtime, Microsoft embarked on the .NET Core initiative. This was a fundamental re-architecting of the .NET platform, resulting in a cross-platform, open-source implementation. C# evolved alongside .NET Core, with new versions of the language introducing features that aligned with modern programming paradigms and took advantage of the runtime's capabilities.

Consider some of the key language features that have been introduced in C# over the years. Generics, introduced in C# 2.0, brought type safety and performance improvements to collections. LINQ (Language Integrated Query) in C# 3.0 revolutionized how we query and manipulate data. Asynchronous programming with async and await in C# 5.0 made it significantly easier to write responsive and scalable I/O-bound code. More recent versions have brought features like pattern matching enhancements, record types for concise data representation, and nullable reference types to help prevent null reference exceptions.

Each of these language evolutions wasn't just about adding new syntax; it was about empowering developers to write more expressive, safer, and more efficient code that could leverage the underlying .NET platform effectively. For instance, the introduction of async and await was crucial for building performant web applications and modern UIs that wouldn't block while waiting for long-running operations, a necessity in the cross-platform world where applications need to be responsive on various devices and network conditions.

Similarly, the .NET platform itself has continuously evolved. The move to .NET Core and now the unification with .NET 5 and later (including .NET 9) has brought true cross-platform capabilities, allowing our applications to run on Windows, macOS, and Linux. The runtime has seen significant performance improvements over the years, with advancements in the garbage collector, the JIT compiler, and the core libraries. The modularity introduced with

.NET Core allows applications to be smaller and more focused, including only the necessary components.

Looking ahead, this trend of continuous evolution is very likely to continue. The C# language will probably see further refinements aimed at simplifying common coding patterns, improving safety, and potentially exploring new paradigms like more advanced forms of concurrency or functional programming constructs. The .NET platform will likely continue to be optimized for performance, scalability, and new application scenarios, including better support for cloud-native development, integration with emerging technologies like WebAssembly for frontend development, and enhanced capabilities for AI and machine learning.

The evolution of C# and the .NET platform isn't happening in isolation. It's driven by the needs of the developer community and the ever-changing landscape of software development. Microsoft actively engages with the community through open-source contributions and language design discussions, ensuring that the platform and the language evolve in a way that meets the real-world challenges faced by developers.

As a .NET developer, staying aware of this ongoing evolution is key. While you don't need to adopt every new feature immediately, understanding the direction the platform and the language are heading will help you make informed decisions about the technologies you use and the skills you invest in. The journey of learning and mastering .NET is a continuous one, and the consistent evolution of C# and the .NET platform ensures that it remains a vibrant and powerful ecosystem for building a wide variety of applications for many years to come.

15.4 Preparing for Future Development Paradigms

Alright, as we wrap up our exploration of modern .NET development, let's look ahead and discuss how you can position yourself and your skills to be ready for the future development paradigms that are beginning to gain traction and will likely shape the software landscape in the coming years. Think of this as equipping yourself with the right mindset and knowledge to navigate the evolving world of software creation, ensuring you remain a relevant and effective developer.

The way we build software is constantly being influenced by new ideas, architectural patterns, and technological advancements. While .NET 9 already provides tools and support for many of these, understanding the underlying concepts and being prepared to adopt them will be key to staying ahead of the curve.

One significant paradigm shift is the increasing adoption of serverless computing. Instead of managing entire servers, serverless allows you to run your code in response to events, with the cloud provider automatically managing the underlying infrastructure, scaling, and billing based on actual usage. Platforms like AWS Lambda, Azure Functions, and Google Cloud Functions enable this. While .NET has excellent support for building serverless functions, understanding the event-driven nature of this paradigm and how to architect applications that can effectively leverage serverless architectures will be increasingly important. This might involve learning about different event sources, designing stateless functions, and optimizing for cold starts.

Another paradigm that's gaining momentum is reactive programming. Reactive programming is a declarative programming paradigm concerned with data streams and the propagation of change. Think of it like an Excel spreadsheet: when

402

you change a cell's value, all other cells that depend on it are automatically updated. Frameworks like Reactive Extensions (Rx.NET) in the .NET ecosystem allow you to work with asynchronous data streams and events in a composable and elegant way. This can lead to more responsive, resilient, and scalable applications, especially when dealing with real-time data or complex event handling scenarios. While Rx.NET has been around for a while, the principles of reactive programming are becoming increasingly relevant in modern architectures.

The concept of decentralized applications (dApps) and blockchain technology, while still evolving, represents another potential future paradigm. While not every application will be a dApp, understanding the principles of distributed ledgers, smart contracts, and decentralized data storage might become relevant in specific domains, particularly those requiring high levels of transparency and immutability. While .NET support for blockchain development is still growing, being aware of this space and its potential applications could be beneficial.

Beyond specific architectural patterns, the way we build software is also evolving. Low-code and no-code platforms are becoming more sophisticated, allowing individuals with less traditional programming skills to create applications. While these platforms might not replace the need for professional developers for complex applications, understanding how to integrate with them or leverage them for certain tasks could become part of the modern developer's skillset.

Furthermore, the increasing importance of AI and Machine Learning in applications will likely continue to shape development. Being comfortable with integrating ML models into your .NET applications, understanding the basics of data science workflows, and knowing how to leverage cloud-based AI services will be valuable skills for the future.

Finally, the emphasis on developer experience (DX) is likely to continue. Tools and platforms that make development easier, faster, and more enjoyable will be highly valued. This includes things like improved hot reloading, better debugging tools, more intuitive APIs, and advancements in IDEs and development workflows. Expect the .NET tooling to continue to evolve in these areas.

Preparing for these future paradigms isn't about becoming an expert in everything overnight. Instead, it's about cultivating a mindset of continuous learning and being open to exploring new ideas and technologies.

Here are a few steps you can take:

- Stay Curious: Read articles, follow thought leaders, and experiment with new technologies that pique your interest.
- Focus on Fundamentals: A strong understanding of core programming principles, software architecture, and data structures will serve you well no matter which new paradigms emerge.
- Learn Incrementally: Pick one new area that seems relevant to your interests or your work and start learning the basics. You don't need to become an expert immediately.
- Build Small Projects: Try building small, experimental projects using new technologies to gain hands-on experience.
- Engage with the Community: Participate in online forums, attend meetups, and connect with other developers to learn from their experiences with new paradigms.

The future of software development is exciting and full of opportunities. By embracing a mindset of continuous learning and staying open to new ideas, you can ensure that you're well-prepared to navigate the evolving landscape and build innovative applications with .NET for years to come.

Conclusion

This book has taken you on a comprehensive exploration of modern .NET development, venturing beyond the surface level to equip you with the knowledge and skills necessary to craft high-performance, cross-platform applications. We began by tracing the evolution of .NET, from its Windows-centric origins to the unified, open-source, and cross-platform powerhouse it is today. This historical context provides a crucial understanding of the design decisions that have shaped the platform and its trajectory.

We then examined the core concepts of C# 13, highlighting the latest language enhancements that empower developers to write cleaner, more expressive, and safer code. From advanced pattern matching to the effective use of record structs and the intricacies of asynchronous programming with async and await, we've equipped you with the tools to leverage the full potential of the language.

A significant portion of our exploration was dedicated to performance optimization, a cornerstone of modern application development. We delved into understanding and mitigating common performance bottlenecks, mastering memory management techniques, and exploring advanced profiling and tracing tools. We also addressed the critical aspects of writing performant C# code and optimizing garbage collection behavior, providing you with the knowledge to build applications that are both fast and resource-efficient.

Recognizing the importance of reaching a broad audience, we dedicated considerable attention to the challenges and best practices of cross-platform development. We explored the architecture that enables .NET 9 to run on diverse operating systems, the role of Target Framework Monikers, and effective strategies for sharing code across platforms. We also provided in-depth guidance on building and deploying applications for the desktop (Windows, macOS, and Linux) and mobile (iOS and Android), acknowledging the unique considerations and tools involved in each ecosystem.

Finally, we looked towards the future of .NET development, discussing emerging trends such as cloud-native architectures, Blazor with WebAssembly, and the integration of AI and machine learning. We also offered considerations for adopting new .NET features and technologies, emphasizing the importance of continuous learning and adaptation in this dynamic field.

By journeying through these chapters, you've gained a holistic understanding of modern .NET development, encompassing not only the technical skills but also the architectural principles, performance considerations, and deployment strategies necessary to build and deliver high-quality applications across a multitude of platforms. The examples and explanations provided throughout this book serve as a springboard for your own exploration and experimentation. The world of .NET development is vast and ever-evolving, but with the knowledge you've acquired, you are well-prepared to tackle the challenges and opportunities that lie ahead.

www.ingramcontent.com/pod-product-compliance
Lightning Source LLC
LaVergne TN
LVHW080111070326
832902LV00015B/2523